ns of Dakar

Ohio University Research in International Studies

This series of publications on Africa, Latin America, Southeast Asia, and Global and Comparative Studies is designed to present significant research, translation, and opinion to area specialists and to a wide community of persons interested in world affairs. The series is distributed worldwide. For more information, consult the Ohio University Press website, ohioswallow.com.

Books in the Ohio University Research in International Studies series are published by Ohio University Press in association with the Center for International Studies. The views expressed in individual volumes are those of the authors and should not be considered to represent the policies or beliefs of the Center for International Studies, Ohio University Press, or Ohio University.

Projections of Dakar

(RE)IMAGINING URBAN SENEGAL THROUGH CINEMA

Devin Bryson and Molly Krueger Enz

Ohio University Research in International Studies
Africa Series No. 101

Ohio University Press
Athens

Ohio University Press, Athens, Ohio 45701
ohioswallow.com
© 2024 by Ohio University Press
All rights reserved

To obtain permission to quote, reprint, or otherwise reproduce or distribute material from Ohio University Press publications, please contact our rights and permissions department at (740) 593-1154 or (740) 593-4536 (fax).

Printed in the United States of America
Ohio University Press books are printed on acid-free paper ∞ ™

Library of Congress Cataloging-in-Publication Data

Names: Bryson, Devin, 1977– author. | Enz, Molly Krueger, 1974– author.
Title: Projections of Dakar : (re)imagining urban Senegal through cinema / Devin Bryson and Molly Krueger Enz.
Other titles: Research in international studies. Africa series ; no. 101.
Description: Athens : Ohio University Press, 2024. | Series: Research in international studies. Africa series ; no. 101 | Includes bibliographical references and index.
Identifiers: LCCN 2024017246 | ISBN 9780896803497 (paperback) | ISBN 9780896803480 (hardcover) | ISBN 9780896803503 (pdf)
Subjects: LCSH: Motion pictures—Senegal—Dakar. | Motion picture producers and directors—Senegal—Dakar. | Dakar (Senegal)—In motion pictures. | Dakar (Senegal)—Social conditions—21st century.
Classification: LCC PN1993.5.S38 B79 2024 | DDC 791.4309663—dc23/eng/20240416
LC record available at https://lccn.loc.gov/2024017246

If Africans do not tell their own stories, Africa will soon disappear.

—Ousmane Sembène

The role of African cinema today is to reflect the vitality of a people—an African people in all its diversity—and through this people, reflect the world.

—Safi Faye

Contents

List of Illustrations
ix

Acknowledgments
xi

Introduction
Beyond Senghor's Shadow
The Role of Culture and Cinema in Senegalese Society and the City of Dakar
1

1
Screening Urban Senegal
Social Interventions through Cinematic Infrastructure, Innovation, and Form
20

2
Shaping the National Body in
Moussa Sène Absa's *Yoolé* and Rama Thiaw's *Boul fallé: La voie de la lutte* and *The Revolution Won't Be Televised*
53

3
Community Responses to Peri-urban Water Mismanagement in Joseph Gaï Ramaka's *Plan Jaxaay!* and Abdoul Aziz Cissé's *La brèche*
98

4
Urban Precarity, Voice, and Contingent Communities in Adams Sie's
Voix silencieuses and Khady Sylla's *Le monologue de la muette*
138

5
Intersectionality, Complexity, and Contradictions of
Senegalese Women's Experiences in Khardiata Pouye's *Cette couleur qui me dérange* and Angèle Diabang's *Sénégalaises et Islam*
169

Conclusion
Cinematic Encounters in the City
Emergent Spaces of Collaboration and Exchange
208

Notes
217

Bibliography
241

Index
251

Illustrations

Figures

I.1. A representation of Cheikh Amadou Bamba on the side of a boutique in Saint-Louis, 2023 — 6

I.2. Hip-hop street art in Pikine, 2013 — 7

I.3. Black Power graffiti mural created by members of RBS Crew in Dakar, 2023 — 7

1.1. The Complexe Cinématographique Ousmane Sembène in Dakar, 2018 — 21

1.2. The logo for the Centre Yennenga in Dakar, 2023 — 33

1.3. Gorée Island's bay with Gorée Island Cinema's headquarters in the background, 2019 — 39

1.4. The screening room at the Centre Yennenga, 2023 — 42

2.1. Pirogues at Ouakam Beach in Dakar near the Mosquée de la Divinité, 2016 — 54

2.2. Fishermen in the Atlantic Ocean with the Dakar skyline behind them, 2023 — 62

2.3. Two wrestlers grapple during a match in Dakar, 2013 — 76

2.4. Wrestlers, trainers, marabouts, and fans prepare for matches in Dakar, 2013 — 82

2.5. Street art portraying Thomas Sankara in Dakar, 2023 — 88

3.1. Residents linger by a catchment basin in Pikine, 2013 — 99

3.2. A resident shows his flooded house in Pikine, July 2013 — 111

3.3. Residents of Pikine navigate flooded streets, July 2013 — 117

3.4. Street art depicting a water spirit in Saint-Louis, 2023 — 123
3.5. The Senegal River in Saint-Louis, 2023 — 125
3.6. The landmark Faidherbe Bridge in Saint-Louis, 2023 — 131
4.1. Passengers board a car rapide in Dakar, 2013 — 157
4.2. The sun sets over city streets in the neighborhood of Point E in Dakar, 2023 — 160
5.1. A cosmetics shop in the Tilène Market of Dakar, 2023 — 186
5.2. An anti-skin-lightening ad in front of a pharmacy in the neighborhood of Mermoz in Dakar, 2023 — 193
5.3. A woman walks along a street in Pikine, 2013 — 200
5.4. Three women walk through the Tilène Market in Dakar, 2023 — 205
C.1. Viewers watch the short film *La boxeuse* at Kenu, 2021 — 210
C.2. The outdoor courtyard and screening area at the Centre Yennenga, 2023 — 212
C.3. One of several editing bays at the Centre Yennenga, 2023 — 213

Acknowledgments

The seeds for our collaborative work and this book were planted during a 2012 Council on International Educational Exchange (CIEE) international faculty development seminar in Senegal entitled "Contemporary Senegal through Literature and the Arts." Organized by Serigne N'Diaye, resident director of CIEE in Senegal, this seminar introduced us to cultural dynamics in the country and to social institutions, filmmakers, writers, artists, and one another. All of these elements have been essential to our scholarship since then as we have endeavored to sustain collaborative, equitable, and publicly engaged work. We would like to thank Serigne for helping us to establish such strong roots for this project.

We've had the opportunity to extend and enrich our work over the years through presenting on panels at the African Studies Association Annual Meetings and the 20th and 21st Century French and Francophone Studies International Colloquia and coediting special issues of *African Studies Quarterly* and *Black Camera*. We express thanks to the editorial teams of these journals at the University of Florida and Indiana University Press as well as to the contributors to the special issues for responding to our initial conceptual frameworks so enthusiastically and with such meaningful scholarship. We also thank the organizers, fellow panelists, and audience members at those conferences. The chance to share developing versions of this book at various stages has been invaluable. Special thanks to the editors of *Black Camera* for granting us permission to include reworked versions of our articles published in volume 9, issue 2, Spring 2018 ("Forging a New Path: Plurality, Social Change, and Innovation in Contemporary Senegalese Cinema," 333–48; "See the Sky: Subjectivity and Social Meaning in Adams Sie's

Filmmaking," 391–413; and "Joseph Gaï Ramaka and Nicolas Sawalo Cissé Promote Change through Cinema: Representations of Flooding and Trash in the Margins of Dakar," 427–49).

Our intellectual partnership over the past decade has been rewarding beyond measure due to our mutual respect, appreciation of one another's important and unique contributions, engaging dialogue, and admiration for Senegalese cultural production. We have had many thought-provoking, enlightening, and challenging conversations over the years during our collaborative ethnographic research in Dakar and while writing and editing. Collaboration has been central to this project, not just with one another but with cultural producers in Senegal. As two white American scholars working at US-based institutions, we acknowledge our privilege and positionality and have attempted to prioritize the voices and experiences of the cultural producers with whom we have interacted and who have been so welcoming to us during many conversations and interviews over the past twelve years. We have worked diligently, and hopefully managed, to center the experiences, perspectives, work, and lives of such individuals in the book. This endeavor would not have been possible without the many people who invited us to their offices, studios, galleries, and homes and gave their time, talent, and thoughts so generously. We express thanks first and foremost to everyone in the cinema community in Senegal, namely all of the filmmakers and cinema workers quoted in the book—Hugues Diaz, Abdoul Aziz Cissé, Coumba Sarr, Moussa Sène Absa, Joseph Gaï Ramaka, Adams Sie, Khardiata Pouye, and Angèle Diabang. Nicolas Sawalo Cissé, Khadidiatou Sow, Moctar Ba, Alioune Ndiagne, and Mor Mbengue also provided invaluable knowledge that was formative to our understanding of contemporary Senegalese cinema. The entire Direction de la cinématographie deserves our gratitude for its sustained help in making introductions, setting up interviews, and including us in various film community events. Amadou T. Fofana has been an essential scholarly collaborator, interlocutor, and supporter of this project as well as a friend. We would like to thank Kamir Délivrance Nzalé and Kalidou "Kals" N'Diaye for their logistical help, cultural insights, hospitality, good humor, and friendship throughout our numerous research trips. We appreciate the entire Becker family for providing us with such a comfortable, sustaining, and intellectually engaging home environment during our many stays in Dakar and especially want to thank Charles and Angélique Becker and Nicole Konaté. We hope this book reflects in some small measure the true value of *teranga* that you have offered us over the years. We extend our thanks to Cheikh Ndiaye and Cécile Fakhoury Gallery for giving us permission to feature the incredible painting Cinéma Awa, Pikine on our book's cover. We are thrilled that Ndiaye's depiction of Cinéma Awa and its urban neighborhood greets readers before they encounter our words. Finally, Ousmane Sène, Mariane Yade, and all the staff at the West African Research Center (WARC) have provided us with our scholarly and welcoming home away from home in Senegal.

We would like to recognize Sarah Osment for her work on the book's index. Thanks to Ohio University Press's editor in chief, Rick Huard, and the entire editorial team as well as two anonymous reviewers who provided insightful feedback and ideas that helped to strengthen our final manuscript. One reviewer referred to our book as "a love letter to Dakar," and this perfectly captures how we feel about our work on and in this city—Dakar is a bustling, dynamic, vibrant capital whose beautiful people, art, and culture have given us both so much professionally and personally.

Devin's research trips to Senegal were supported by a number of generous faculty awards and grants from Illinois College: Engelbach Endowment for Peace Studies Faculty Award, Dean Carole Ann Ryan Faculty Award, C. Reed Parker Professional Development Grant, and Malcolm F. Stewart Award. I want to thank my colleagues in the Department of Global Studies at Illinois College for their kindness, understanding, and support in research, teaching, and all of the ups and downs of academia. I also express gratitude to my entire family for their excitement and encouragement for this project, their patience as I left home and missed important events for research trips, and all of their love and laughter, especially Emily, Quentin, Greta, and Edith. You make all of this worth it.

Molly's research for this book has benefited from the generous support of the Fulbright US Scholar Program as well as various funding sources at South Dakota State University, including the School of American and Global Studies, the College of Arts, Humanities and Social Sciences, and the Office of Research Assurance and Sponsored

Programs. I had the wonderful opportunity to establish connections with several Senegalese cultural producers during study abroad programs in 2014, 2016, 2019, and 2023 that I led for students from South Dakota State University in collaboration with the West African Research Center. I am appreciative of WARC for organizing such enriching programs and of my students for their curiosity, openness, and enthusiasm. Many colleagues and friends supported and encouraged me throughout the duration of this project, and I would like to thank in particular Hilary Hungerford, Eileen McEwan, Christine Garst-Santos, Becky Kuehl, Luz Angélica Kirschner, Eckhard Rölz, and Barbara Syrrakos. I am immensely grateful to my parents, John and Patricia Krueger, for instilling a love of learning and encouraging me to pursue my passions, and to my siblings, Sarah, Kate, and Mark, for always being there. My heartfelt thanks go out to Greg for his constant support and for taking care of everything at home while I was away in Senegal for weeks or months at a time. Finally, I express profound gratitude to Grace and Maya, who did not hesitate to leave their friends and family for a semester to join me in Dakar and enroll in a new school. I am deeply appreciative of how you embraced the city and everyone you met there. It was a true gift to be able to explore and experience Senegal together.

Introduction

Beyond Senghor's Shadow

The Role of Culture and Cinema in Senegalese Society and the City of Dakar

Following Senegal's independence from France in 1960, the country quickly gained international prominence due to the leadership of its first president, Léopold Sédar Senghor. A well-respected poet, a member of the French colonial government, a subsequent agitator for independence, and one of the founders of the literary, intellectual, and political Negritude movement, Senghor knew the importance of articulating a national identity for Senegal and then communicating that identity globally. He employed the arts as a principal tool to accomplish this feat. Senghor's government allocated significant portions of its budget to the Ministry of Culture and established several cultural institutions that served as artistic infrastructure for the creation and dissemination of Senegalese cultural productions. A number of scholars have emphasized the centrality of culture to political and social life in early postcolonial Senegal and its continuing influence on the Senegalese citizenry's conceptualization of its relationship to its government and its ability to engage with the social and political fields in Senegal.[1]

Although not all contemporary Senegalese cultural producers, including filmmakers, use their art to consciously respond to or intervene in the cultural ideology established by Senghor, they nevertheless work as agents for social and political change "in Senghor's shadow," which is Elizabeth Harney's expression for the influence of early postcolonial cultural ideology.[2] Postcolonial Senegalese society has constructed cultural producers in the country as social and political actors. Many of them embrace this opportunity to advocate for change in their country and on their continent through their work, including through visual art, music, dance, literature, television, and cinema.

Senegalese economist, philosopher, author, and public intellectual Felwine Sarr has convincingly and prominently argued for the continued importance of cultural producers to be socially engaged. In his book *Afrotopia*, Sarr argues that "thinking the continent of Africa is an arduous task, enshrouded in a fog of treacherous clichés, stereotypes, and pseudo-certitudes."[3] Despite the all-too-common pessimistic view of the continent as a "haven of misery," he believes that Africa must engage in "the efforts of critical reflection in regard to oneself, one's own realities and situation in the world: to think oneself, to represent oneself, to project oneself" in order to promote transformation.[4] Sarr prompts reflection on the continent from within its borders, and cultural producers play a critical role in the reimagined vision of Africa that will lead to a better future for its inhabitants: "Thought, literature, music, painting, the visual arts, cinema, television series, fashion, pop music, architecture, and the lively energy [*élan*] of cityscapes are the spaces where the future forms of individual and social life are sketched out and configured."[5] Working from the socially engaged cultural foundation established by Senghor and elaborated and extended by many subsequent cultural actors, the Senegalese filmmakers analyzed in this book exemplify Sarr's "arduous task" of transforming African societies through their cinema, which represents and projects contemporary Senegal within local and global contexts. As scholar Mbye Cham argues, African film serves as "a crucial site of the battle to decolonise minds, to develop radical consciousness, to reflect and engage critically with African cultures and traditions, and to make desirable the meaningful transformation of society for the benefit of the majority."[6] African filmmakers who represent the social, political, economic, and cultural concerns of the residents of their countries use cinema purposely as a tool to create a better life for their compatriots.

In this book, we highlight the audiovisual creations and practices of Senegalese filmmakers who are living, working, and distributing their work primarily, if not exclusively, in Senegal. As Frieda Ekotto and Kenneth Harrow remind us in their introduction to the edited volume *Rethinking African Cultural Production*, cultural capital that is possible within "African cinema" or "world cinema" is often unevenly distributed in favor of those filmmakers who are primarily situated outside of the continent or those who "'qualify' to pass borders in both directions more easily."[7] In order to combat that inequity, we seek to articulate, as Ekotto and Harrow encourage, the specific conditions of production for twenty-first-century Senegalese filmmakers working and living on the continent.

We are particularly interested in the ways that the work of these filmmakers is shaped by and reimagines the realities of contemporary urban Senegal. According to Harrow in *African Cinema: Postcolonial and Feminist Readings*, a shift in African cinema from the general postcolonial to the local urban occurred during the 1980s and 1990s. As cities in Africa witnessed a deterioration of life conditions, such as fewer jobs, a rise in crime, and a lack of city infrastructure, African filmmakers crafted "a new vision for survival . . . that would go beyond such terms as *engagement* or commitment, one that would engage the conditions of life on a local scale."[8] In what Harrow refers to as "post-engagement cinema," African filmmakers shifted from portraits of global postcolonial systems of power to depictions of current and internal problems, often highlighting marginalized urban locations such as bidonvilles or shantytowns.[9] As filmmakers turned to their own realities, they became more implicated in using film on a local level. The films that we study in *Projections of Dakar: (Re)Imagining Urban Senegal through Cinema* exemplify this wider cinematic shift because they center urban Senegal and primarily the capital, Dakar. Characters and narratives represent urban identities, existences, exchanges, and dynamics. We analyze how these films reveal and contribute to how people live in the city, relate to one another, build their lives, advocate for change, find joy and meaning, and create community. They also articulate more just, equitable, and inclusive forms of these actions in the context of Senegalese cities. Furthermore, the filmmakers themselves navigate urban contexts in order to make and distribute their films. In this way, their filmmaking strategies are products of specific urban conditions in twenty-first-century Senegal. Their work is a direct intervention in the urban dynamics of the country, imagining and reimagining existence for a variety of Senegalese residents.

Dakar as a Global Cultural Capital, 1960–99

The unique, dynamic relationship that exists between Dakar and the cultural work produced in and from the city dates back to the early postcolonial period. Through the federal funding of cultural projects under Senghor, Dakar was transformed into an internationally recognized capital of African culture and arts soon after independence. It became dotted with presses, theaters, museums, art schools, archives, and workshops. Senegal's capital city "hosted annual salons, sponsored internationally traveling exhibitions, and provided a generous system of bursaries and civil service jobs" within the visual arts community.[10] The National Dance Company and the National Ballet were formed in the year after independence and took up residence in prime locations within the city. Cinematic productions from the 1960s and 1970s were often set and filmed in Dakar, most notably Ousmane Sembène's *Borom sarret* (1963), *La noire de . . .* (1966), *Mandabi* (1968), and *Xala* (1975) and Djibril Diop Mambéty's *Touki bouki* (1973), all of which received international acclaim and brought depictions of Dakar's urban life to global audiences. The prime example of Dakar's preeminence as a site within cultural and artistic communities, both national and global, in the early postcolonial period occurred in 1966, when Senghor and Alioune Diop organized the First World Festival of Negro Arts. Over 2,500 cultural figures and representatives from over thirty countries gathered in Dakar for almost a month for performances, colloquia, and collaboration. David Murphy articulates the political import of the festival when he writes that it created "a space in which multiple versions of Pan-Africanism and the African Renaissance could be performed."[11] It is not incidental that this festival was held in the capital city of Dakar, both for its political importance and cultural dynamics. While Senegalese postcolonial cultural ideology has been challenged and renegotiated over the subsequent decades, it irreversibly established Dakar as an essential urban site in Africa for the intersections of local and global cultural concepts, practices, and forms. These artistic currents have then had an intractable influence on Senegalese urban lives, exchanges, and communities. Since Senghor's presidency, the urban, the political, and the cultural have been inextricably entwined in Senegal.

Senghor's successor, Abdou Diouf, appeared ready to continue Senghor's cultural policies and discourse upon taking the presidency in 1981. However, due to increasingly dire economic circumstances from the effects of neoliberal economic structural adjustment, market-driven globalization, and political stagnation, Diouf significantly decreased the government's support of the arts as well as basic governmental services during his tenure, which lasted until 2000. The areas of health, education, culture, and sanitation were completely abandoned by the federal government, leaving them to be provided by underprepared local governments. Rural inhabitants, looking to escape the droughts that were ravaging their livelihood, streamed into the city. As a result of these changes, cityscapes became dirty, decrepit, and overcrowded. Urban riots marked the national elections of 1988 as the opposition claimed corruption and vote rigging. University strikes led to an entire academic year being canceled in Dakar. Under Diouf, urban infrastructure, both cultural and social, deteriorated. As funding from the government dried up, cinema faced its own challenges during this period. Theaters closed, while filmmakers increasingly looked outside of the country for funding, production support, and shooting locations. However, the root cultural ideology continued to manifest itself among urban dwellers. In her book *Art World City: The Creative Economy of Artists and Urban Life in Dakar*, Joanna Grabski summarizes the various visual arts that increasingly became part of the Dakar cityscape in the late 1980s and early 1990s, including the Set/Setal murals and sculptures, the iconography of religious leader Cheikh Amadou Bamba, and hip-hop street art and graffiti (figs. I.1, I.2, and I.3).[12] As organic, grassroots forms of artistic expression, as opposed to state-sanctioned and state-commissioned art, became more prominent and omnipresent in the city, other individuals and communities in Dakar were inspired to culturally engage with their urban milieu. This was especially pertinent for urban residents as economic and infrastructural limitations in Dakar became more pronounced in the 1980s and 1990s due to economic readjustment. The people of Dakar had an increasing need for social and political engagement in their city, which was most accessible through cultural forms.

FIGURE I.1. A representation of Cheikh Amadou Bamba on the side of a boutique in Saint-Louis, 2023. Photo by Molly Krueger Enz.

FIGURE I.2. Hip-hop street art in Pikine, 2013. Photo by Devin Bryson.

FIGURE I.3. Black Power graffiti mural created by members of RBS Crew in Dakar, 2023. Photo by Molly Krueger Enz.

Dakar as "Palimpsest City," 2000–Present

The endurance of cultural ideology in Dakar was evident upon the election of Abdoulaye Wade as Senegal's third postcolonial president in 2000. He won the presidency largely due to his engagement with urban youth, both by promising them greater economic opportunities and garnering the public support of urban hip-hop artists. Once elected, Wade was conscious of the need to reinforce how he differed from his predecessor Diouf. One of the principal ways he did this was by affirming his commitment to the arts and implementing prominent infrastructural projects, both social and cultural. For example, he undertook large-scale road projects that connected various Dakar neighborhoods, including its peripheries, as well as the city and rural areas. In 2002, Wade modified the constitution to inscribe the president as the "primary protector of arts and letters." He announced ambitious *grands projets culturels*, planning to construct seven cultural sites in Dakar, including museums, a national theater, a national library, a national archive, an architectural school, and the Monument de la Renaissance Africaine. In December 2010, forty-five years after Senghor's Festival of Negro Arts, Wade revived the concept and secured Dakar as the host for the third iteration of the festival, inviting representatives from dozens of countries. Wade's eager public engagement with culture in urban space demonstrates once again the continuation of the cultural ideology established by Senghor in the shaping of Dakar. However, instead of concretely supporting the arts, Wade more often than not used hollow rhetorical maneuvers and unfeasible plans of cultural construction to consolidate his power and to enlarge his personal coffers. Only three of the cultural projects were ever completed during his twelve years in office: the Place du Souvenir Africain, the Grand Théâtre, and the Monument de la Renaissance Africaine. Faced with his inability to decrease the unemployment rate among urban young people, Wade "attempted to mask his failure to create jobs by promoting wrestling, dance, and music, which are extremely popular, especially in urban areas."[13] While this superficial adoption of culture to retain political capital worked for some time, young people living in Dakar eventually became fed up with Wade.

Their displeasure with Wade's indifference to urban residents under the screen of cultural engagement came to a head in 2011, when the president attempted to rewrite the Senegalese constitution in order to seize a third term in office. Many Senegalese in Dakar and its urban periphery responded through artistic and cultural modes, bolstered by protests in the streets, rather than through codified political opposition structures and figures. While they utilized artistic tools to combat Wade's grasp for further control of the country, their tactics were not simply political. Instead, these urban dwellers used their cultural strategies and rhetoric to express their generalized and accumulated frustrations about city life in Dakar and to call other Dakarois residents to greater engagement with their urban space. The diverse groups of protestors comprised "artists, writers, or 'parliamentarians of the street,' those popular singers, those numerous 'carriers of signs' (which sometimes contained whimsical messages) who took over public space to craft demands that were tied up with wants of the central political system. . . . This new avant-garde was built from the arts."[14] These artistic protesters specifically occupied urban space for their social and artistic interventions. Among the many actors protesting against Wade through the arts, the most visible group was the Y'en a Marre (French for "fed up") movement, formed when several journalists and hip-hop artists from the Dakar suburbs banded together during a too-frequent power outage. Using music, written manifestos, oratory, and striking visual imagery in urban spaces, Y'en a Marre quickly garnered the support of Dakar residents from various walks of life and successfully contributed to organizing a more socially active urban citizenry and preventing Wade from regaining office. According to journalists Vieux Savané and Baye Makébé Sarr, "it [the group] knew how to unite a community of young people who had been broken by the steamroller of unemployment. Young dynamic managers, journalists, the unemployed, workers, students, musicians, basically all social categories were part of their cry of revolt."[15] While artistic strategies had been deployed for social and political ends for decades in urban Senegalese communities, the 2012 presidential election proved to be a flash point at which the tactics and discourse of urban cultural producers across mediums congealed into a recognizable, socially engaged artistic community. Dakar hip-hoppers, filmmakers, and writers recognized their shared aesthetic and social investments, adopting a strategy of collaboration, collectivism, and artistic exchange. Their actions once again reminded us of the central role cultural productions can play in strategies to transform urban African societies, especially within

Senegal. The dynamic urban history of Dakar since independence has constituted the city as the primary site and inspiration for cultural production in Senegal during the early twenty-first century.

Dakar has persisted since independence as an essential site in the negotiation and renegotiation of the parameters of belonging within Senegalese, African, diasporic, and global networks. Furthermore, these negotiations in Dakar have consistently taken place through and within artistic and cultural forms, symbols, and discourse. Therefore, *Projections of Dakar: (Re)Imagining Urban Senegal through Cinema* contributes another component to the long history of Dakar as a unique urban African context for the intersections of culture, social inclusion, political participation, and international exchanges. Sarr calls Dakar "the very prototype of the palimpsest city," meaning that "several layers comprise the mingled sediment of the cityscape so as to furnish it with its current face. Its colonial history is blended together along with its semilegendary and semi-mythic history. Dakar is a city in movement that is constantly in the midst of creating itself. . . . The social, economic, and demographic dynamics have become superimposed, and we are producing an unplanned, undreamed-of city that is growing in an anarchical manner."[16] The filmmakers examined in this book are distinct products of and contributors to this "unplanned, undreamed-of city." They engage with these urban dynamics fully in their filmmaking practices and in the aesthetic forms they create on-screen. Our work contributes to the larger scholarly reconsideration of contemporary African cities that has been such an essential recent contribution to African studies.[17] Dakar has been an especially fertile site for scholars of urban Africa, and the Senegalese urban context has been the milieu for a number of important studies of cultural productions and artistic creation.[18] Similarly, in our study of cinema in Dakar, we draw on the rich lineage of cultural dynamics within urban Senegal that extend back to Senghor and Sembène and that gained global attention through Y'en a Marre. We specifically analyze twenty-first-century cinematic creation within Dakar that came directly from urban means of production and circulated among urban viewers and that depicts dimensions of contemporary life in the capital city. Our approach draws heavily from the concept of the African city as "a place of manifold rhythms, a world of sounds, private freedom, pleasures, and sensations."[19] The films studied are products of, representations of, and interventions in these urban cultural currents and practices in Dakar.

Dakar and the World

Grabski's conceptualization of Dakar as an "art world city," referenced earlier, is especially informative to our study of cinema because it speaks to Dakar's international connections and the ways those connections shape and are shaped by urban cultural productions. Sarr writes that "Dakar functions as a city understood as a perpetual construction site where international immigrants (from Italy, the United States, and France) have become the creators of new neighborhoods, adding their own idiosyncratic aesthetic to the city and populating the city with new creative styles."[20] These intersections have created a vibrant urban center that is rich with cultural diversity, which then rebounds back out into the world in various forms and directions. Grabski deploys the expression *art world city* to characterize Dakar as "a multiscalar, urban site for artistic production, mediation, and transaction ... [and a] paradigm to account for the imbrication of the creative economy and the urban environment as well as the interplay of local and global dynamics shaping Dakar's art world."[21] Grabski uses the term *art* to refer specifically to the visual and plastic arts produced in Dakar, but we argue that her concept can be extended to cinema. The filmmakers in our book depict Dakar as a "worlding city," as defined by Ananya Roy and Aihwa Ong: "Worlding in this sense is linked to the idea of emergence, to the claims that global situations are always in formation. Worlding projects remap relationships of power at different scales and localities, but they seem to form a critical mass in urban centers."[22] The films we study are both creations and representations of the city as well as of the complex dynamics between Dakar and "multiple elsewheres," as referenced in scholarship by Achille Mbembe and Sarah Nuttall and by Mamadou Diouf and Rosalind Fredericks. Just as Mbembe and Nuttall emphasize the African continent's interconnectedness with other places in the world, Diouf and Fredricks insist on the African city as a particular site of global connection and exchanges. All of the filmmakers in this book represent the urban capital city "while fleshing out connections with multiple elsewheres—other cities, 'home' villages, the global."[23]

While these filmmakers live and work in Dakar, their films may not be shown internationally or even on the big screen. However, this does not mean that they do not play a critical role in global cinema. Grabski contends "that the global art world is not limited to blockbuster museum exhibitions, biennales, or art fairs in Europe or North America. In Dakar, far more artists earn their livelihoods from making and selling art than are known to the curators, critics, or decision makers associated with global art world institutions."[24] Since we began our research on contemporary Senegalese cultural production and our fieldwork in Dakar in 2012, we have noticed the same phenomenon regarding cinema. Filmmakers working in Dakar may not regularly screen their films at international film festivals such as Cannes or the Festival panafricain du cinéma et de la télévision de Ouagadougou (FESPACO), but they are often well known within the Senegalese cinematic community, are crafting international networks outside of the standard film festival circuit, and are creating works that are socially and politically engaged at both the local and international levels in an attempt to better their city, country, and continent. The films manifest a deep understanding of the ways the world shapes life in Dakar as well as the potential of Senegalese urban dynamics to renegotiate global networks. According to contemporary Senegalese filmmaker Joseph Gaï Ramaka, whose work we analyze in this book, "global cinema cannot exist without the individual. It is necessary to think about both."[25] As much as Senegalese films examined in this book are products of and reflections upon their local dynamics, they are also interventions within global exchanges situated in and around Senegal as a geographical and conceptual site.

Our focus on Dakar, its films and filmmakers, and their connections to other sites draws on and contributes to recent scholarly concepts about the African city. Mbembe and Nuttall write of the importance of Africanist scholarship in defying the predominant narratives of Africa as "an object *apart from the world*."[26] They highlight reasons why present-day scholarship has failed to represent "the embeddedness in multiple elsewheres of which the continent actually speaks" and to "describe the novelty and originality of this continent in all its complexity."[27] One of their suggested strategies for redefining the image of Africa is to reimagine it as "a space of flows, of flux, of translocation, with multiple nexuses of entry and exit points. . . . The continent [they] have in mind exists only as a function of circulation and of circuits. It is fundamentally in contact with an *elsewhere*."[28]

Similarly, in the introduction to the published proceedings of the first Ateliers de la pensée, a four-day gathering of African and Afro-diasporic intellectuals and artists held in Dakar and Saint-Louis in 2016, organizers Mbembe and Sarr establish one of the foundational tenets of the symposium as "the intertwining and the community between Africa and the world," which deteriorates the illusion of "a long-standing and supposedly inherent separation between the symbolic 'Africa' and the space of the world."[29] Such thinking informs our study of urban Senegalese cinema in dialogue with cultural production from other global urban sites and communities. While cinema from urban Senegal is decidedly a product of specific local conditions of creativity, infrastructure, and belonging, it is simultaneously a contributor to the global flows of cinematic productions and discourse that shape meaning about urban Senegal, Africa and its cities, the world, and the relations between all of these sites.

Margins and Belonging

Contemporary Senegalese cinema and its exchanges with international, rural, and other urban contexts are especially important for rethinking the city as they become archives for inequities and imaginative spaces for greater inclusion and freedom. As the filmmakers in this book offer critiques and alternatives through their films and their filmmaking practices, the city opens up to a range of individuals and communities who have been generally marginalized and excluded from dominant discourses, opportunities, and practices of urban space. These filmmakers directly depict the realities of that exclusion, yet their cinematic work becomes an avenue through which citizens of the city might transcend, however provisionally, those realities, whether as cinematic subjects or as spectators. Throughout the book, we examine films that interrogate the lines separating the boundary in Dakar between inside/outside, self/other, and community/strangers.

Scholars have recently countered the heretofore prevailing view of African cities as sites for the confluence of personal misery, political malfeasance, and infrastructural decay. They argue that such a focus on urban problems is limiting and ignores the great amount of dynamism, creativity, and grassroots problem-solving that is essential. Mbembe and Nuttall posit that the African city "has been reduced in most recent (and less recent) literature to an experience of the pathological and of the abnormal" and point out that studies often forget "that the city always also operates as a site of fantasy, desire, and imagination."[30] Of course, African cities have their share of social ills, which often lead to entrenched inequities and urban residents living on the margins. Those harsh realities of exclusion and marginalization are certainly part of contemporary urban dynamics in African countries, including Senegal, and the filmmakers in our book are attuned to those inequities and invested in starkly depicting them. The films we study often serve as despairing cris de coeur that lay bare the difficulties for residents in navigating inequitable urban spaces. In this way, they are significant social and political interventions that provoke local residents and communities to enact change for greater inclusion.

However, the filmmakers and their films cannot be viewed simply through the lens of social problems. Their ability to imagine and reimagine the potential of Dakar and other Senegalese urban spaces for belonging, citizenship, community, and ingenuity, even as they directly depict urban injustices, marks this group of filmmakers as unique. The recent scholarship that denounces a prevailing miserabilist paradigm for African cities has also reconceptualized and redeployed the role of individuals, their relations with one another, and their human creativity and collaboration in delineating the parameters of urban existence, even outside of sanctioned social and political contexts. Urban dwellers are not simply subjected to the exclusion perpetuated by hegemonic power dynamics and political indifference, with the state as their only recourse. Instead, they are able to craft their own inclusive relations and social structures. Again, the recent scholarship on African urban dynamics emphasizes human potential to transform urban spaces to be more equitable, just, and inclusive.[31] African cities, while sites for hierarchal privilege and exclusion, can also be generative of interpersonal relationships, collective creativity, and communal resilience, which, in turn, counter exclusively pathological paradigms of African cities that center inequities. The filmmakers in our book work directly to prioritize inclusion and collaborative participation in their filmmaking practices as well as in their filmic depictions of Senegalese urban life. Through their filmmaking and films, they emphasize the life and vibrancy of Dakar and its residents and propose inclusive, equitable possibilities for urban existence that transcend harsh realities. Our approach to the work of these filmmakers is especially informed by Diouf and Fredericks's concept of "arts of citizenship." They use this term to describe "forms of experimentation, adaptation, and negotiation surrounding claims to the rights and rewards of the city" that produce "spaces of belonging," which are not always politically or socially codified.[32] We show that the filmmakers examined in subsequent chapters are contributing to this process in Dakar.

Much of our research for this book has come from extensive and consistent fieldwork since 2012, including visits to cinematic sites in Dakar (movie theaters, government offices, filmmakers' home studios, television production offices) and sustained visits and interviews with filmmakers. This ethnographic research figures prominently in chapter 1, where we provide a comprehensive overview of the production, financing, distribution, and viewership realities for twenty-first-century cinema in Dakar. The participant observations threaded throughout the book highlight the ways those in the film community are consciously navigating and renegotiating the cinematic infrastructures of Dakar, from development and production to distribution and audience engagement. We show how they are creating alternative cinematic networks and institutions that work around those failings of the officially sanctioned infrastructure. The infrastructure of urban Senegalese cinema can often frustrate, block, and limit filmmakers, films, and viewers in Dakar. While we account for the challenges to sustainable existence and cinematic creation in urban Senegal, we emphasize the productive possibilities that persist alongside those challenges. These innovations, in turn, often spur improvement and change within the official institutions of cinema. In this way, we argue, members of the twenty-first-century Senegalese cinematic community parallel urban residents, whose human ingenuity is continually on display as they engage with and overcome their own social deficits and exclusion.

Along with highlighting the contemporary ingenuity and problem-solving in Senegalese cinema through our ethnographic research, chapter 1 details the historical trajectory of Senegalese cinema within the context of the postcolonial creation of Dakar as an essential site for

Senegalese cultural production. These cultural dynamics have endured into the twenty-first century and provide an ideological paradigm in which contemporary filmmakers create and work. We then proceed to a comprehensive overview of the production, financing, distribution, and viewership realities for twenty-first-century cinema in Dakar, pointing to its challenges but also the various ways that filmmakers, government officials, theater owners, and other members of the cinematic community are confronting those difficulties. Finally, we discuss the documentary form in African cinema and its importance to contemporary cinema in enacting social and aesthetic change. All of the films that we study are documentaries, and thus we frame our corpus within this larger cinematic form on the continent. Although the documentary is often minimized within global cinema culture in favor of feature films, it is a readily accessible, socially meaningful form of cinema in Africa. We argue that it is precisely because of this fraught positioning of African documentary filmmaking within global cinema that it merits direct critical attention. The tension surrounding its importance in African societies and cinemas in relation to its general devaluation on a global scale produces insights into the ways that urban dynamics on the continent interface with global currents and how cinema can intervene in and shape those relations.

Chapter 1 provides an important cultural, social, political, and cinematic context for the filmmakers and their films that we analyze more closely throughout the chapters that follow. In chapters 2–5, we detail the conceptualizations and attempts of our filmmakers to fashion reconfigured cinematic dynamics in Dakar, which, in turn, contribute to the possibilities for widespread renegotiation of urban life. In each of these chapters, we highlight two filmmakers who have been key figures of Senegalese cinema in the twenty-first century, often drawing from our interviews to foreground their filmmaking practices and conceptualizations of contemporary cinema in Dakar. We have intentionally chosen to analyze filmmakers who were born and/or raised in Senegal and who have primarily lived and worked in Dakar, with the goal of centering local issues, perspectives, and communities through the voices of those on the ground. The films we examine intervene in a specific dimension of contemporary urban life in Senegal, including strategies of community building in migration, wrestling, hip-hop, and social protest; natural resource management; extreme urban precarity; and intersectional feminine identities. We argue that, despite facing challenges in the Senegalese cinema industry, these filmmakers are using innovative ways to bring attention to critical urban social issues and to take on the "arduous task" set forth by Sarr to create a stronger, more inclusive society and country.

Chapter 2 details urban actors' reshaping of national belonging and lineage through migration, wrestling, hip-hop, and social activism. The national body is significantly conceptualized and structured through values, practices, relations, and tropes of masculinity. The residents of Dakar who aim to reconfigure the body politic in the aforementioned cultural areas, as well as the filmmakers documenting these subjects, thus engage with and reframe notions of masculinity. We present this argument through analysis of three films: Moussa Sène Absa's *Yoolé* and Rama Thiaw's *Boul fallé: La voie de la lutte* and *The Revolution Won't Be Televised*. We argue that urban realities, compounded by global narratives and hierarchies, can leave urban Senegalese men, especially young ones, feeling impotent to transform their lives and communities. This, in turn, can provoke young urban residents to undertake perilous journeys abroad. Sène Absa's documentary explores the reasons why the migrants undertake these journeys in the first place and undercuts many of the predominant narratives and ideologies of these migrant men.[33] He emphasizes the failures of the Wade administration to provide for its citizens and how the government pushed young Senegalese in particular to emigrate in search of opportunities abroad. Sène Absa emphasizes throughout *Yoolé* that other tactics are possible for urban Senegalese. Similarly, Thiaw presents a number of additional alternatives in her two films, including social activism, wrestling, and hip-hop. Both *Boul fallé: La voie de la lutte* and *The Revolution Won't Be Televised* document the realities for Dakarois men of peri-urban exclusion and political corruption, but they also reconfigure through innovative cinematic techniques the gendered and social possibilities that are produced within these urban domains.

Chapter 3 examines how water management impacts urban and rural residents alike in Senegal yet in different ways. In Joseph Gaï Ramaka's *Plan Jaxaay!*, residents living in a peripheral suburb of Dakar are manipulated and abandoned by Wade and his administration after a water redistribution plan leads to flooding in their neighborhood. Ramaka's film details their own local engagement with this problem and often criticizes the government for its disregard while focusing on alternative, organic solutions. Abdoul Aziz Cissé's *La brèche* considers the area around the city of Saint-Louis. The documentary, like *Plan Jaxaay!*, captures the aftermath of the national government's miscalculation in keeping ocean water from flooding Saint-Louis. Their project to breach a section of the land surrounded by the water leads to the destruction of a rural, coastal community. The film, like Ramaka's, acknowledges the devastation that occurs but is more invested in showing how local, indigenous knowledge, practices, and traditions are essential for the sustainability of rural Senegalese communities, even as the national government privileges urban knowledge and locales.

In chapter 4, we study a film by Adams Sie and another by Khady Sylla. Both filmmakers amplify the voices of those in the extreme margins of urban life in Senegal. In *Voix silencieuses*, Sie examines street children, while Sylla films maids and houseworkers in *Le monologue de la muette*. We witness the severe economic and educational marginalization that the dynamics between Dakar and other sites enact upon these nearly invisible urban residents. Yet these films also reveal the communities, subjectivities, and voices that are forged, even provisionally, within urban precarity. These phenomena include cinematic and artistic articulations as well since the filmmakers, in both films, equally implicate their own identities and actions as urban residents and as filmmakers. Sie and Sylla articulate their own subjectivities and consider that they themselves, for all of their privileges, share and participate in the social exclusion that their subjects face and might even exacerbate it through their filmmaking.

In chapter 5, we use an intersectional lens to look at two films that document women's experiences with marginalization and acceptance. While in chapter 1 we consider how women filmmakers are uniquely situated to document social exclusion in Senegal and how they often do so through the documentary form, in this chapter we focus more deeply on these issues through an examination of Khardiata Pouye's *Cette couleur qui me dérange* and Angèle Diabang's *Sénégalaises et Islam*. Pouye's documentary examines the societal pressure Senegalese women feel to lighten their skin and exposes the medical dangers associated with this practice. She powerfully evokes the scope of this practice, called *khessal* in Wolof, showing how it functions within domestic, private space, as well as the way it continues to exist due to international economic relations and global standards of beauty. Like Pouye, Diabang also creates a site where the multiplicity of women's voices is heard and witnessed, using interviews with Muslim women about their views on Islam and their gendered experiences. The female interviewees speak about diverse topics, such as veiling, the intersection of beauty, desirability, and modesty, gender equality, Islam's influence on politics and social relations, Islamic extremism and Sharia law, and the possibility of an understanding between the West and predominantly Muslim countries or Islamic states. Both Pouye and Diabang use the artistic form of documentary to treat social issues that impact women in particular but that are often silenced or ignored in society and on-screen.

Our book provides insights into the complexity and variability of quotidian and creative existence within urban Senegal and cinema's potential to create societal change. We profile the imaginations, practices, and realities of those filmmakers who live and work in Dakar and who place the imaginations, practices, and realities of the city's residents on-screen. The creative and the quotidian, the cinematic and the material, the lived and the imagined: these all hold a place in our understanding of how contemporary cinema has intervened in the city of Dakar specifically and the country of Senegal generally. Our book contributes to the important and sustained scholarship on African cities and their dynamic, essential roles in ongoing global relations and issues. Through an analysis of original and creative films that amplify the voices and experiences of those who inhabit Senegalese urban and peri-urban areas, we show how Senegalese cinema has the power to help create "a new civilization that will place humanity at the center of its preoccupations, by proposing a healthier balance between the different orders, be they economic, cultural, or spiritual."[34] We argue that Dakar, originally the birthplace of African cinema, now stands as one of the foremost centers of urban cinematic innovation on the African continent.

1

Screening Urban Senegal

Social Interventions through Cinematic Infrastructure, Innovation, and Form

In May 2018, when we were in Dakar conducting ethnographic research on Senegalese film culture, we were invited by the Direction de la cinématographie, under the Ministry of Culture, to the national premiere of the documentary *Poisson d'or, poisson africain* by Thomas Grand and Moussa Diop. The screening was held at the newly inaugurated Complexe Cinématographique Ousmane Sembène along the Atlantic coast, off the corniche and adjacent to the Magic Land amusement park (fig. 1.1).[1] The impressive complex features three theaters, a discotheque with a capacity of eight hundred people, a restaurant, and a gaming room. After the screening, filmmakers, leaders in the cinema industry, and guests all gathered in the area near the restaurant to socialize. The event provided an opportunity to view an award-winning Senegalese film and for those in the film industry to network and engage in dialogue within a sparkling new cinematic complex, representing the vitality and strength of community within contemporary Senegalese cinema in Dakar. The premiere seemingly refuted the narrative of crisis about Senegalese cinema that has been prominently voiced during the

FIGURE 1.1. The Complexe Cinématographique Ousmane Sembène in Dakar, 2018. Photo by Molly Krueger Enz.

twenty-first century by concerned members of the cinematic community and outside observers and critics.

During a 2012 interview with Agence France-Presse, Senegalese filmmaker Mamadou Ndiaye offered a bleak, if not entirely despairing, outlook: "I see Senegalese cinema not as something dead, but as something which is diseased, on the operating table, in a coma of course. Now will this sickly thing wake up . . . or will it die?"[2] In a 2013 article promoting a screening of Moussa Touré's *La pirogue*, the British Film Institute couldn't resist framing the film as a rare outcropping of hope amid the barren landscape of Senegal's waning film industry.[3] CGTN Africa reiterated Senegalese cinema's problems in 2017, and a 2018 article published on the site Africa Is a Country announced in its title that "Senegalese Cinema Doesn't Exist."[4] This perceived crisis extends beyond issues related to production and distribution; it can also be seen though the emphasis on-screen of supposedly African problems. Manthia Diawara notes the development of "social problem films," which are driven by the imbrication of European funding and misperceptions of African societies. Diawara articulates the disconnect between the production sources of such films and the lived experience of Africans: "Many of the films were made on order for European institutions which thrive on portrayals of Africa's tragic situation, but possess little understanding or desire to meet people on the ground."[5] Crisis has become a lens through which many people perceive and understand the cinema of Senegal. Events organized by the Direction de la cinématographie like the premiere of *Poisson d'or, poisson africain* and the creation of the resplendent Complexe Cinématographique Ousmane Sembène in a prominent location help to reshape and alter the perceptions and narratives of cinema in Dakar that have tended to focus on problems. However, although there is a desire and an effort among those working in the industry to reimagine Senegalese cinema, it is undeniable that significant obstacles exist. These challenges have been on full display for any urban moviegoer in Dakar who has eschewed a *cinéma de luxe*, like the Sembène theater, in favor of a screening at one of the city's smaller movie houses during the first two decades of the twenty-first century.

In June 2016, we visited two local theaters, though we were unable to attend screenings while there. First, in the crowded, working-class neighborhood of Gueule Tapée, we eventually located the Bada Ciné.

While we had found the address online, it was still difficult to be sure if we were entering the right building since there wasn't any visible signage. Proceeding with caution but hoping that we were in the right place, we went up a narrow, twisting staircase and entered an antechamber where piles of neglected video cassettes were stacked against the walls. This was our first sign that we were in some type of movie location. We had still not encountered another person, let alone an employee asking us to purchase a ticket or directing us to the screening room. We decided to go through a curtain at the other end of the antechamber, and there we found the screening room. A film—it appeared to be an Indian movie—was playing on a relatively small screen in the rather cramped room that contained just a few tiny rows of battered theater seats. There was only one moviegoer in the room along with the theater's single employee, who grabbed our hands and, seeing that we were *toubabs*—the West and Central African term meaning "Westerner"—took us directly to the office of the theater's owner.

Later that same month, we visited the Cinéma Awa in the Dakar suburb of Pikine. We were accompanied by our friend who lived in Pikine, so the taxi driver knew exactly where to go. The theater was decidedly less hidden than Bada Ciné, with a prominent sign atop the tall, white building. Out front, there were easily accessible ticket windows that overlooked a spacious plaza, which was quite full of people. Cinéma Awa was seemingly more popular than Bada Ciné. While we stood in front of the theater talking to its manager, a good number of young men were milling around us, listening in on our conversation, many of them buying tickets to enter. We thought we might join the audience as well. However, as our conversation with the manager wound down, our friend subtly but decidedly steered us away from the theater and into a taxi. He quickly told us that the cinema is a well-known location for crime and drugs, and his impression was that many of the young men were going in to participate in these activities rather than to view the film. He suspected that those who seemed invested in eavesdropping on our conversation about the current state of movie theaters in Dakar were potentially targeting us as robbery victims. While our visits to these theaters might not have been representative of moviegoing for typical residents of Dakar since our trips were certainly shaped by the fact that we are white Americans who don't speak Wolof, it is clear that the infrastructure of Senegalese cinema, as represented by these two small neighborhood theaters, faces severe issues. These challenges have become even more apparent since our 2016 visits, as both theaters have subsequently been shuttered.

Our experiences with movie theaters in Dakar, from the energy and comfort of the premiere at the Ousmane Sembène Complex to the dilapidation of the Bada Ciné and the criminal repurposing of the Cinéma Awa, demonstrate the duality within contemporary Senegalese film culture. On one hand, challenges exist in all areas of urban Senegalese cinema. On the other, life and dynamism are central to this film culture. From our consistent ethnographic work on Dakar's film industry, we have come to an in-depth, sustained understanding of both the challenges and successes within contemporary Senegalese cinema produced and distributed in Dakar. Due to these experiences, we argue that the narrative of crisis surrounding Senegalese cinema is incomplete. Through this chapter, we complicate and nuance the perspective that Senegalese cinema is dying, or doesn't even exist, by showing the wide range of innovative solutions to cinematic problems proposed by members of the film community in Dakar. From the Direction de la cinématographie, owners of local theaters, filmmakers, festival organizers, and directors of cultural centers to other cinematic participants, those in contemporary Senegalese film culture are consistently aware of the challenges they face and persistently engaged with potential solutions to those problems. In this way, our view of Senegalese film culture in Dakar is aligned with that of filmmaker Khady Sylla. Sylla admits that there are certainly challenges in Senegalese cinema but that they can be overcome: "Senegalese cinema is sick, it's true, but not as seriously as it may seem. There is still hope for healing, I think."[6] Sylla adds that cinema is an art form that requires patience.[7] In order to discover appropriate solutions necessary for this healing process, it is important to take the time to continue fighting for change, which members of Dakar's film community are demonstrably doing.

The media elaboration of a despairing view of Senegalese cinema that ignores the ingenuity and creativity of that same film culture parallels the scholarly and critical perceptions of African cities as sites of perpetual failure, lack, and inequities that we identified in our introduction. Just as African urban centers, including Dakar, are too often seen only through the lens of crisis, contemporary Senegalese cinema has been overly understood exclusively through its problems. Like the scholars of African cities who we referenced in our introduction and who have helped shift the paradigm in African urban studies from crisis to ingenuity, from restriction to opportunity, from problems to possibilities, we attempt in this chapter to contribute to a reassessment of twenty-first-century urban Senegalese cinema that centers the creativity, collaboration, and innovation present in film production, distribution, viewership, and form while still accounting for the film industry's challenges. To this extent, we both echo and repurpose Caroline Melly's conceptual tool of *embouteillages*, or "bottlenecks," for understanding mobility and belonging in contemporary Dakar: "At the very same time that bottlenecks strained flows and limited mobility, they also held the promise of future movement. . . . To speak of embouteillage, then, was to emphasize one's expectations for a resolution of impasse, for renewed movement and for future inclusion. In this sense, the bottleneck was an instance of potential energy."[8] While throughout the rest of the book we study the work of specific filmmakers who reimagine urban life in Senegal, we devote this chapter to our ethnographic study of film culture in contemporary Dakar not only to point to the difficulties that are determinedly present but more importantly to demonstrate the ingenious solutions that members of the Dakar film community are continually crafting from their work, lives, and experiences in urban space. We begin with a historical overview of Senegalese cinema to provide context and perspective to the contemporary situation. Although Senegalese cinema of the twenty-first century faces unique challenges, as well as distinct successes, the entirety of Senegalese cinema history is marked by the tension between highs and lows. The discourse of crisis surrounding contemporary cinema is shown to be accurate but less acute than it first appears when considering the historical context of persistent challenges and sustained proposals for solutions; it is also generative of new approaches to Senegalese cinema in the twenty-first century.

The Historical Trajectory of Cinema in Senegal, 1960–2000

Léopold Sédar Senghor helped catapult Senegal to the fore of African cinema through his political and financial support of Senegalese filmmakers; he regarded cinema, alongside other artistic forms, as a tool of nation building and cultural enrichment. As a result, during the country's first decade of independence, Senegal quickly became a leader in African cinema, and a number of filmmakers emerged, most of whom produced documentaries commissioned and funded by the state and that reflected their mastery of European filmic techniques. However, the cinema of 1960s Senegal has become synonymous with Ousmane Sembène, widely considered the father of African cinema. In 1961, after establishing a successful literary career, Sembène abandoned literature in favor of cinema. He reasoned that he could reach more Senegalese people through film due to the high rates of illiteracy in Africa and the difficulties of publishing and disseminating literature in Wolof. The viability of cinema to reflect Africans back to themselves, to represent their experiences, and to articulate their challenges as well as possible solutions to those problems remained a constant throughout Sembène's cinematic career.[9] While he disagreed, publicly and vociferously, with Senghor on various political and cultural points, Sembène shared the president's view of the centrality of culture in shaping Senegalese society.

Sembène's international success and acclaim continued into the proceeding decades and served as a standard that the entirety of Senegal's national cinema strived to attain. The Senegalese governmental Ministry of Culture created a Société de cinéma (SNC) in 1973 in order to encourage and fund national cinematic productions of a greater variety than found in the 1960s. According to Manthia Diawara, the SNC's purpose "was to encourage national production in fiction and documentary films. Filmmakers were requested to submit scripts on topics ranging from juvenile delinquency and urban problems to literacy campaigns. The best scripts were selected by a group of readers who were designed by the president of the SNC."[10] The SNC also collaborated with the Association des cinéastes sénégalais to support young directors of short films. Due to sustained national support for cinema throughout the 1960s and early 70s, many filmmakers rose to prominence, including documentarians Safi Faye and Samba Félix Ndiaye. Djibril Diop Mambéty, the most notable among these filmmakers, brought new aesthetic and narrative techniques to film culture in the country. This time period also saw the proliferation of government-owned and government-supported movie theaters. Amadou T. Fofana explains that, in 1973, the community of Senegalese filmmakers was able to pressure Senghor into nationalizing Senegal's movie houses and creating a governmental body, Société sénégalaise d'importation, de distribution et d'exploitation cinématographique (SIDEC), to oversee cinematic distribution and screenings.[11] Throughout its two decades of existence, SIDEC "thrived and spread cinema nationwide by building theaters in most secondary Senegalese cities. By the late 1980s, Senegal had as many as eighty functional theaters."[12] Senegalese cinema was flourishing, and it appeared that the foundation, with its cinematic forefathers, national financial support, and global attention, was set for continued growth and recognition.

Despite this momentum, economic crises across the continent quickly put the brakes on the nation's cinematic progression as the state withdrew funding for cinematic projects and theaters across the nation began to close. James Genova highlights the impact of the global economy on the destruction of the arts, especially cinema, in West Africa: "Since the mid-1970s the entire African continent has been dealt a series of economic shocks, each of which has enabled outside agencies and governments to gain a greater control over the continent's material and creative wealth."[13] Established filmmakers, such as Sembène, continued to work but primarily with financial sustenance from international production companies. Diawara has pointed to the ways that such filmmakers have been consistently forced to rely on international funding, production, and distribution partners: "African filmmakers are directly affected by the lack of national and international industries that include the structures of production, distribution, and exhibition.... Francophone directors are not only forced to depend upon the French Ministry of Coopération and similar offices for the production of their films, but they also face problems of programming the films in movie theaters in their own countries and distributing them elsewhere."[14] As a result of the lack of theaters, oftentimes the films made by African directors were never screened in their home countries. Diawara posits that francophone filmmakers from the continent "have been fighting to change this situation, which Tunisian filmmaker Tahar Cheriaa calls 'les écrans colonisés,' and to set up new plans for the development of film industries in Africa."[15]

While established filmmakers working from the late 1970s onward became increasingly reliant on international film partners, burgeoning filmmakers were no longer able to learn their trade, hone their skills, produce their films, and distribute them within their native country. In 1995, Elizabeth Mermin observed, "The excitement and motivation of the 1970s, when the industry was new and money was available for productions, film school abroad, and distribution, have vanished."[16] The dearth of new Senegalese filmmakers in the late 1970s, the 1980s, and most of the 1990s becomes readily apparent in Françoise Pfaff's historical overview of Senegalese cinema in her book *À l'écoute du cinéma sénégalais*. Ending her description of the fertile period of the 1970s with references to Mambéty and Ndiaye, she transitions to the proceeding decades with the very general but telling sentence, "Then, Senegalese cinema continues with change and continuity."[17] This seemingly antithetical description points to the fact that, just as there have always been successes and challenges and highs and lows in Senegalese cinema, change and continuity are its defining characteristics. Pfaff mentions a number of filmmakers and their films that have subsequently contributed meaningfully to the continuation of the country's film culture. However, she only includes one film from the 1980s (Cheikh Ngaïdo Ba's *Xew xew* from 1983) and the films of three cineastes from the mid to late 1990s. Due to the financial exigencies of these decades in Senegal, there exists a noticeable gap in the history of the country's film culture during which filmmakers became increasingly rare.

Movie theaters suffered a similar fate during the last two and a half decades of the twentieth century. Fofana writes that the national government was forced to divest from theater ownership, selling the movie houses to private investors who quickly turned the properties into real estate projects. Genova explains another factor of the time period that transformed cinema viewership: "The late 1970s saw the introduction of video technology, which presented another outlet for viewing movies independent of the public space of the theater."[18] As a result, viewers began watching shows and films in the privacy of their homes, changing the way in which images were consumed and resulting in "a different form of socialization than the movie theater."[19] Consequently, "by the mid-1990s, only a handful of theaters remained in activity in Dakar, and as of 1995, there were fewer than ten operational theaters nationwide."[20] Filmmakers and viewers alike had experienced substantial constrictions and transformations of Senegalese film culture by the close of the twentieth century.

Governmental Funding and Support for Cinema in the Twenty-First Century

With the turn of the twenty-first century, Senegal found itself with a new president. Abdoulaye Wade and his administration quickly proposed myriad new initiatives, including the adoption of a revised constitution. The twenty-first century promised to be an epoch of change and improvement for Senegalese citizens, and Dakar was the epicenter for this shift. The promise for change extended to Senegal's film industry, most notably in the creation of the Direction de la cinématographie under the Ministry of Culture and Communication in the national government. This administrative body was inaugurated in 2000 with the broad objective of regulating and promoting the cinematic and audiovisual sectors. Its mission includes developing training opportunities, providing technical and financial support, coordinating international collaboration, and conserving, restoring, and valorizing the cinematic and audiovisual heritage of Senegal. Two years later, just as President Wade was announcing and undertaking his momentous urban construction projects in Dakar, he signed a law intended to regulate and support the cinema industry. The legislation created the Fonds de promotion de l'industrie cinématographique et audiovisuelle (FOPICA) to review and oversee competitive bids from filmmakers, distributors, production companies, theater owners, and other members of the film industry for government funding support. These financial grants, awarded and managed by the Direction de la cinématographie, were intended to support cinematic and audiovisual production in Senegal of all genres (documentary, fiction, animation, web creation, video games, etc.) and lengths (short films, medium-length documentaries, feature films, etc.).[21] The FOPICA was also created to address the financial and infrastructural needs of theater owners, distributors, and festival organizers. In short, the FOPICA was envisioned as a corrective to the government's financial abandonment of Senegalese cinema in the 1980s and 1990s due to the country's economic problems.

While the government was unable to financially support Senegalese cinema at the end of the twentieth century, Senegalese filmmakers continued to make and produce films. However, facing the realities of cinematic funding and infrastructure in the country, many of these filmmakers followed the example of Sembène and relied increasingly on European funders, distributors, and audiences. Some acclaimed Senegalese directors who have followed Sembène and Mambéty, such as Joseph Gaï Ramaka, Moussa Touré, and Moussa Sène Absa, undertook their cinematic formation in Paris and have been forced to rely heavily on European financing to produce their films, which are typically distributed through international film festivals and rarely in Senegal.[22] Wade's creation of the FOPICA was partially intended to bring such filmmakers home, providing them with the financial and technical support necessary to produce their films in Senegal and to show them to Senegalese audiences. However, similarly to many of the president's construction projects, the law was never put into effect, and Senegalese cinema continued to struggle through the first decade of the twenty-first century.

Finally, Wade's successor, Macky Sall, made the decision to augment the FOPICA to one billion West African CFA francs (FCFA) in 2014 (US$2 million), which allowed the grants to become a viable source of support for filmmakers.[23] As the FOPICA was being put into place, the then minister of culture, Abdoul Aziz Mbaye, announced in May 2014 that 11.5 million FCFA (US$23,000) would be dedicated to the rehabilitation of four movie theaters in the capital city of Dakar. The theaters selected for renovation included the aforementioned Awa in Pikine, Bada Ciné in Gueule Tapée, Cinéma Christa in Grand Yoff, and Médina in Tilène. Mbaye stated, "It was an effort that we made so that the movie theaters revive themselves. After that, it is necessary to help the theaters acquire new technologies. However, this will be in the context of a public-private partnership."[24] This augmentation in funding for filmmakers and theater owners to encourage the (re)growth of cinema in Dakar was part of the Ministry of Culture's five-year plan for Senegalese cinema launched on February 24, 2015, at the Grand Théâtre National. The project proposed various actions that were "concrete, planned, and budgeted for the period of 2016–2020."[25] Unsurprisingly, interest in the FOPICA from members of Dakar's film society was immediate and has only increased since then, leading to the creation of a management committee and individual office space for the FOPICA in the Maison de la Culture Douta Seck, apart from the Direction de la cinématographie.[26]

The Direction de la cinématographie and the FOPICA have initiated institutional and infrastructural changes, aimed to improve the conditions for theater owners, spectators, and filmmakers, and created a visibly vibrant film community, as evidenced by the premiere of *Poisson d'or, poisson africain* that we attended in 2018. Abdoul Aziz Cissé, former head of the Division des études, industries techniques, formation et planification within the Direction de la cinématographie and current head of the management committee of the FOPICA, is a well-regarded filmmaker himself. He told us that when he was offered his position in the Direction de la cinématographie in 2012, he was encouraged to accept it by fellow filmmakers because they believed he would be in a unique place to advocate for and enact administrative changes that would be in the best interest of filmmakers. Indeed, he and the Direction de la cinématographie have implemented a participatory model of advocacy and leadership, which involves as many filmmakers as possible in the deliberations and decision-making process. This has allowed Cissé to be an intermediary, particularly for the rising generation of filmmakers, helping them advance their careers. Cissé's analysis of the current state of Senegal's movie houses also maintains a filmmaker's perspective.

Despite the barrier created due to the closing of theaters, Cissé explained in 2016 that a solution was underway to deal with the lack of venues in which to view films and to renew the presence of a national cinema. Since 2011, the Direction de la cinématographie had been acquiring servers and was in the process of collecting films to create a "memory archive."[27] Ideally, large cities in Senegal would each have a cinema complex where local citizens could view films. This project is an early example of the general transformations offered to Senegalese cinema by the growth of digital technology and the innovative attempts to harness them by members of the industry. Former director of the Direction de la cinématographie, Hugues Diaz posits, "Cinema, as an art, industry, and technique, experienced numerous upheavals throughout its history. . . . Foreseeable or not, the mutation linked to digital technology is inscribed in the continuity of the technical."[28] He adds that the focus should be on the promise of these changes rather than complaints about the obstacles facing moviegoing due to technological advances: "We should interrogate and decipher the digital era, which is ours, through a communal will to serve as stakeholders and actors in this change."[29] Contemporary administrators of Senegalese cinema, while aware of the challenges and difficulties in the industry, do not share in the discourse of crisis that has prevailed for too long. They are thinking creatively and collectively to propose solutions to the problems that do exist, without allowing them to predominate Senegalese film culture.

The need to think creatively, remain patient, and continue fighting, as proposed by Khady Sylla, had perhaps never been more evident than during the early months of the COVID-19 global pandemic. Project filming and production were suspended both in Senegal and internationally, which meant that those involved in the film industry at all levels found themselves without work for an extended period of time, exacerbating the industry pressures that were already present and possibly setting back hard-won progress. Despite the undeniable burden placed on the Senegalese cinema industry due to COVID-19, the early period of the pandemic was a moment for cinematic actors in Senegal to once again deploy adaptability and ingenuity. While government subsidies helped to alleviate the financial strain of having to suspend film projects and the inability to publicly screen films in theaters, other interventions required more innovation. One positive outcome that resulted from the national curfew and quarantine in Senegal during the pandemic was a joint initiative by the Direction de la cinématographie and the national television channel RTS to screen Senegalese films on weekends. The series *Senegalese Cinema at Home* provided an opportunity to promote the work of Senegalese directors on the small screen. While film productions could not continue under the curfew, Diaz and the Direction de la cinématographie found the potential within these conditions to repurpose television for cultivating cinephilia among Senegalese. Lindiwe Dovey and Estrella Sendra highlight similar efforts by the Centre Yennenga, a filmmaking and cultural center in Dakar founded by Franco-Senegalese filmmaker Alain Gomis. During the early days of the pandemic in April 2020, when film festivals were being canceled and movie theaters were closing around the world, the Centre Yennenga was "a pioneer in offering an online film program."[30] Members of the Centre Yennenga's staff disseminated details about films in an impromptu fashion, followed by links and passwords so that viewers could watch them streaming online over a forty-eight-hour period. As was true for

Screening Urban Senegal

FIGURE 1.2. The logo for the Centre Yennenga in Dakar, 2023, that sits above the entrance and features legendary princess Yennenga, a brave warrior who is considered the mother of the Mossi kingdom. Photo by Molly Krueger Enz.

the film industry, which faced so many challenges during the pandemic, "it was not easy for the Centre Yennenga to undertake such a venture. They had to convince African filmmakers to let them share their films online."[31] However, the Centre Yennenga carefully organized its programming, and African filmmakers generously agreed to share their work due to a "collaborative and activist spirit."[32] Instead of highlighting the inherent crisis of the virus, the Senegalese film community focused on retaining and reinforcing its strengths and opportunities. These efforts aimed to help Senegalese cinema survive the pandemic and eventually heal and grow. The response to the COVID-19 pandemic and its impact on Senegalese cinema by the Direction de la cinématographie and the Centre Yennenga are just a few examples of how resilient, innovative, and adaptable the cinema industry has become through the first two decades of this century. The difficulties previously faced by the film industry, far from being moments marking the death of Senegalese cinema, have prepared it to respond creatively and effectively to almost any challenge it encounters.

The progressive support for cinema at the national level during the twenty-first century has seemingly opened a new path that will only bring more opportunities for urban filmmakers, spectators, and theater owners. However, as is so often the case with infrastructural, top-down "solutions" to widespread social problems, there are limits, challenges, and debates to these undertakings. For example, some theater owners stated that they did not receive the announced funds allocated to the revitalization of local theaters, claims reinforced by the closure of those sites such as the Bada and Awa. Directors have argued that there is a lack of transparency around the funds offered and distributed by the FOPICA.[33]

Despite these issues, recent government efforts have certainly gone a long way to combat the view of Senegalese cinema as dead or dying, as evidenced by the international success of films partially funded by the FOPICA. Alain Gomis's *Félicité* won the Jury Grand Prix at the 2017 Berlin International Film Festival and was shortlisted for the Best Foreign Language Film at the 2018 Academy Awards as the official entry from Senegal. *Atlantique*, written and directed by French Senegalese director Mati Diop, Djibril Diop Mambéty's niece, was in competition at the 2019 Cannes Film Festival—the first feature directed by a Black woman to compete. The festival's jury ultimately awarded *Atlantique* the Grand Prix. Shortly after Cannes, Netflix acquired the film for worldwide distribution. By the end of the year, *Atlantique* was on numerous lists across the globe of the best films of the year, including Barack Obama's, it was shortlisted for the Best International Feature at the 2020 Academy Awards as Senegal's entry, and Diop had done scores of interviews with the international film press during which she spoke directly about contemporary Senegalese society.

However, the reimagination of Senegalese cinema in Dakar goes beyond sanctioned forms of funding and infrastructural support and the international success of directors like Gomis or Diop—both of whom were born and raised in France. We prefer to focus the rest of this chapter and subsequent ones on the urban cinematic practices of those who choose not to, or are unable to, participate in the "migration of cultural capital in an age of globalization" articulated by Ekotto and Harrow.[34] As they argue, this development in the cultural field within postindependence Senegal has led to significant issues and challenges for those culture makers, including participants in film culture, who are "left behind." Urban Senegalese film participants who are located in Dakar and whose cinematic practices and conceptualizations are distinct products of and interventions in the processes of the capital city are often neglected—by critics, viewers, and funders—in favor of Senegalese or Franco-Senegalese filmmakers who have cachet in Europe. This inequitable comparative view centered around Europe coincides with the conceptual framework that has far too often judged contemporary urban Africa as inadequate in relation to cities of the Global North, refusing to understand it on its own terms.

Therefore, in the next section we turn away from official governmental interventions in Senegalese cinema to highlight the reconceptualization of cinema viewing practices proposed by theater owners, distributors, filmmakers, and other invested members of the cinema culture in Dakar. As they work with the support of the Senegalese government and/or international partners, they focus on the lived experiences and social realities of urban residents in providing greater access to cinema. We reveal that the strategies and discourse of these cinematic actors have been essential counterexamples to the discourse around Senegalese cinema's inadequacies in the twenty-first century by demonstrating its vibrancy, adaptability, and ingenuity. Even as infrastructural challenges persist in Senegalese cinema and governmental solutions to those problems proliferate, contributors to Dakar's film culture continue to prioritize local, homegrown, urban interventions in cinema.

Cinema Beyond Theaters:
Film Festivals, Urban Screenings, Mobile Cinema, and Television

Despite the difficulties in infrastructure and funding faced by owners of local movie theaters in Dakar, they have envisioned great potential for cinema that is anchored in the specificities of the urban neighborhoods that they occupy. While these theaters have since closed, the owners' conceptualizations of the roles of cinema and of movie theaters in local communities capture the circulation of innovation and reimagination that persists in Senegalese cinema in Dakar. One of the central areas of creative thinking undertaken by the management of these theaters was the films that they screened. In an interview with Fofana, Malick

Aw, former owner of Cinéma Christa, argued that the local population is most interested in films that provide an escape: "When they watch a western movie, they do not even notice the passing of time. They forget about the present, they travel, they see other settings, and it makes people feel good. . . . I keep telling other producers that we need to be mindful of the images we show, that we should stop showing images of our dirty streets, and show beautiful scenery instead. Let's show another image of Senegal, not the usual, but positive images, and let people see that, 'hey, Senegal can be clean.'"[35] In order to "fulfill public expectation," he primarily showed action, martial arts, and police films, as did the owners of the Bada Ciné and the Awa.[36] More significantly, the theater owners conceived of their movie houses as integral contributors to and distinct products of urban communities. They emphasized selecting their films based on intimate knowledge of the neighborhoods' preferences. Despite their financial and infrastructural limitations, the owners envisioned making their theaters open, inclusive sites of belonging and community building. In particular, this included young people whom they saw as the future of local communities and the nation and thus deserving of images that resonated with their particular experiences and perspectives. Although the Cinéma Christa, Bada Ciné, and Cinéma Awa have all closed, cinema remains an essential part of the social landscape of Dakar as a localized urban tool for social change. The ways in which young people access and view films may have evolved, but the critical role of cinema in providing a way to examine and discuss social issues, gather as a community, and gain new perspectives has not changed.

One important way to offer a variety of images to the local population that doesn't have access to movie theaters and to feature the work of Senegalese and African directors is through urban film festivals. Scholars have argued that local film festivals, due to their continued sustainability, vibrancy, and nonhegemonic structure and functioning, offer opportunities for connection, dialogue, networking, and training among those working in the film industry.[37] As a result, this has led to the growth of African cinema cultures. Beti Ellerson writes, "Local festivals play the vital role of audience-building and cultivating the skills of local talent, particularly in countries with little or no infrastructure, due to the lack of movie theaters for film viewing as well as learning institutions for film training. . . . Undeniably, the realistic presentation, interconnected spirit, and popular character of continental African film festivals assume an alternative 'glocal' space to the internal events where African presence is minimal if not absent. Hence performing a vital function in interpreting and restoring the perception of community into cultural, social, and political engagement."[38] Given the essential influence that localized festivals can have on film cultures, Dovey and Sendra argue that public focus should turn more regularly to such festivals as a contribution to decolonizing cinema: "It is important to note that the majority of the film festivals in the world are audience-oriented, smaller festivals—however, it is the large festivals that continue to attract the most attention from filmmakers, the media, and scholars, due to their prestige. These stakeholder groups (including those of us who are academics) thus *also* need to take responsibility for helping usher in decolonized film festival worlds through turning our attention elsewhere."[39] This is especially pertinent for Senegal, which has hosted over one hundred film festivals in the twenty-first century.[40] While festivals were a key component of the early postcolonial cultural ideology and practice of the Senegalese state, such as Senghor's First World Festival of Negro Arts, they have contemporaneously been returned to the public as the state has had to make difficult economic choices. These smaller, grassroots festivals serve as "an active agent in forging a new cinephilia and wave of young filmmakers in Senegal, rooted in the socio-cultural context of Dakar and in the historic trajectory of the cinema produced since the early sixties."[41] Festivals are therefore another essential site for locating the contemporary urban dynamics of resiliency, problem-solving, community building, and innovation that are prevalent within Senegalese cinema.

One of the most prominent film festivals in Dakar is Image et vie, which was founded in 1999 and has been occurring annually since 2001. Despite the fact that Image et vie is much smaller than other African film festivals such as the Festival panafricain du cinéma et de la télévision de Ouagadougou (FESPACO), it has gained national and even international notoriety, underlining "the significant contribution of small film festivals to growing local film cultures and industries" in urban Senegal.[42] The festival includes film screenings and also promotes panel discussions with the filmmakers and debates about the issues presented in the films, providing the dialogic and collective dimensions that festival scholars have identified as being essential to film cultures on the continent. The Image et vie organization's credo is to promote education through images and cinema. Khalilou Ndiaye, former president of Image et vie, said in 2019 that the organization has hosted activities beyond the film festival throughout the year, including cinema clubs for kids in order to expose them to and educate them about cinema. Children not only view films but are also encouraged to develop their critical thinking skills, form their own opinions about the images they see on-screen, and then defend these views. Ndiaye posits that this critical perspective has been missing in Africa, where "people decide in our place, make choices that concern us in our place, and we remain a passive spectator."[43] He emphasizes the critical role of young people in creating a positive future for their societies and argues that they have a lot to say and should be consulted. Viewing films and thinking critically about them helps to empower the youth to raise their voices about social and political issues in their country, as well as to strengthen Senegalese cinema for future generations. This exemplifies how organizing bodies of film festivals in Africa use the festival as a way to sustain and extend the community, communication, and education that are produced from it.

The festival Films Femmes Afrique was created in 2003 with the goal of valorizing women through cinema and is funded and supported by various national and international organizations, including the Senegalese Ministry of Culture, the FOPICA, the French Embassy, and Canal Plus, demonstrating "the important function African women perform as founders, organizers, curators, and stakeholders of film festivals . . . as well as the significance of film festival practices in the promotion, advancement, and the making visible of African women in cinema, visual media, and screen culture over the past fifty years."[44] The multiweek cultural and citizen event of Films Femmes Afrique is free to attend and offers encounters with filmmakers and exchanges with various professionals (teachers, health professionals, attorneys, environmental activists) about the topics presented in the films. The festival's theme varies from year to year, but films are screened in Dakar and its suburbs as well as in various Senegalese cities such as Fatick, Kaffrine, Kaolack, Louga, Rufisque, Saint-Louis, Thiès, and Ziguinchor. The films are of various genres, including feature films, fictional shorts, and

FIGURE 1.3. Gorée Island's bay with Gorée Island Cinema's headquarters in the background, 2019. Photo by Molly Krueger Enz.

documentaries, and all highlight the subject of women's resistance but from differing perspectives, with the goal of contributing to gender equity in Senegal.[45]

In 2015, filmmaker Joseph Gaï Ramaka organized a groundbreaking film series held regularly on the beach of Gorée Island in partnership with the mayor's office. The unique event was free and open to the public, with additional ferries traveling to and from Dakar and the island to facilitate access. The application process to screen a film was open to any and all filmmakers, and this procedure offered a way for young filmmakers to raise awareness about their work and for new talent to be discovered. The screenings included events and concerts, as well as occasional discussions with the filmmakers. The film festival served as a way to both honor the past and bring people together around contemporary filmmaking in an innovative way while also decidedly linking the essential and distinct Gorée site and community to wider urban Dakar and its cinematic dynamics.

Ramaka's connective vision for film screenings has also extended out of Dakar, bringing the urban capital into cinematic contact with other regions of Senegal. Ramaka stated in our conversation with him that he has envisioned strengthening cinema in Ziguinchor, a city in Casamance, the southernmost region of Senegal.[46] Ramaka believes that making cinema more accessible and visible in a region of Senegal like Casamance, which has faced separatist violence and internal strife, would be an essential "tool for peace."[47] He says that Senegalese citizens, particularly those in Dakar, would become more aware of the residents of Casamance and the issues they face and that they would be less likely to dismiss those fellow Senegalese and their concerns as part of something "over there."[48] Ramaka envisions productive dualities between the urban capital and other Senegalese sites rather than restrictive oppositions that only compound social problems. In his visionary reinvention of film distribution in urban Senegal, Ramaka illustrates that urban cinema of the twenty-first century becomes a "place of exchange" that connects with the world and the country as a whole, without losing any of its effectiveness as an intervention in the context of the urban local.[49]

Other innovators in the film industry have looked beyond Dakar in an attempt to expand the typical audience for cinema by overcoming the inequities in access to cinema. One such group, Cinéma numérique ambulant (CNA), takes digital copies of movies to the poorer suburbs of the capital or rural communities through its mobile screening setup. Created in Benin in 2001, with national iterations in a number of francophone West African countries, the association refers to itself as a "friend of African cinema" that is committed to offering both entertainment and education to Africans who would otherwise lack access due to their geographic or socioeconomic marginalization.[50] In addition to screening African films, CNA also offers opportunities such as mobile vaccination and birth registration at its events.[51] As a cultural tool, CNA "opens up possibility and access to a collective imaginary, a source for reflection, and oral testimony and dialogue among the populations regarding different traditional practices and their evolution."[52] Coumba Sarr, director of Senegal's CNA, states that the program's objective is to allow villagers a chance to discover cinema as well as their own culture.[53] Since so many movie theaters have closed, CNA offers a way to reach remote areas with eighteen mobile units in West Africa, including two in Senegal. During the film, a moderator with a microphone helps viewers understand the plot and themes, a service intended especially for those who are illiterate. Afterward, there is a "community debate" where everyone is able to "express and enrich themselves" with a "sense of sharing."[54] Sarr argues that CNA represents "a citizen spirit" and highlights "an acknowledgement of African culture by the African population."[55]

Screening Urban Senegal

As most movie theaters in Dakar have closed, been unable to afford distribution rights, and faced dwindling numbers of customers, innovative film-viewing models that produce equitable viewing opportunities for both urban and rural residents are essential. They provide a potential spark for the dampened yet still flickering passion for film among all Senegalese, as well as for cinema's social and community import for the entire nation. Such innovations are essential for addressing the lingering question of the health of Senegalese cinema because they connect the urban capital of Dakar to rural areas in the country.

Just as the Direction de la cinématographie turned to television as an alternative means to distribute Senegalese films and cultivate an interest in cinema among Senegalese citizens during the coronavirus pandemic, other members of the Dakar film community have worked on strengthening and promoting Senegalese cinema through Senegalese television. Filmmaker Adams Sie is one such figure. After directing a number of documentary shorts and one full-length feature, in 2016 Sie created and produced a reality TV series named *Summer pencc*, which featured teams of teenagers who were first trained in filmmaking techniques and then who made short movies about current social issues pertinent to their lives—drug abuse, menstruation shaming, genital excision, teen sexuality.[56] After each team produced its own short, the audience then voted for the finished films, with one team's film being awarded as the season's winner. While the program was broadcast on the television station RTS, the content of the show and its relationship to its urban audience were directly focused on cinema. In the inaugural season, the various teams were named for well-known Senegalese filmmakers, such as team Djibril Diop Mambéty and team Khady Sylla. Sie had three goals for the project at its beginning: to empower the teenage participants in self-expression, to inspire young viewers to engage with social issues through art and technology, and for Sie to gain industry recognition from television that is not typically possible through film in Senegal. He was particularly interested in attracting young women to the seventh art, contending that there are more men than women in the Senegalese film industry.[57] Throughout the show's run, Sie remained thoughtful, adaptable, and purposeful, making various adjustments between seasons to sharpen its impact on urban viewers and their engagement with filmmaking. These developments in the show provide another example of the various innovations in film distribution and viewership that members of the Dakar film community have undertaken in the twenty-first century, which, in turn, motivate and empower the official structures and institutions in the Senegalese film industry. Estrella Sendra has argued, "Contemporary film production, particularly in the past five years (2015–2020), has been significantly shaped by grassroots initiatives. These have eventually been transformed into a structure and encouraged the implementation of FOPICA ever since 2014."[58] CinéBanlieue and Centre Yennenga are two significant grassroots cinema organizations in Dakar that have organized festivals, neighborhood screenings, and other alternative viewing options, as well as educational and informational activities. Sendra identifies that they "have had two main political implications: firstly, they have provided the government with a visible platform for the practical application of their cultural policies, such as FOPICA; secondly, they have encouraged the government to enhance its support of film and screen media production."[59] The arena of distribution and viewership exemplifies the complex dialogic dynamics found throughout all of contemporary urban

FIGURE 1.4. The screening room at the Centre Yennenga, 2023. Photo by Molly Krueger Enz.

Senegalese cinema. Governmental disinvestment from cinema has produced infrastructural challenges, but cinema actors have responded to those difficulties with unique innovations. These innovations, in turn, cycle back to the official sectors of Senegalese cinema, spurring them to codify and systematize various forms and conceptions of these popular creations. While urban neighborhood theaters might infrastructurally and financially falter in Dakar, the minds behind those theaters and other forms of cinematic dissemination are never limited in their conceptualization of Senegalese cinema.

Documentary as a "Product of Its Period": Rising Voices and Representations of Urban Social Issues

Those working in cinematic access and distribution are not the only industry players who exhibit ingenuity and creativity. In the chapters that follow, we study contemporary urban films from eight innovative filmmakers who are all living and working in Dakar and its environs: Moussa Sène Absa, Rama Thiaw, Joseph Gaï Ramaka, Abdoul Aziz Cissé, Khady Sylla, Adams Sie, Khardiata Pouye, and Angèle Diabang.[60] Each of their careers is exemplary of the interplay between cinematic limitations and innovation that we've shown to be a hallmark of Senegalese cinema throughout its history but that has been particularly acute in the last three decades. All these filmmakers began and established their careers during the period of limited domestic opportunities prior to the full funding of the FOPICA: Sène Absa and Ramaka are the earliest, with their debut films being released in the late 1980s; Sylla began making films at the end of the 1990s; and Thiaw, Cissé, Sie, Pouye, and Diabang all released their inaugural films in the first decade of the 2000s. With a lack of financial and infrastructural support in Senegal during the early stages of their careers, all of these filmmakers have incorporated creative, mutable, organic strategies into their filmmaking. As we previously mentioned, Sène Absa and Ramaka turned to France as a cinematic resource at the beginning of their careers.[61] However, these filmmakers have increasingly anchored themselves, their films, and their filmmaking practices in Senegal, as demonstrated by Ramaka's creation of the Gorée Island film series and conceptualization of expanding cinema in Casamance. The subsequent filmmakers in our group have been even more decidedly centered in Senegal throughout their careers and have been equally innovative and flexible in overcoming the challenges and difficulties of the Senegalese film industry, as exemplified by Sie's creation of *Summer pencc.*

Although the complete filmographies of these filmmakers illustrate the ingenuity of contemporary Senegalese cinema culture, we focus our analysis on their specific films that most fully embody that creativity because they represent and intervene in urban Senegalese issues. In particular, all the works highlighted in our chapters fall into the category of documentary. Sylla posits that "cinema shows reality" and serves as "literature that represents liberty," especially for those who cannot read or write.[62] This is particularly true for the documentary form. Furthermore, technological developments in filmmaking and the distribution of films during the early twenty-first century have increased the global production and prominence of documentary films. According to Aida Vallejo, "The 2000s witnessed a 'golden age' for documentary marked by the digitization process. The increase in production and exhibition grew in parallel, and documentary festivals appeared as a natural response to the lack of a distribution infrastructure."[63] Despite the greater accessibility and visibility of documentaries for African filmmakers in the twenty-first century, the historical inequities in filmic representation continue as the realities of contemporary African history, society, and culture have often been misrepresented and mocked by Western documentarians. African film scholar N. Frank Ukadike contends that ethnographic and anthropological documentaries made by Western filmmakers are "mere spectacles" that have only portrayed "fragments of reality."[64] He adds that documentaries by African filmmakers aim "to interrogate the African experience.... The social issues, cultural values, and politics of the African world are portrayed with both sensitivity and realism. It is this connection between the documentary and the real circumstances depicted, between the filmmaker and the subject/audiences, that is the most distinctive characteristic of this genre."[65] All the documentaries that we study in our chapters specifically speak to the reality of urban social and cultural issues in Senegal. This relationship between the urban and the documentary mode of filmmaking is not unique to contemporary Senegalese cinema. Since the early period of cinema, "the documentary, the preferred mode of political film, was also intended to do more than represent this new urban world of social upheaval, speed, movement and transition. Above all it was to bring the viewer into a different and critical relationship to it."[66] Contemporary Senegalese filmmakers extend and expand this critical intervention of documentary filmmaking in urban realities in distinct ways. As we will show, the filmmakers rely on their close connections with their subjects, often filming individuals and communities that are part of their daily lives, to accurately portray and to critically reflect upon the urban society in which they live. Ukadike elaborates on four central characteristics employed by African filmmakers that are used to combat oppression: authority, transparency, immediacy, and authenticity.[67] The documentary form represents the reality of a particular time and place, functioning as "a product of its period."[68] From this anchoring in contemporary Senegalese urban realities, the documentary mode of filmmaking then allows the filmmakers in our book to more directly intervene in the globalized system of image making that surrounds Africa.

Bertrand Cabedoche argues that contemporary documentaries from Africa also "align more and more the social 'I' with the individual 'I'"; they provoke their audiences so that "social norms are therefore reconsidered," and within them we find "hybrid identities [that] provoke rhetorically the collective to interrogate their foundational characteristics."[69] The filmmakers in our book examine the unique challenges of urban life in Senegal but also consider the rural and isolated areas of the country in order to refashion Senegalese subjectivities and society. They situate Senegalese history and social problems within a local urban context and connect them to global circumstances and the contemporary practices of transnational communities. Instead of putting social issues unambiguously on the screen, they render complex, tense representations of the problems and suggest that solutions cannot be imposed from outside actors. Rather, they must be found within the community on-screen and by its own members. They also render their subjects, the spaces they occupy, and the communities in which they live with great aesthetic attention and purpose. As much as the films we study exemplify the social engagement dimensions to African documentary filmmaking, they are not strictly socio-realist depictions of Senegalese urban problems. Instead, the filmmakers carefully capture the beauty and vibrancy that exist within the lives and communities of their subjects and intentionally make their own aesthetic creations from the images of urban existence. In this way, they emphasize and contribute visual pleasure and beauty to our collective reimagination of Senegalese urban space. The cineastes analyzed in the following chapters depict through the documentary form the inherent duality of despair and hope, problem and solution, social ill and social change, and dilapidation and beauty in present-day urban Senegal.

The documentary form not only portrays the full scope of urban realities; it also permits our filmmakers to amplify the voices of those who are the most marginalized in contemporary Senegalese society. They pay particular attention to how those marginalized figures persevere and overcome difficulties in urban spaces and the ways those experiences are shaped by and contour similar situations in rural and global sites. In the films we study, rural communities are sacrificed for the needs of the urban populace; the urban poor often see no option to change their lives but to flee their country; women face limited social options and outright exclusion; street children arrive in the city from rural areas, only to be abandoned and exploited. Yet the individuals and communities experiencing these stark situations are rarely depicted merely as suffering subjects. Instead, these documentaries center the entirety of their experiences, including oppression and resistance, joy and pain, restrictions and solutions, and persistence and circumvention. Furthermore, the documentaries represent their subjects with aesthetic intention and vitality and allow them to articulate their own experiences. This follows with recent scholarship that African documentaries are "inevitably activist" by giving full cinematic expression to previously ignored or excluded identities, experiences, and cultures.[70]

This documentary focus on marginalized urban figures is often and uniquely undertaken by women filmmakers, such as Thiaw, Sylla, Pouye, and Diabang. Scholars have convincingly argued that documentary filmmaking in Africa has come to be dominated by women for significant reasons. Of course, the film widely recognized as the first from a sub-Saharan African woman director is a documentary (Thérèse Sita-Bella's *Tam-tam à Paris* from 1963), while the most celebrated early female African filmmaker, Safi Faye from Senegal, worked primarily in documentary films, especially socially engaged ones.[71] Through her persistence in making films even as she was often the only woman noticeably doing so, Faye "charted the path for feminine cinema: that of engagement."[72] Ellerson claims that African female filmmakers often turn to the medium of documentary to raise awareness about issues they find important: "Telling stories through documentary... has been a dominant mode among African women, perhaps out of a genuine interest in addressing the pressing issues in their societies and relating stories that otherwise would not be told."[73] She finds a wide range of themes and approaches in their work: "autobiographical, experimental, hybrid, consciousness-raising, sociopolitical, as well as within translocal and transnational spaces."[74] Elsewhere, Ellerson points out that since FESPACO started a separate competition category for documentaries in 2007, women have been the predominant recipients of the award, something they have never done in the category of best film.[75] Documentary filmmaking then becomes an ideal form for women to prioritize female voices and experiences in order to instill a sense of authenticity and urgency, raise awareness about the variety of experiences of Senegalese women, and ultimately inspire social change among their viewers.

Women filmmakers' work in the documentary form is also understandable given the limitations women have often faced within African cinema. Women's own cinematic marginalization, compounded with their social exclusion, can attune them to document other forms of social marginality in their films. In her extensive annotated bibliography on women in African cinema, published in *African Cinema: Postcolonial and Feminist Readings*, Emilie Ngo-Nguidjol states, "The general omission of African women in works devoted to African cinema, women in general, Third World women, and women's studies led me to conclude that either experts in these areas are not aware of the literature available, or they do not consider issues concerning African women important enough to include in their scholarship."[76] Although the bibliography was published in 1999, the situation in regard to publications on West African female filmmakers has been slow to change.[77] It is our aim to contribute to the rectification of this gendered blind spot that persists in African cinema studies and the cultivation of greater gender equity in African cinema scholarship. As our book demonstrates, Senegalese women have been making innovative, socially meaningful documentaries that stand alongside any cinematic work produced by men. This is not only true of documentaries, as evidenced by the 2018 edition of *Senciné*, published by the Direction de la cinématographie, entitled "Le cinéma au féminin." Just the cover alone features images of thirty-two Senegalese female filmmakers. In the introduction to the issue, Baba Diop writes about "the tremendous cohort who, since the early 2000s, expands the ranks and dares to attack cinematic genres such as comedy, ... musical comedy, ... urban culture. Senegalese cinema is currently rich with these female filmmakers."[78] The documentary form, then, is just one of the cinematic modes of expression undertaken by Senegalese women filmmakers. Yet, as we argue in a number of our chapters, documentaries have been particularly important for Senegalese women filmmakers as a way to advocate for social change, to navigate through the film industry in Senegal, and to produce a viable career.

Finally, it is worth noting that the documentary films we study share some common characteristics in their funding, production, distribution, form, and reception that mark these cinematic works as distinct. As previously mentioned, all of these films were produced and released before the FOPICA was more fully funded by Sall's administration. Therefore, these documentaries are funded through various coproduction agreements between international film companies, private Senegalese cinema producers, cultural institutions, social organizations, and Senegalese television channels. Furthermore, the four youngest filmmakers—Cissé, Sie, Pouye, and Diabang—all spent time at the now defunct but much beloved Media Center of Dakar. This local, grassroots film school was founded by Moussa Gaye and provided training, equipment, studio and editing space, and partnerships for screenings, including within the context of their Festival du quartier, or Neighborhood Festival, in which they set up temporary outdoor screenings of their students' films in various urban neighborhoods. Additionally, many of these filmmakers share cinematic topics and interests beyond the ones we identify and examine in our respective chapters. For example, Cissé and Sie both made documentaries about the devastation to rural communities in the Senegal River basin due to water mismanagement.

Most of the documentaries in our corpus were screened and often won awards at international film festivals outside of Senegal. Yet they are also easily accessible to those within the country; Ramaka and Sie, for instance, have posted their films on Vimeo and YouTube in the hopes that a wider audience will access them, especially among Senegalese. Similarly, Pouye's film that we study, *Cette couleur qui me dérange*, was coproduced by the major Senegalese television station RTS, where it was also broadcast. While these films are seemingly within the legible cinematic tradition of African documentaries that highlight social problems, they are generally "unapologetically local, . . . made without an external white gaze, . . . mak[ing] no effort to make [themselves] legible to any audience apart from [their] original constituents in Africa."[79] They are so anchored in local urban dynamics, histories, and experiences that the "social issue" current within these films may not readily translate to international spectators. The filmmakers prioritize Senegalese subjectivities in their films and in their conceptualization of their audience, forcing non-African viewers to find their own entry points into the films. The documentaries highlight Senegalese urban social issues while resisting global narratives of African problems that center around poverty, misery, hunger, civil war, and underdevelopment. The Senegalese writer Hamidou Anne characterizes this narrative approach from African artists as a tactic of "lucidity [that] necessitates breaking from categories of optimism or pessimism and documenting the continent as it is."[80]

Finally, all but one of these documentaries (Thiaw's *The Revolution Won't Be Televised*) are midlength films, which could potentially make them seem like minor works within the filmmakers' filmographies given the heightened focus by both critics and audiences on features. However, this form can provide the advantage of easier circulation on television and online for quick, local consumption, overcoming the limits on accessing feature films that many Dakarois face due to finances, infrastructure, and leisure time. Overall, the common characteristics of these documentaries demonstrate once again the malleable filmmaking practices deployed by these filmmakers in order to navigate through the vicissitudes of the Senegalese film industry. Recent Senegalese cinema has not been in an interminable crisis but has instead generated its own internal responses to its problems.

Additionally, these documentaries represent the dynamism of contemporary African urban space. Felwine Sarr points to the social, cultural, and demographic changes that are perpetually taking place within African cities and sees them as constitutive of the flexible aesthetic and creative expressions produced by urban residents: "These various dynamisms contained within the city are directly linked to the worldviews of the people who not only live in the cities but *inhabit* them."[81] Abdou-Maliq Simone more precisely articulates those worldviews as ones of "preparedness and readiness to switch gears."[82] Achille Mbembe and Sarah Nuttall go so far as to call the African city "an aesthetic project" whose order and structure arise not from design, purpose, and foreseen hierarchies but rather improvisational imagination, creativity, provisional subjectivities, and dialogue.[83] The documentaries we study in the remainder of our book are exemplary products of these urban dynamics in Senegal and aim to shape those currents for more just, equitable ends.

However, even as these films provoke and demonstrate the life of urban spaces, they are decidedly focused on the exclusions, margins, and inequities that haunt urban life in contemporary Senegal and lay bare the lives that are diminished because of local and global power imbalances. In this way, these films are part of Harrow's critical unpacking of trash as a thematic, social, aesthetic, and political concern in African cinema. In *Trash: African Cinema from Below*, Harrow writes, "Trash, above all, applies to people who have been dismissed from the community, marginalized and forgotten.... Trash encompasses the turning of that reduced status into the basis for revolt, change, and the turning away from regimes that produce definitions of trash to newly formulated regimes that force us to reconsider the criteria for assigning value, not only to people, to culture, but to African films in particular."[84] The films analyzed in our book aim to contribute to such social, political, and ideological shifts for urban Senegalese. They also add to the changing value given to the full range of African films, as referenced by Harrow at the end of the above passage. *Trash: African Cinema from Below* draws our attention to the diverse forms and thematics at work in African cinema to emphasize the power inequities within African societies and that those societies face on the global stage.

Acknowledging the rise of Nollywood in the 1990s, the important critical studies devoted to this popular form of entertainment, and other scholarly works that have diversified and complicated our notions of African cinema, Harrow recounts the genesis for his book: "We had to be shaken out of our historical need to read African cinema in narrow political terms, as subject to the exigencies of nation building, of meliorism, of Truth, with serums delivered by Authentic African voices performed by Griots. I felt we need to expand our critical readings beyond the educational imperative, and African cinema needed to become something other than dogmatic. . . . This book began by wondering about trashy aesthetics, graffiti, popular cinemas, and imperfect cinemas that enriched our reactions to African visual culture."[85] The films that we study similarly suggest alternative ways of understanding African cinema of the twenty-first century because they occupy a distinct yet fluid and unstable space within recent African cinema.

While these films are not popular forms of entertainment like the video films from Nigeria and Ghana, neither are they decidedly FES-PACO art films or auteur cinema of West Africa.[86] Thus, how can we adequately classify and understand the documentary films examined in our book, some of which were partially funded through European sources and entered in FESPACO but which were created in highly localized urban contexts and are now readily accessible through online streaming services? In many ways, the films we've included in our analysis occupy the margins of contemporary African cinema, just as their Senegalese subjects reside in liminal urban spaces. They linger within overviews of recent cinematic trends but are rarely central to these studies. Scholarly works that focus exclusively on auteur cinema, like James S. Williams's *Ethics and Aesthetics in Contemporary African Cinema*, privilege features over other cinematic forms, including many of the documentary midlength films that we study.[87] In his chapter on Senegalese cinema, "Screening Dakar: Locating Beauty in the Afropolis," a project seemingly related to ours and thus ripe for extended study of many of the films we include in our book, Williams makes brief, early mention of Sylla's films and then explicitly states that he wants to focus on fiction features, which he does for the bulk of the chapter. This seems like a lost opportunity since, as we will demonstrate, Sylla's films directly engage the African city and provide prolonged moments of engagement with the beauty that is possible in Dakar. It seems that, just as the films we study often defy the conventional bounds of the representation of African social issues for Western audiences, they resist being easily situated within the dominant paradigms of African cinema. Just as these films center revolt from Senegalese citizens against the inequities that arise from urban dynamics, they also suggest a reconfigured understanding of contemporary Senegalese cinema that "frees us from conventional cinema readings of dominant western forms of commercial or of auteur cinema."[88] This, we argue, is exactly why they are so essential for understanding contemporary Senegalese cinema. They offer new avenues into cinematic practices, representation, and aesthetics in Dakar and other Senegalese cities, while also documenting the reshaping of Senegalese politics, social structures, and access to resources that are constantly part of these cities. Harrow's call to shed our accepted understandings of African cinema and to give serious consideration to the aesthetic forms, social insights, power realignments, and cinematic reconfigurations proposed by those cinematic works that can be too easily disregarded as minor, vulgar, unimportant, or trivial—"imperfect cinemas"—guides us in our consideration of these Senegalese documentaries and their relationship to contemporary urban life.

2

Shaping the National Body in Moussa Sène Absa's *Yoolé* and Rama Thiaw's *Boul fallé: La voie de la lutte* and *The Revolution Won't Be Televised*

Walking along the numerous shorelines in Dakar, one constantly encounters pirogues—long, narrow, colorfully painted dugout canoes. It is impossible not to notice them docked on the beaches or to spot them in the distance on the expansive ocean (figs. 2.1 and 2.2). Along with their visible presence, their comings and goings help shape daily life in the city as they carry urban inhabitants out to fish early in the morning. Their return later in the day announces the possibility of buying the fresh catch for dinner that night. With the colors they exude into the cityscape, the smells of fish and ocean they bring back to shore, and the financial and culinary options they afford citizens, the pirogue is one of the most meaningful symbols of the Senegalese nation and people. As Caroline Melly engagingly details, Senegalese cultural narratives emphasize the pirogue's importance for life and community in the precolonial period, as well as its symbolic importance in the postcolonial era for national solidarity that synthesizes ethnic and religious differences.[1] In more recent years, the pirogue has become the image par excellence of migrant men who are supposedly fleeing desperate economic conditions, the network

FIGURE 2.1. Pirogues at Ouakam Beach in Dakar near the Mosquée de la Divinité, 2016. Photo by Molly Krueger Enz.

of smugglers and middlemen profiting from their migratory attempts, and what is often labeled as an "unresolvable crisis" in the country. It is no surprise, then, that the origin myth for the name Senegal states that it derives from the Wolof expression *suñu gaal*, meaning "our pirogue."[2] The pirogue becomes the metaphoric vessel for the Senegalese people's national identity, unity, and possible future.

Physical pirogues are ubiquitous in Dakar, seemingly available to anyone. Yet, who is able to board the symbolic pirogue of national unity and progress toward a seemingly better life and who must remain behind or seek out alternative paths for personal and collective development? How do the dynamics of inclusion and exclusion in these journeys shape national identity and collective belonging? How are the coinciding narratives of nationality and lineage created and disseminated, and by whom? We propose answers to these questions surrounding issues of inclusion, exclusion, nationhood, and identity in contemporary Senegal through our analysis of three documentary films by contemporary Senegalese filmmakers Moussa Sène Absa and Rama Thiaw. In Sène Absa's *Yoolé* (2010) and Thiaw's *Boul fallé: La voie de la lutte* (2009) and

The Revolution Won't Be Televised (2015), these filmmakers contribute to contemporary narratives of Senegalese national identity, belonging, and lineage that include the full scale of the national body and its empowerment.[3] They interrogate and ultimately reject narratives of national belonging that narrowly envision the body politic and the possibilities for the nation. In an interview with us in June 2021, Sène Absa stated that, in his cinema, he likes "to blend into the country, the people, . . . to show society through a view that sets out the issues at stake, the contrasts, and the paradoxes."[4] Sène Absa particularly aims to represent "the anonymous, everyday heroes," giving them "flesh and spirit."[5] Similarly, Rama Thiaw has documented contemporary Senegalese social dynamics with an aim to contribute to the national posterity's understanding of its history: "It was really important to have these facts that future generations could rely on when they want to know about their history. Because all the facts and images that we have about our history have been made by white men. We need to tell our history with our own voice."[6] While *Yoolé* was initiated from a migratory incident with a pirogue, neither Sène Absa nor Thiaw limits their work to migration as the only national pathway open to Senegalese citizens to improve their lives. Instead, as we argue in this chapter, these filmmakers evoke an expansive, dynamic pirogue of national belonging and lineage in their films, showing the multifarious ways that the people of Senegal have recently invested in and reimagined their society, especially from and within urban contexts, and what such work means for the inheritors of the country.

Of course, conceptualizations of national belonging and cohesion are often constructed through the complex interplay between various discursive forces, which results in contested understandings of nationalism. The films in this chapter carefully account for and reflect on these discursive dynamics and their influence on the Senegalese national body. In *Imagined Communities: Reflections on the Origin and Spread of Nationalism*, Benedict Anderson famously characterizes the nation as "an imagined political community," wherein individuals who will never interact and who live within structures of inequality nevertheless feel a sense of unity and cohesion with one another, defined against those of other nationalities.[7] Nationality is relational in this view, its definition dependent on a system of differences and similarities, both within the borders of the nation and in comparison to other nation-states.

Subsequent theorists of nationalism have articulated various currents that compose but that can also disrupt the imagined community of the nation, including gender and sexuality. Sidonie Smith and Gisela Brinker-Gabler write, "Various forms of nationalism secure and in turn depend upon specific constructions of femininity, masculinity, and normative sexuality. . . . Different forms of nationalism promote and depend upon different forms of sexuality, and the discourses of nationalism invoke various, sometimes contradictory, discourses of gender."[8] They continue on to detail the various sites of gender and nationality's mutual constitution: language, land, families, governance, public space. Of particular relevance to our present study, periods of supposed national crisis or instability are narrativized through the gender binary: "If the right working of the nation is the right working of masculinity enforced, threats to the nation are represented as emasculating."[9] Invading forces, whether they be militaristic, viral, or migratory, are often depicted as weak, feminized, and vulnerable, while typically masculinist values of strength, courage, and determination are imbued through the national body. National problems come to be understood through images and narratives of gender. Within this dynamic interplay between gender and nationality, masculinity consistently looms large. Tracing the rise of European nationalism in the nineteenth century, George L. Mosse has offered "the idealization of masculinity as the foundation of the nation and society."[10] Theorists of other sites of national belonging have identified similar prominences of masculinity. Melly posits that "postcolonial nation building and male migration constantly re-center male movements and actions."[11] Stefan Helmreich views diaspora as a "system of kinship reckoned through men."[12] This discursive field of gender identity and national belonging is therefore complex and contested for the body politic, with the collective and the individual confronting hegemonic forces but also reformulating gendered positions and values within the national body.

Sène Absa's *Yoolé* and Thiaw's *Boul fallé: La voie de la lutte* and *The Revolution Won't Be Televised* all document and contribute to the discursive social conjunctions between nationalism and gender and especially engage with the formation of masculinity within national discourses in Senegal. As we have shown in our introduction and in chapter 1, narratives of crisis have predominated in contemporary Senegal, in urban life, in cinema, and certainly in regard to Senegalese men, most publicly represented by those who have undertaken perilous journeys by pirogue to Europe. Observers often explain those migratory trajectories through the economic and social emasculation of Senegalese men in contemporary Senegal. In turn, this dearth of men in the country contributes to the further weakening and passivity, incapacity, and impotence of the body politic. Thus, the migratory experience comes to be perceived as "a crisis of masculinity."[13] Many recent discursive threads surrounding Senegal posit a dual crisis of masculinity and the nation, with a particular focus on economics.[14] However, as we demonstrate through our analysis of the films in this chapter, "poverty, unemployment and the desire for higher incomes are thus one-sided, inadequate explanations" for the current state of Senegalese men and their masculine practices and actions.[15] Other value systems, social forces, and networks of belonging contribute to men's understanding of and actions for themselves and their communities. These alternatives to the trope of crisis are even present within analysis of migrant flows from Senegal since "migration has long been a reality of life for many Senegalese in a country where social status is often attributed to migrants."[16] Furthermore, expressions and practices of masculinity do not exclusively channel through migration, and other gender identities contribute to the nation in essential ways in those endeavors. The pirogue as the symbol of national community is crafted by complex gendered dynamics, resulting in varied experiences of belonging, relations, family, and identity for those in and out of the vessel.

The three documentary films highlighted in this chapter interrogate the cultural construction of such gendered dimensions, documenting the implications of these gendered relations for various social spheres and collective identities in urban Senegal and expressing through distinct cinematic practices the innovative responses from Dakar men to such forces. *Yoolé*, *Boul fallé*, and *The Revolution Won't Be Televised* question and identify alternatives to masculine social impotence or crisis in contemporary Senegal. They counteract "exaggerated, mediated and also fundamentally flawed popular ideas of desperate and poor Africans trying to reach the shores of Europe," in which "migrants appear as passive pawns who are being pushed out of their countries and their continent by macro-level factors" while those who remain are elided and silenced as social actors.[17] In place of such narratives, these films highlight the work being done by a wide range of urban Senegalese residents to reimagine masculine worth, investment, and inheritance. The documentaries also underline the structures of belonging that arise from those gendered processes, given the country's current social realities.

Sène Absa's documentary *Yoolé* examines the circumstances surrounding a pirogue full of eleven dead Senegalese men that washed ashore in Barbados in 2006 while the filmmaker was temporarily residing on the island. Although the film emotionally archives and mourns for those lives lost, Sène Absa does not shoot the dead bodies or the horrors within the pirogue. Instead, *Yoolé* opens up to a pluralistic view of migration from Senegal, thus disrupting the monolithic economic narratives of contemporary migration that circulate in public discourse, including in literature and cinema. Furthermore, the film documents the tragedy with great attention to both its Senegalese and global sociopolitical contexts and illustrates the full range of despair and frustration of early twenty-first-century Dakar, especially for men, but it also shows the stirrings of revolt against this paradigm. Additionally, with an intriguingly diverse array of cinematic and artistic choices, Sène Absa expresses the full humanity of those implicated in the incident and the possibilities for new gendered dimensions through aesthetic expressions. *Yoolé* proposes contemporary urban masculinity as actively reconstructed through cinematic aesthetics, social engagement, and political activism in the face of severe social restrictions. While the film neither documents nor offers full resolution of those limitations, it does catalog the potentialities embedded within contemporary urban Senegal for gendered social change that narratives of transatlantic crossings too often elide in the public imaginary.

Rama Thiaw's *Boul fallé* captures the same relative time period in Dakar as *Yoolé*. Whereas Sène Absa's film centers on the sociopolitical engagement of Senegalese men in response to their sense of social impotence, Thiaw's film documents the men implicated in the titular social movement that arose in the late 1990s through hip-hop and wrestling. As we show in our analysis of *Boul fallé* later in the chapter, the film highlights Senegalese rap pioneer Didier Awadi of Positive Black Soul and a young Thiat of the group Keur Gui, who will figure prominently in *The Revolution Won't Be Televised*. The cultural areas of hip-hop and wrestling became the means for young men to express their desire for generational distinction and individual agency in the face of economic restrictions and social stagnation. Although *Boul fallé* documents parts of the hip-hop scene, it most powerfully and distinctly conveys men's involvement in the popular wrestling culture in the urban periphery of Dakar. It prioritizes the physical preparation and interior reflection required for wrestling rather than its outcomes in the ring. While only hinting at the socioeconomic limitations that draw the wrestlers, gym owners, and promoters into the industry, the film captures men's bodies in movement and action, both aesthetic and physical, exhibitive and reconstructive. *Boul fallé* suggests that men in limited social conditions in Senegal can reinvent their social standing through their physical selves; the individual body acts as the connective tissue to the social body. Long the province of action, power, and control, masculinity in the film becomes the site for beauty, desire, and performance, offering new possibilities for Senegalese men to establish cultural worth. Through its connections between the wrestling and socially engaged hip-hop communities in Dakar, the film depicts all of these men as seeking out a better life in the city through work, investment in available resources, and community building. While some men, in an attempt to overcome their feelings of social powerlessness, might choose to abandon their homes, families, and even their lives by migrating to Europe, Thiaw's film powerfully and artistically demonstrates the other avenues for reimagining masculinity and national belonging within contemporary urban Senegal that do not put their lives at risk.

Both *Yoolé* and *Boul fallé* provide viewers with significant insights into the social realities of contemporary Dakar and consider the alternatives for reinvention of that society, especially in relation to masculine identities, that many Senegalese men undertake instead of migration. These social currents documented in 2009–10 seem to come to full realization in Thiaw's second film, *The Revolution Won't Be Televised* from 2015, which strikingly shows that revolt and change in Dakar are not just latent potentialities but ongoing projects of Dakar men that can have immense impacts. The film documents the participation of rappers Thiat and Kilifeu, collectively known as Keur Gui, in the Y'en a Marre movement; their participation includes rapping but also public protests, organizing, verbal denunciations of those in power, and even violence and imprisonment. *The Revolution Won't Be Televised* reveals the full flowering of the seeds of revolt that Sène Absa's film detailed but that were also embedded within the *boul fallé* (roughly translated from Wolof as "don't worry") movement evoked in Thiaw's earlier film. This film draws out a legacy of masculine protest and revolt that Y'en a Marre has inherited in urban Senegal. However, it also opens up that inheritance to feminine predecessors, which makes *The Revolution Won't Be Televised* an extension of the aesthetic reformulation of Senegalese masculinity that Thiaw initiated in *Boul fallé*. The national community thus shifts from one in crisis to one in productive investment, which proceeds specifically from a rearticulation of the nation's gendered lineage. Just like in her first film, Thiaw uses deft cinematic choices to move her documentation of important masculine-centric domains of contemporary Senegal into more innovative reconsiderations of the role of gender, inheritance, and social engagement in the country.

These three films acknowledge the social, political, and economic difficulties that many men in contemporary Dakar face and the implications of those challenges for families, local communities, and the nation. Yet they also trace a social trajectory of hope for Senegalese men and their sites of belonging, from the death archived in Sène Absa's film, through the localized work of the wrestlers in *Boul fallé*, culminating in the sustained, impactful, national, and international revolt of Keur Gui in Thiaw's later film. The films of Sène Absa and Thiaw convey the subversion that Dakar residents enact on the disempowering, miserabilist paradigm so often imposed on them by hegemonic masculinity. Additionally, these three films are uniquely attuned to how such gendered forces impact all urban Senegalese residents, whatever their gender. They document the collective, creative, artistic, and revolutionary responses to gendered realities and ideologies that men and women in Dakar have articulated, pointing to further possibilities for the reimagining of national belonging, relations, and identity in Senegal.

Yoolé: Men Adrift

Moussa Sène Absa was born in 1958 and raised in the Tableau-Ferraille neighborhood of greater Dakar. This upbringing gives his cinematic work a peri-urban focus, as Sène Absa himself insists: "All of my stories tell the stories from my childhood. I gather them."[18] Along with his own childhood, another source of inspiration is his open-air studio and home on the shore of Popenguine, a city seventy kilometers to the south of Dakar. Sène Absa says of being in that location, "I become a sponge that takes in all of the local stories and that allows me to write. I can't write anywhere else."[19] These dynamics between the director's childhood and his current locale, between urban and peri-urban life, between the city and other Senegalese sites are represented strongly in Sène Absa's well-known feature films. However, these recurring tropes also appear in his sole documentary film to date, *Yoolé*. As we show through our analysis, this film, then, stands as a product of the filmmaker's ongoing concerns about contemporary Senegal but also as an outlier in his filmography due to its form and production.

Even as Sène Absa's *Yoolé* proceeds from the tragic death of the eleven men in the pirogue that washed up on Barbadian shores, the film opens with a turn toward the sky, with its epigraph pulled from the Senegalese national anthem, written by Senghor: "Sun upon our fears. Sun upon our hopes." The image of the sun returns throughout the film, and introduced with this line that expresses national cohesion through crisis and progress, it serves to remind the viewer of the migrants' enduring links to Senegalese national identity. As long as the defining feature of the sun touches them, even as they drift out to sea in a desperate attempt to find hope in Europe, these men belong to the national body of Senegal. *Yoolé*'s gesture to rejoin these lost souls to the body politic of the country stands in contrast to many narratives of Senegalese migrants that situate them as disruptive actors or products of a pathological social context. Yet Sène Absa's film accomplishes this re-membering without ever flattening or narrowing its portrayal of contemporary Senegalese social realities. Instead, *Yoolé* documents the extensive variety of migratory impulses and experiences—including contradictory ones—which refute homogenizing narratives of national crisis, migration, and masculinity. It reassembles dispersed Senegalese urban residents under the impetus to improve the country, shifting the focus from fears offered by migration to the hopes afforded by investment in social change. As the director stated in our interview with him, people understand that there must be "other visions, other universes, a rupture, a future to build, a little dreaming."[20] In his view, if people are ready to die in the ocean, they are ready to die for their country.

FIGURE 2.2. Fishermen in the Atlantic Ocean with the Dakar skyline behind them, 2023. Photo by Devin Bryson.

Through this film, Sène Absa adds revolt as one of the national characteristics embodied by the pirogue.

Of course, even as *Yoolé* works to reformulate national belonging, cinema plays a key role in strengthening and perpetuating cultural narratives of crisis. A number of twenty-first-century films from across the world, including from Senegal, have centered on African migrant men's harrowing experiences in attempting to reach Europe and integrate into European societies upon arrival.[21] Senegalese filmmaker Moussa Touré's 2012 renowned feature, *La pirogue*, is one such example. The majority of the film locks in on the community in the titular pirogue, shows the tension between life and death in the vessel, and highlights the horrific outcomes from such tension for the majority of those who try to cross. Despite the tragic conclusion to the journey, the pirogue still stands in the film as the site of national unity and identity, as individuals with ethnic, linguistic, and regional differences join together in their attempts to leave Senegal and find a better life in Europe. Certainly, there exist very clear divisions between those in the pirogue, but the passengers are united in their need to flee West Africa. Yet this community is only possible due to the stark limitations that exist within the body politic back in the country and that necessitate departure in the film. In particular, *La pirogue* depicts a bleak economic landscape for men living and working in Dakar. Despite its deployment of the powerful national idiom of the pirogue, Touré's film does little to offer alternative possibilities for national identity, belonging, and inheritance, instead relying on normative gendered views of the masculine dimensions of social problems and their possible solutions within Senegalese national ideology.

Sène Absa's *Yoolé* similarly reflects on the pirogue as a site for national belonging but additionally takes up exactly those issues that Touré's film neglects, demonstrating the radical potential that the "minor" documentary films of our corpus contain to rewrite normalizing cinematic impulses. Instead of taking the social impotence of the migrant men found dead in the pirogue in Barbados as an unquestionable reality, the documentary aims to evoke the full scope of social forces that bore down on the individuals in that vessel, as demonstrated by the first shot of the film. After the epigraph, the initial shot is not of the pirogue in Barbados nor of the families of the victims nor of photos and video of the deceased themselves, as might be expected in a film invested in plumbing the dramatic depths of the tragic transatlantic migration of Senegalese men. The film begins with a shot of Senegalese president Abdoulaye Wade at a rally asking for young people to support him in the 2000 election. This election was the first legitimate opportunity since independence for a change in the governing party, and in the footage, Wade encourages young voters, "Come with me to change Senegal!"[22] The footage provides another example of the rhetorical and imaginative power of images of movement, of trajectory, and of propulsion toward something better in the country. However, as the rest of the film argues, nothing had changed with Wade as president between 2000 and when the bodies in Barbados were found in 2006, nor in 2010 when the film was released. Various Senegalese men are interviewed throughout the film about what might drive young men to migrate, and they all indicate a sense of betrayal by Wade and his administration. A young man named Thierno states, "The way politicians rule the country, they rule it badly, wrong governance." Ibrahime more directly calls out Wade, "If we could find a job here, we wouldn't leave. Wade has to know that." The social and political policies implemented by Wade obfuscate any possibilities for a prosperous future, forcing Senegalese men, like those found in Barbados, to believe they have no choice other than to migrate across the Atlantic. Although many have lost hope, it was not inevitable that those men were to leave Senegal. In fact, as *Yoolé* demonstrates, many men have chosen to remain and to invest in their country. The film becomes a site for those other options, documenting the social and political activism of Senegalese men, expressing the full range of the gendered relations between migrant men and the women they leave behind, and proposing regendered variations of national belonging and cohesion. With this film, Sène Absa contributes to the body of cinematic work that "looks to counteract the mediatized and political discourse associating migrants with social outcasts, delinquents, or invaders" by restoring to those caught up in the forces of migration "their density, their fragility, and their human dignity."[23]

The director uses a number of methods to capture the various dynamics, characteristics, and social forces of contemporary Senegal that produce sentiments of social impotence and thus migration. In fact, Sène Absa employs so many different techniques and styles in the film that it is ultimately a disjointed and fractured work. This approach, though, serves the political and social ends of the film well. The uneasy conjunction of styles in *Yoolé* reflects the fracturing of Senegalese society provoked and exacerbated by Wade that the interviews document. It also conveys the impossibility of ever having a coherent view of the Senegalese body politic and therefore complete, stable answers to why people migrate from Senegal. As the film shows through its interviews with Senegalese citizens and its discordant style, people of a wide range of views, backgrounds, and positionalities belong to the Senegalese nation. The decision to migrate for any of them is produced through a complex, even contradictory confluence of personal, local, national, and global forces. It can never be reduced to one simplistic narrative. *Yoolé* adopts a restless perspective to try to understand and convey the causes, even as it acknowledges that it never will fully, that evoking the fracture is all it can hope to do. It is clear that the film was made in the aftermath of the discovery of the boat, and the emotional impulse from that discovery—anger, confusion, sadness, mourning—drives the film rather than cold, logical observation and analysis. Yet the emotional engine of the documentary is never aimless or performative. Set within the larger social context of contemporary Senegal portrayed in the film,

Yoolé proposes "emotion as a form of cultural politics or world making."[24] Wade made an emotional appeal to young voters in the opening clip from 2000, asking them to marshal their affective investment in their nation in support of his candidacy. Sène Absa constructs his film in line with this affective economy, cataloging and expressing the affective responses of those now disappointed, angry, and disillusioned citizens. Sara Ahmed has argued that "attention to emotions allows us to address the question of how subjects become *invested* in particular structures."[25] Sène Absa's eschewal of objective social and political analysis, and preference for emotional subjectivity, reveals the affective investment that Senegalese individuals have made in their nation and their communities. Given that investment, the film asks, How can those emotions be systemically directed into more constructive, socially equitable ends and away from the affective manipulation by political leaders like Wade that results in a sense of social impotence?

Even those Senegalese citizens who migrate in the film are emotionally tethered to their nation. As mentioned, Sène Absa uses a variety of cinematic approaches to convey the emotional resonance of this incident and its attendant social context. He especially employs fiction film techniques to distinguish his representation of the migrants who died stranded in the ocean and eventually washed up in Barbados. Using the fact that a note was found in the pirogue indicating whom to contact back in Dakar if the migrants were to die and the boat was found, Sène Absa reconstructs the experience of those migrants. These intermittent sequences are constructed around subjective visuals from the perspective of the migrants and a voice-over that is supposed to be the writer who left the note. These sequences eschew portraying the brutal horrors that those migrant men must have experienced in the pirogue in favor of drawing these men back into the national body through cinematic artistry and the poetic power of the voice-over. The first of these sequences arrives in a long, elevated shot of the streets. The color film transitions to black and white and the voice-over of the migrant writer from the pirogue enters. The man addresses his mother, providing details about the departure from Tableau-Ferraille, the number of passengers, and their expectations for the journey to only last ten days. Yet they are now stranded in the middle of the ocean, which is unfortunate, as the writer notes, since he can't swim. As the voice-over proceeds, there are varied shots, all in black and white, of young men walking through Dakar streets. The camera eventually arrives at the shore, and as it pans out to the ocean, the film transitions back to color. The transition in the color of the film marks the first of these reconstructive sequences as a palimpsest in the film's documentation of urban life. The men in the pirogue are part of the national community, not aberrations. Just as the camera shots remain consistent but the color simply transitions into and then out of black and white, the migrants are an expansion and adaptation of the national collective. The difficult circumstances in which they find themselves within the pirogue are not simply their problem; they are an issue embedded within the national body, for all Senegalese to understand and to confront.

These sequences return intermittently throughout the film, always with images that insist on these men's inclusion in the national community and the voice-over that reminds viewers of the gendered dimensions of migration, those left behind, and the national project of social change. The voice-over continues to be the writer addressing his mother; while he departs for Europe in a pirogue, she remains behind to worry about him and face the consequences of the tragic outcome of his journey. However, the mother is honored and valued in the voice-over, not set as just an artificial interlocutor for communicating masculine concerns to the audience. In one of the later sequences, the writer addresses his mother in Wolof over shots of kids surrounding a woman; he says that even if she doesn't speak French well, he dedicates the following poem to her, which is written by their beloved ancestor Mame Senghor. Writing and art connect the migrant writer to his mother back in Senegal, just as cinema reinserts the actual migrant men back into the wider social and political context of their country. Cross-gender communication and collaboration are articulated through these sequences to counteract exclusively masculinist notions of nationalism and economic migration.

The visuals of these sequences also emphasize this reconstruction of national belonging. Many of the shots from the later subjective sequences, when the pirogue has been adrift at sea for many days, are from the perspective of someone inside the pirogue, like the writer of the supposed note. Thus, there are a number of shots of the ocean, which, as the film conveys elsewhere, is the traditional source of food and income, through fishing, in Senegal. Sène Absa also films the sky repeatedly, which echoes the line from the national anthem in the epigraph that expresses how the sun shines on the national body in times of despair and of hope. The film refuses to embody and physically depict the dead migrants. Instead, it turns to imaginative, artistic evocations of their passage. The true experiences of such men are unknowable and unrepresentable. *Yoolé* visually emphasizes the migrants' belonging to the social body. The men in the doomed pirogue are essential components of the national collective, having left behind people they love and with whom they've created lives; they represent the significant social problems of the country as well as the potential for future change. Their deaths should strengthen the national body's resolve to address the source of their fate rather than to see them as national aberrations.

These cinematically imaginative reconstructions rest disjointedly but purposely beside the more standard documentary components of the film. The bulk of *Yoolé* is composed of interviews with Senegalese who are implicated in migration in a variety of ways, including men who migrated to Europe but who were then expatriated to Senegal, a psychologist who diagnoses the social malaise that contributes to feelings of despondency and impotence and then migration, villagers who rely on fishing to sustain themselves and their families, people who have lost family members in their migratory attempts, individuals in Barbados who dealt with the aftermath of the pirogue's arrival, and Senegalese who have migrated to other countries. These interviews show the reach of migration in contemporary Senegal but, more significantly, the underlying social and political causes of its prevalence. Senegalese from all segments of the population are discontent and seeking options for improving their lives, their communities, and their country. Migration is just one of the options that the interviewees voice because of multifarious social issues. As Thierno, one of the illegal migrants who was returned to Senegal, insists, "Don't tell me we're crazy or suicidal.... We're clear-headed men who decided to go!" *Yoolé* restores agency back to Senegalese who decide to migrate but also launches a full-throated critique of all of the social structures in Senegal that limit options for its citizens. Thierno says that those who migrate are carefully assessing their society and making an informed, conscious decision in response to the dimensions of contemporary Senegal that are not allowing them to live as full and rich of a life as they deserve and as they were promised by Wade. Another of the returnees with Thierno, Ibrahime, makes the connection between the threats of migration and the failures of Wade explicit in his interview: "Everybody knows it's dangerous to cross the ocean. Wade has to admit he's done wrong." The content of the interviews returns repeatedly to the blame that should be cast on Wade for the various forms of damage he has produced in Senegal and the betrayal of the citizens' trust he has enacted. That is the primal source of Senegalese social disenfranchisement and migration in *Yoolé*.

Sène Absa's shooting style of the interviews also works against some of the typical impulses of migrant narratives and documentation. He shoots these citizens—who have experienced despair, rage, and loss brought on by the corrupt governance of Wade—in a visual style that captures the full dimensions of their communities and their place within them. The men of Dakar are often on the roofs of buildings, with the cityscape behind them. Others are interviewed in the streets, surrounded by the bustle of the city and hanging out with rap artists who give their musical versions of the challenges of urban life. Sène Absa also includes interstitial shots of men on the beach and walking in the streets of Dakar. These men, many of whom attempted to leave the city for other countries at the risk of their lives, continue to think, act, speak, and live within the urban community. Similarly, the director portrays the sense of belonging, and its disruption by current social challenges, in a village. After an extended focus on the men of Dakar and another excerpt from a speech by Wade, Sène Absa shoots a pirogue on shore surrounded by people. Once again, the pirogue is the communal hub. This time, though, it represents more than just an abstract notion of community and belonging, as the film documents the difficulties for a fishing village to sustain itself with that vessel. The villagers place blame on Europeans, referred to as "the plunderers," as well as the Chinese and Koreans who overfish their waters and "use techniques that spoil the sea." The men who rely on fishing to sustain their lives in Senegal have been made vulnerable by the inequities produced by global economic forces. Sène Absa's visual portrayals of the positionalities of Senegalese men in their sites of community and belonging reinforce their verbal claims that they and other migrants never wanted to leave Senegal but that they ultimately felt like they had no other choice in the face of political neglect on the part of Wade.

Besides linking urban and rural Senegalese men visually through their shared sense of community as well as verbally through their common feelings of despair and anger at those in power, *Yoolé* expands gendered national belonging to include women. The film documents women's social discontent that is equal to men's. It also portrays women beyond their typical roles in public narratives of migration as helplessly abandoned, grieving mothers and widows. It complicates and deepens women's engagement with both of these areas of contemporary Senegalese national community that are too often constructed as exclusive domains of men. Ousman Abdul Azis, one of the early urban interviewees, admits that he understands how illegal migration appears unethical from a European perspective, but in Senegal, "it's your own mother that sends you away," implying that women are not simply passive victims of men's economic decisions to migrate but rather active participants in the careful calculation of the process. Azis's rapper companion takes up the idea in song, claiming that they will return with money from their journeys to the Global North to "give pride to [their] mothers." The film reinforces this dimension later with an interviewee who claims that women push their sons and nephews to migrate because women face social pressures to expect material possessions as markers of their personal and familial worth. *Yoolé* frankly depicts the complex, even contradictory gendered dynamics of migration while avoiding blame for economically driven men or women. The film constantly contextualizes these personal examples within the wider social, nationalistic, and gender forces that shape contemporary Senegal, showing individual members of the body politic to be actively reconstructing and negotiating that discursive terrain. Further on in the film, Sène Absa interviews a wife, Maam Jaara, who was left behind by her husband when he migrated. Her perspective contradicts Ousman Abdul Azis's argument, as she indicates that she didn't want her husband to go because they were sustaining themselves economically with his work as a tailor. Yet her husband felt compelled to leave due to fraternal relations. His younger brother had decided to migrate, and Maam Jaara's husband couldn't let his brother attempt the crossing alone. Both of the men died at sea, leaving Maam Jaara in a more tenuous situation in Senegal than before her husband's departure. While this personal story comes the closest in *Yoolé* to confirming dominant narratives of migration, with an absent husband and a suffering wife, it undermines such narratives in some key ways. Masculine relations, not economic necessity, construct this particular instance of migration from Senegal. Additionally, Maam Jaara's suffering expressed in her interview is juxtaposed with the next shot of women gathering and dancing together, demonstrating female solidarity and perseverance, even joy, in the country. Again, *Yoolé* works against typical gendered narratives of migration from Senegal that construct men as the sole agents in the process, working from narrow economic concerns and leaving women as helpless bystanders to the men who need to provide for their families. The social and political contexts that the film documents engage both men and women but in distinctly intersectional ways. While the social landscape of the country and hegemonic masculinity often leave Senegalese men feeling as though they have no other option than to migrate, they can also position women as beneficiaries of the social and economic capital that comes from migration. *Yoolé* opens up its depiction of the Senegalese body politic in the context of migration to include both men and women as active navigators of community bonds and social relations, with both genders adopting and rejecting complex, even contradictory forces and outcomes of social impotence and migration.

Similarly, the film accounts for those Senegalese who have migrated from the country and have established lives in Europe and elsewhere and documents the complexity of their ongoing ties to their home country. European countries are the prominent destinations for migrants, and the film accounts for that extension of the national community. Yet it also highlights components of the Senegalese diaspora that are less visible, which serves to again displace and complicate public narratives of migration from Senegal. As Melissa Thackway argues, "Flows and migrations often produce an opposition or a contrast between African and European spaces."[26] However, as she continues on to show, cinema can work to complicate and disrupt such binaries. Sène Absa accomplishes this in *Yoolé* by making Barbados the imaginative, productive site of origin for the film yet also a triangulating point in the migratory trajectory between Senegal and Europe. Moudou Diagne, one of the first individuals we encounter in the film, is a Senegalese migrant who resides in Barbados. He contributes his own views to the discovery of the deceased in the pirogue. In a later sequence of the film, he says that most Barbadians have a negative view of Africa, envisioning it as a "hard continent" where hunger and war prevail. The pirogue's washing up on the shores of the country only confirmed those perspectives for Barbadians. Diagne articulates his difficulties in counteracting these perceptions in his interactions with Barbadians: "I just didn't know how to explain to them that Senegal, you know, is a wonderful country, that people are happy, and why are they all leaving, why are they all trying to find a better life, or to get more material things ... that they are ready to die, I don't understand it." Even as the dead migrants confirmed certain narrow views of Africa for the people in Barbados, the film itself counteracts the symbolic weight of the deceased with its portrayal of the words and lived experiences of a Senegal migrant in Barbados who continues to feel and express a sense of national belonging, even outside of the country.

Late in the film, Sène Absa does finally provide those perspectives of Senegalese migrants who have achieved "the dream" of establishing a life in Europe. However, the reality the film documents is once again contrastive to the narrative construction of such experiences. The first shots of Senegalese migrants in Europe in *Yoolé* are of Senegalese men selling African masks and necklaces on the streets of Portugal. Ousseynou is one of those men, and his interview reveals the disconnect between the life in Senegal that he left behind and what he experiences now in Europe. He says that he had a stable life and a good income that allowed him to care for his family. In short, he was able to satisfy the demands of normative nationalized masculinity. Nevertheless, Ousseynou still felt compelled to migrate to Europe for the potential of a better life. However, since he arrived in Europe, he no longer earns enough to provide for his needs and to continue to support his family. He calls Europe "a lure" and says, "Things that were easy for me to manage in Senegal, here I can't." This statement, particularly in contrast to Ousseynou's emphasis on the stability of his life in Senegal, implies that his masculine identity has been disrupted far more by the threat of impotence and vulnerability in Europe than it ever was by economic distress in Senegal. The film documents other considerations, such as family relations, stability, and a sense of home, that might not be fully accounted for by potential migrants before their journey but that become especially visible in the midst of the migratory experience in Europe. It is unsurprising, then, that Ousseynou and his compatriot Laye say that they want to go back home as soon as they can. Their departure has only sharpened their sense of belonging within Senegalese national identity. However, neither man is looking to return to the life they previously had in Senegal. Both of them are pointedly critical of the social values and inequity within the country. They say, "Senegal has nice aspects, but the bad side is bigger. The rich have no mercy for the poor, that's the problem." Their solution to this is still to return to the country and rejoin the work of improving the situation: "The idea is to work for your country. But this kind of immigration . . . no . . . One day it will be fine." While both Ousseynou and Laye were taken in by the lure of Europe as the site for improving their masculine contributions to their families and their country, they now realize their masculine worth can come from being present in Senegal to shift its values and to make a good life more accessible to all. They have hope for positive change in their country and want to be part of it. *Yoolé* presents Europe as an almost inescapable draw for potential migrant men from Senegal due to the problems in their home country and the power of Eurocentrism, but it surpasses the inevitability of these dynamics by documenting the Senegalese who have been swept up in that process yet who still envision an escape from it that permits them to both return to and reinvest in Senegal.

The end of the film suggests, like the opening, that there is hope amid the frustration with Wade and the lack of economic opportunity in urban Senegal. Oumar, another migrant in the film, says that the only solution is that "everyone must take to the streets," which echoes Sène Absa's view from our interview that Senegalese youth are fed up. Sène Absa indicates that *yoolé*, the titular Wolof word, means "sacrifice" and refers to the way in which Senegal is sacrificing its young people, which he calls "a true genocide of youth."[27] However, he adds that the youth is conscious of this sacrifice. He predicts that although it takes time, "young people are going to take the power and no one can stop them."[28] This idea of youth who take their future, and their country's future, into their own hands contradicts the stereotypical representation of a continent, nation, and film industry in crisis. In *Yoolé*, Sène Absa turns away from portrayals of despair and hopelessness that are often associated with migration and instead points to images of hope, revolt, and reclaiming power, belonging, and a sense of nationhood.

Boul fallé: Men in the Arena

Rama Thiaw was born in 1978 in Nouakchott, Mauritania, to Mauritanian and Senegalese parents. Although she moved between France and Senegal during her childhood, she grew up primarily in the Dakar suburb of Pikine. This location is also the setting for her first film, and the poverty of the neighborhood that Thiaw knew during her youth seems to have set her cinematic interest in urban areas and their sociocultural challenges: "Up until the last two or three years there was no power, and before 2004–2005, no water, we had to go to the public tap."[29] Despite these conditions, Thiaw obtained a master's degree in international economics from the Sorbonne in Paris and then a second master's degree in filmmaking from the University of Paris–Saint-Denis. She began her career in cinema by making a short film about youth and religion in France and was hired to produce short episodes for the television station Zaléa TV. However, she ran into obstacles because no one believed in her or her work.[30] She returned to Senegal in 2005 and wrote her film *Boul fallé: La voie de la lutte,* which highlights hip-hop but especially focuses on wrestling as a possible resolution for social impotence and generational crisis and documents young people in Pikine and their attempts to improve their lives and set themselves within the national body through the sport.

In 2013, we were invited by a friend to be part of his family's and community's support of his brother's upcoming wrestling match. Arriving at the family's home in Pikine, it was quickly evident that this was an event for the entire neighborhood. Numerous people were gathered in the family's courtyard as the wrestler undertook physical and spiritual preparations. Many more occupied the neighborhood streets and looked into the family courtyard from nearby roofs. The wrestler consulted with spiritual advisers, known as marabouts, who performed rituals in order to strengthen and protect him for the match. After a couple of hours of this preparatory work and communal strengthening, we loaded into cars and vans for the trip to the stadium located in the center of Dakar. A caravan of vehicles rushed through the packed streets of Pikine, honking and waving at pedestrians and other motorists in order to clear the road but also to announce the impending match of the community's homegrown wrestler. Once we arrived at the toll road that connects Dakar's peripheral neighborhoods, including Pikine, with the city center, we continued our blaring approach, demanding that other vehicles make way for our wrestler and his supporters. Having arrived at the stadium, the wrestler took his own entrance while the rest of us joined the mass of decidedly young spectators. Each segment of the crowd was clearly in support of specific combatants as the event progressed through various matches. As these proceeded, upcoming wrestlers undertook their various preparations with the support of marabouts, trainers, dancers, and musicians. Spiritual rites were offered over and over again in order to give the specific wrestler the best chance of being victorious. While our wrestler ultimately lost, the entire experience was a striking example of the collective investment in wrestling in contemporary Dakar. In 2018 a national wrestling arena was inaugurated in Pikine by Macky Sall and Chinese president Xi Jinping. Paid for by the Chinese and constructed in just twenty-eight months, this stadium seats twenty thousand and provides a way for people to enjoy wrestling, as well as other sports such as boxing or martial arts, in a larger venue.[31] The national arena illustrates the importance of wrestling for Senegalese cultural identity, especially among young people and marginalized or peripheral communities.

While wrestling was immensely popular and the subject of artistic and academic works by the time Thiaw began *Boul fallé*, she finds a unique entry point into the culture and individuals of the sport and its social implications.[32] Much of the reflection on Senegalese wrestling has focused on the dynamics between tradition and modernity. While some writers have insisted on the indigenous origins and historical development of the sport, others have emphasized the contemporary dimensions of capitalist globalization, commercialization, and cultural hybridization.[33] In *Boul fallé* Thiaw doesn't avoid this binary nor does she adopt a particular side. Instead, she upends the standard perceptions of this athletic industry and its participants by displacing the social and economic questions embedded within the sport in favor of personal development, masculine physicality, collective belonging, and social investment. The sport's complexity and social utility are set as background to the film's focus on the individual men who are attempting to navigate these complexities and their immediate social circles that support them in these endeavors. The film suggests that wrestling might be a beneficial arena for contemporary Senegalese men in urban contexts not due to how it allows them to strengthen their "authentic" Senegalese identities or to what they might be able to extract from the industry—money, fame, social status, economic mobility—but rather how the sport might permit them to invest in themselves and their communities in new ways, producing social capital for the participants. Thiaw emphasizes the personal agency of the men to work through the dualities and complexities of not just wrestling but contemporary urban Senegal. Wrestling is just the unique site in which these men are attempting to accomplish this working through, and Thiaw strives to understand and document these men within that context as urban actors. In this way, Thiaw's film aligns with the views of scholars of Senegalese wrestling who insist that the sport is a complex amalgamation of various components within contemporary urban Senegal: "Dakar society is hybrid, composite, and complex. Its current outcomes emerge from rising individualism and communal identities, recomposition and reinterpretation of traditional social relations. . . . Wrestling in Dakar is not just a matter of sport, culture, politics; it is all of those combined and even other things."[34] *Boul fallé* does not attempt to capture all of those elements, but it does take that complexity as a given and then narrows its focus onto the lived realities of the men struggling to be wrestlers.

Just as with migration, masculinity functions significantly within this field because the sport is almost exclusively composed of men. *Boul fallé* engages with masculinity's functioning within wrestling and its milieu of urban Senegal through three primary elements: the wrestlers' bodies, their subjectivity, and their social bonds. Thiaw describes how her film becomes a sort of sensual homage to the bodies of these men so carefully preparing to wrestle: "Well-built, hefty men, they're not my type! But I find them beautiful. It was important to show it. The black man is beautiful. We are always into models that are not our own. Let's show positive role models, it is important to change the images."[35] Besides counteracting white hegemonic conceptualizations of beauty, the film's attention to the wrestlers' corporeal selves suggests that the reshaping and implementation of the male body in wrestling might allow young men of the urban periphery to distinguish themselves from the social body but also to become valid members of it. Drawing on the work of Marcel Mauss, Cheikh Tidiane Wane insists that a focus

FIGURE 2.3. Two wrestlers grapple during a match in Dakar, 2013. Photo by Devin Bryson.

on the body and bodily techniques in wrestling is essential for understanding its engagement with the cultural values and historical lineage of Senegalese society: "Man's first object and resource is his body. Man will achieve the totality of his personhood through the resources of his body."[36] Wane continues on to apply a corporeal framework to the ethnic and national negotiations that wrestlers perform.[37] In her film, Thiaw undertakes a similar approach but for the purposes of considering spatial and socioeconomic lines of belonging and differentiation for urban Senegalese men.

Like with the epigraph of *Yoolé*, the first line we hear in *Boul fallé* evokes the national community and questions of belonging. Speaking to a gathering of university students, a man says, "We are Senegalese."[38] He speaks about the generation of young people in the 1990s, named boul fallé, who demonstrated strong skepticism toward political leaders and enacted protests against them, using cultural forms like public art and the musical genre mbalax. The man in the opening scene encourages the students to follow the example of that collectivity by taking leadership and a participatory approach rather than waiting for others to lead. This speaker is not a politician or civic leader, or even a wrestler, but the renowned Senegalese hip-hop artist Didier Awadi. His famous group Positive Black Soul had a 1994 hit song "Boul falé," featured on the album by the same name, which popularized the movement. Awadi is accompanied in his presentation by a younger rapper, Thiat of the hip-hop duo Keur Gui. Thiat adds to Awadi's encouragement, telling the students that they are the hope and future of the country and the entire African continent. The opening sequence evokes important dynamics of lineage and inheritance, especially in relation to community building and social change for African men. Although Awadi states that they are Senegalese, he adds that they are also the children of Thomas Sankara, Patrice Lumumba, and Nelson Mandela, thus expanding their identity to a broader African context.

Besides their prominent position within boul fallé, socially engaged hip-hoppers like Awadi were prominent in Wade's reelection bid in 2007, with most rappers coming out publicly against the president. By the time of their visit to Cheikh Anta Diop University in Dakar, which is documented in the film, hip-hop was a well-established domain for political contestation and social change, and hip-hop artists were viewed as important social critics. The opening sequence sets the conceptual foundation for the rest of the film's primary focus on peri-urban wrestlers. By beginning in the country's most respected university, located in Dakar, with the words of a well-known, socially engaged hip-hop artist, especially the one who popularized the term *boul fallé*, the film challenges its viewers to see the wrestlers within a similar context of social engagement and investment through cultural forms, even as it emphasizes the personal and physical components of wrestling.

By the time of the film in 2009, the boul fallé movement had declined significantly in prominence and popularity, although the social causes, collective emotions, and public objectives of the movement were still very much pertinent to younger Senegalese, as demonstrated by Awadi's speaking to the university students and their eager reception of his message. The film thus raises questions of who will continue the social engagement previously performed under the aegis of boul fallé and what form it will take. Besides the students in the audience, Thiat, as the younger, less visible rapper, stands as the inheritor of Awadi's work. Awadi introduces Thiat to the students as someone who has done a significant amount of work in his neighborhood of Kaolack and encourages the students to listen to what he as to say. The full results of this fraternal relationship of mentoring are not known until the events documented in Thiaw's next film, but the importance of continuing as well as adapting the heritage of social investment through masculine social relations is emphasized in the initial sequence of *Boul fallé*.

The next sequence then starts to connect these aspects of social change and masculine lineage in hip-hop to wrestling at the local level. A Pikine rap collective named Coalition Naimu Bmaam performs for the camera and then talks about what boul fallé means to them. Like Awadi, they refuse to be subservient to those in power, instead encouraging action: "Get up and fight!" However, while the more well-known rapper insists that boul fallé is about taking on leadership for one's own community, the Pikine rappers focus on the personal strength and focus that boul fallé expresses: "You don't care what people say, what they do. . . . Take your own path!" They then mention the popular and successful Senegalese wrestler Tyson, who is the other national figurehead of boul fallé, saying that they used to see him training in Pikine. Tyson, whose real name is Mohammed Ndao, is originally from Kaolack and gained recognition in the 1990s due, in part, to Senegalese singer Bada Seck's CD release *Génération boul falé*. The album includes a *bàkk*, or short poetic narrative that commemorates an important historic or societal event, to his hero Tyson.[39] Rather than choosing to train with an established gym for wrestlers, known as an *écurie*, Tyson decided to train alone and identified with the "don't worry" slogan of the boul fallé movement, which was his response to those who stood in the way of his goals.[40] Boul fallé eventually became the name of Tyson's wrestling team and signified the way in which he entered the arena before his matches, performing a "new dance, called 'bul faale dance' and executed to the rhythm of the tam-tam."[41] The young rappers are clearly amazed that Tyson is from their community and that he won the national championship and gained fame, wealth, and importance. He is described as a symbol because of how he innovated his sport: "He modernized wrestling because he injected the boul fallé spirit; he modernized a tradition." His success is all the more striking to the rappers because, as one of them says, the neighborhood of Pikine "won't give you anything. If you wake up and don't have anything to eat, you don't show it. You stay focused and follow your path." While the university students might be able to adopt boul fallé as a call for freethinking, leadership, and community building, as Awadi encourages them to do, the rappers of Pikine use it as a strategy for navigating their dire economic and material circumstances. Boul fallé is clearly a widespread ideology that continues to inspire many in urban Senegal in the first decades of the twenty-first century. Yet, it has been adapted and transformed to fit distinct social settings, resisting co-optation and homogenization. From its opening, Thiaw's film is attentive to its subjects' own understanding of their experiences and the social strategies that they adopt. However, although the title derives from the social movement and documents the cultural areas that figured most prominently within it, *Boul fallé* ultimately presents a situated version of the ideology, capturing how its legacy has continued but also how it has been adapted and personalized to various social circumstances.

While the opening of the film references the two most important figures of boul fallé with Awadi and Tyson, the film never features the wrestler; he is only mentioned by members of the wrestling community in Pikine as a figure in their memories or as an example of what is possible through the sport. Thiaw had initially intended to film Tyson, but when she approached him, he had already starred in the film *L'appel des arènes* by the Senegalese director Cheikh Ndiaye, and she was not able to pay his desired salary. Therefore, she decided to focus on a lesser-known wrestler known as Nguer, a member of the Boul Fallé wrestling team in Pikine. She also shoots other unknown local wrestlers, their training regimes, and the community in which they live. Thiaw stated, "One may find the spirit of Boul Fallé in hip hop. It is made of liberalism, resistance and involves taking the freedom to one's own work. To take charge while thinking of others, which is what Tyson did, by investing his money in Pikine to train other young people from the same disadvantaged backgrounds."[42] While Tyson has clearly inspired the rappers of Coalition Naimu Bmaam and some of the wrestlers in the later part of the film, it is important to note that by the time of the film's release in 2009, Tyson had suffered three significant defeats and was even in the midst of a three-year ban from competing in the sport. Furthermore, his adoption of boul fallé as a slogan was, as Jean-François Havard has argued, not so much a cry of social protest against limiting social norms, expectations, and economic marginalization as a self-aggrandizing articulation of his self-made success by defying the harmful, belittling biases of his elders.[43] While his individualism did amplify a general social desire among young Senegalese of the late 1990s to break with tradition and exercise their own agency, as Havard claims, Tyson's appropriation of boul fallé primarily emphasized neoliberal and capitalist possibilities for Senegalese men, as demonstrated by his becoming the first wrestler to pitch a variety of consumer products, flaunting his wealth with luxury goods, draping himself in the flag of the United States for his matches, and becoming a spokesperson for the ruling Socialist Party. Instead of emphasizing the exceptionalism of a man like Tyson in wrestling, the film documents the ways that young men in Pikine, both unknown rappers and wrestlers, are inspired by and learn from the example of a nationally renowned figure like Tyson but also personalize those lessons to their own situations, dropping those values and actions that do not work for them. One of the Coalition Naimu Bmaam rappers articulates this well when he claims that their version of boul fallé "isn't individualism or indifference" but a foundation for the fact that "man is the only medicine for man." The film shows early on that social strategies like masculine inheritance can take many forms. There is an ongoing need in urban Senegal to borrow from predecessors but also to reconceptualize Senegalese society, national belonging, and social relations for each successive generation according to their own urban contexts.

The next sequence in the film introduces the viewer to what such a personalized form of work and engagement looks like for a young, hopeful wrestler in contemporary Pikine. The transition from the interview with the rappers to the images of a wrestler beginning his day is abstract and dreamlike. While one of the rappers continues to speak, Thiaw cuts from a close-up of his hands to a tracking shot focused close on the reddish sand of the beach. This shot then cuts to a darkened image of some curtains blowing, accompanied by the sound of wind or the sea. Another quick edit follows, this time to a running tracking shot of the shoreline, with ocean waves jutting occasionally into the frame. Music accompanies this shot, with thudding drums figuring prominently. The film then cuts to a still shot of a man sleeping in his bed. This is one of the two primary wrestlers who we will follow throughout the rest of the film: Cheick-Tidjane Nguer. In this sequence we see him arise from his bed, stretch and wake up, wash, and then pray. Thiaw's camera follows him closely, but we don't hear Nguer speak except for when, over the shot of him praying, he says, "God said, 'the nose that has breathed life has already breathed death.' Our death is the first thing that we write in the book of life. We all signed it and we are on Earth to discover the meaning of that agreement." Thiaw cuts to an out-of-focus shot of some red fabric and a banging door, with the drum music returning. Then, Nguer is running on the beach, beginning his training regime for the day. While the opening sequences of the film with Awadi, Thiat, the university students, and the Pikine rappers introduce the social stakes of the boul fallé movement and have clear import for the wrestlers who we will follow throughout the rest of the film, Thiaw marks this shift to wrestling with distinct visual and musical cues. We are clearly in a different cinematic realm than what we experienced in the opening sequences, which were shot in a traditional documentary style. A wrestler like Nguer is looking to change his social situation, just like the rappers and students, but the film's introduction of him through abstract visuals and occasional musical accompaniment also conveys the personal, even spiritual importance of wrestling to the young man. In a voice-over, the narrator indicates that boul fallé began in Pikine, "our miserable neighborhoods" where there was no hope, but this led some to wrestling in order to "rediscover who we are." Again, Thiaw's film reactivates the potential of boul fallé to express social frustration and to discover social engagement as an accessible, equitable social ideology. While the filmmaker could have accomplished this by focusing exclusively on hip-hop, wrestling is a unique site for the boul fallé ethos because it allows so distinctly for simultaneous individual and collective reconfigurations: "Wrestling, particularly because it has weak institutions and still few constraints from external norms, . . . is an especially productive site for providing insight to this dialectical movement of the invention of modernity through the reinvention of tradition."[44] Nguer's articulation of his endeavor to discover his spiritual destiny through wrestling emphasizes this dialectical movement on a personal level. He is clearly not interested in simply earning wealth and fame but rather in discovering who he is, his place in society and life, and how he relates to others. Thiaw captures this dialectic throughout the film by centering unknown young men, situating them within their social milieu, and documenting the communities to which they belong.

FIGURE 2.4. Wrestlers, trainers, marabouts, and fans prepare for matches in Dakar, 2013. Photo by Devin Bryson.

Boul fallé also sharpens its perspective by narrowing in on the physical work that the wrestlers accomplish, filming the corporeal surface of the individual that links him to the social body. The camera lingers on Nguer's displayed body as it trains, pulling in closely to his chest and face. Later sequences highlight wrestlers' hands, arms, legs, and backs as they are worked on through training but also as they embrace other men's body parts in practice matches. The other central wrestler in the film, Dam Sarr, also from Pikine, is similarly introduced primarily through his physical form. Thiaw presents him through a close-up from the bare waist up, and we see his muscular chest and determined face. There is then an extended sequence of Sarr's body in action as it engages with other bodies in practice matches, with the trainer giving guidance on how to position and maneuver his body. Physical work, performance, and visibility are the central means of understanding and identification with Thiaw's subjects in the film.

The individuals documented in *Boul fallé* are never only depicted as bodies, however. Thiaw allows the wrestlers to express themselves in interviews, through voice-over, and in captured conversations, with the images and sound underlining their subjective experiences, as in the introductory sequence to Nguer. When they speak, the men often express worries or hesitancies of the importance or outcomes of their work in wrestling. They feel the pressure to perform well in the ring for their families and communities; they express the social implications of their physical work. The film portrays wrestling as a pursuit in which the socially transformative outcomes of work on the masculine body are less important than those of subjective and collective development. Oumar Ndao insists that wrestling is "above all else, an art of perspective and thoughtfulness."[45] Thiaw doesn't undertake a standard documentary of the wrestlers and their actions and accomplishments in the ring. Instead, she moves toward an understanding of their motivations, their hopes, their fears and struggles, and she conveys how that interiority relates to the work they are doing on their physical selves, drawing together the superficial and the subjective. A number of scholars of twenty-first-century Dakar have proposed masculine bodies as essential sites for combating men's economic disempowerment, social marginalization, and global exclusion. They analyze the ways that men's investment in physical visibility, beautification, exposure, and perfection reifies their self-importance, social worth, agency, and mobility.[46] In many ways, these tactics defy the strictures of normative masculinity, which often interdicts attention to the superficial pleasures of masculinity and limits the wholistic alignment of the physical and the interior for men, prioritizing instead one over the other for masculine identities. As Tshikala Kayembe Biaya writes, "New imaginative possibilities for masculinity are currently being formed in African cities."[47] *Boul fallé* expresses a number of those possibilities for urban Senegalese masculinity through an alignment of the physical and subjective components of wrestling.

Along with documenting the physicality and interiority of the wrestlers, the film also documents the collectivity of wrestling, emphasizing it as a local site to articulate belonging and to build community in ways that might be distinct from the homogenizing impetus of the national body. Thiaw shows the camaraderie, support, and mutual respect between the athletes, and the film itself becomes a space of local connections as Thiaw forged a particular relationship with her wrestler subjects because she herself was raised in Pikine and had faced the neighborhood's limitations. *Boul fallé* also lingers on the physical bonds that are formed between wrestlers as they train alongside one another, embrace one another in sparring, and set their bodies in confrontation with one another in their matches. Much of the communal dimensions to wrestling in the film center on the écuries in Pikine, the local gyms and wrestling clubs that gather wrestlers together under a common trainer, training regime, and purpose. They serve as "the nerve center of the neighborhood, a home for socialization and education. They often stand as a second family for the wrestlers."[48] These training centers bring together the men to wrestle, but they also produce links between the friends, family, and community members associated with the wrestlers. In Thiaw's film, the body is the manifestation of and the site for work on the self, but it is also the surface for contact and connection with the community. She doesn't extensively document the families and communities of the wrestlers outside of the écuries and the other networks built around them, such as managers and promoters. The sites of social relations in the film are wrestling spaces and networks. The physical reshaping that takes place within those spaces then produces a reconsideration of one's sense of belonging, affiliation, and even familial links. This process thus has implications for the national body as a whole since the potential for national recognition and connections percolates throughout wrestling culture. Thiaw's film uniquely considers Senegalese masculinity in urban space by depicting the almost spiritual nature of these powerful male bodies and the bonds drawn between them, as well as the collective reverberations of these personal pursuits and relations. *Boul fallé* emphasizes how wrestling provides a way, outside of migration, to combat social impotence, reimagine the body politic, and promote a sense of pride and national identity for urban Senegalese men.

Although the film almost exclusively portrays these masculine spaces centered around the gym and training, there is a focus on the collective body. As the men train, they chant and clap together in unison. In the suburb of Pikine, they do not have the option to be indifferent. Because life in the banlieues is hard, they have to stay focused. In one shot, Nguer is walking on the streets of Pikine, and as he gets on the bus, he witnesses an argument over someone stealing from a woman. His friend says that their parents suffered to educate them with dignity, and "now, it is up to us to continue their work." Wrestling is not only a way to augment one's station in life, but it's also a Senegalese tradition that can be passed along from generation to generation. This emphasis on lineage can be seen in a shot of a woman who is lying in a bed with a baby and a young child sleeping next to her. As the camera moves across the room, Nguer gets up out of bed and puts on his shirt. He then leaves his house and runs out into the dark. He runs along the crowded city street until he reaches the beach. We then see a close-up of his chest, wet and covered in sand, and other shots of his body parts in close-up as he continues his training. In a voice-over, Nguer says, "I am proud to be from Pikine" and that he wants to succeed in the place he was born. He details the familial responsibility that he carries with him into the ring: for his parents as the eldest son, for his wife and children, and also for his brothers and sisters. He says that he trains and fights for all of them with faith. Nguer uses his physical body, shot in close-up, to improve the material, emotional, and spiritual conditions of the familial body evoked in the voice-over. Unlike in *Yoolé*, where young men see no hope or reason to stay in their home country, *Boul fallé* depicts men like Nguer, Dam Sarr, and the rappers who are proud of their communities and fight for them so that their children and future generations can prosper.

The culmination of this individual and collective work in the écuries and on the beaches arrives at the end of the film as we pass into the arena for the official match between the two primary wrestlers who we have followed in the film: Nguer and Dam Sarr. This moment has been anticipated throughout the film as we have come to understand that in a peri-urban Senegalese community like Pikine, as Nguer states, "You have to fight to achieve your goals. Here in the urban periphery, life is hard. There's no other choice than to fight." An official match seems to be the ultimate test of that ability to fight, both in society and in wrestling, as personal work is put on public display. In various scenes threaded throughout the film, we have seen the network of trainers, gym owners, managers, and promoters prepare and negotiate for the spectacle of this event. The sequence of the match builds slowly as Thiaw shows us, first, a match between two young boys who are compared to Tyson. In this shot, the mentoring and lineage of wrestling for boys and men in Pikine are clear. Next, Thiaw shoots a match between Touba Dakar and Leopold. We watch their preparations and the guidance they receive from their training team, which includes marabouts.

The match itself is shot in close-ups of the bodies, making it difficult to distinguish the two men. Already Thiaw is signaling her idiosyncratic cinematic approach to this supposedly culminating event of the film as she obscures the individualization of the wrestlers and shoots them as almost a single, joined entity. We then cut to the match between Dam Sarr and Nguer; again, we see their extensive, elaborate preparations, with the crowd chanting, dancers undulating, and musicians pounding on drums. The anticipation mounts as the announcer asks, "Who will be the winner of the flag?" The role of divinely appointed identity is again highlighted as chants and drums resound: "Show me your divine gifts, show us what God gave you, show us who you are." The wrestlers don't necessarily fight just for prestige or glory but to represent their country, where wrestling is a long-standing tradition, as well as their family and community. Thiaw shoots this match, which is supposedly a battle between two individual men, with an emphasis on the social import of their combat for the wrestlers as well as the community. Wrestling allows resignification, revaluation, and reconfiguration of the individual and social bodies. Right as the two wrestlers enter the ring and prepare to seize one another, a woman's voice-over states, "The warrior's worth doesn't come from the outcome of the fight, but from his capacity to get ahead of his destiny." Thiaw then cuts from the arena to a shot of a boy running through city streets, never showing us the much-anticipated match between Dam Sarr and Nguer.

Thiaw refuses the narrative pleasures that would come from the match, forcing her viewers to return to the preparatory physical work, the personal investment, and the social dynamics of the wrestlers to find closure and meaning from the film. By leaving the match perpetually contingent and open, the filmmaker forecloses the social trends around wrestling that might compel co-optation and competitive individuation, as they did for Tyson. With the communal preparation of the men's bodies before entering the ring, the woman's voice-over about destiny, and the child running, the role of family and community is emphasized. Wrestling provides a way for individual families and local communities to grow and prosper, but it also promotes distinct, alternative forms of national belonging and unity. Thiaw retains the individual agency and collective possibility that her wrestling subjects have attained through their physical training and that boul fallé originally articulated, and she then diffuses them toward her audience and their own social positions and desires for social improvement with that final shot in which we are back in the urban streets of Pikine, running alongside a young boy who has his whole life ahead of him. Whether he eventually enters the wrestling arena or not is ultimately beside the point; his community on the periphery of Dakar will provide him with opportunities and support for carving out his own identity and place of belonging.

The Revolution Won't Be Televised: Men in the Streets

Thiaw extends her documentation of Dakar rappers, their social investment, and personal development in her award-winning 2015 documentary, *The Revolution Won't Be Televised*, by following two of the primary hip-hop members of the Y'en a Marre movement, Thiat and Kilifeu, collectively known as Keur Gui. The mentorship of Didier Awadi toward Thiat that we observe in *Boul fallé* evidently comes to fruition in this later film as the two rappers come to combat the antidemocratic move of President Abdoulaye Wade to secure a third term in office. *The Revolution Won't Be Televised* also continues Thiaw's interest in reconfiguring community, identity, and belonging through social activism along gender lines. Again, Thiaw primarily turns her camera toward men in Dakar. Whereas she resignified masculinity in a number of ways in *Boul fallé*, she explicitly imbues the predominantly masculine communities of hip-hop and Y'en a Marre in Dakar with a revolutionary mother figure in *The Revolution Won't Be Televised*.

The film opens with a close-up shot of Senegalese author and filmmaker Khady Sylla in a dark room, writing and reflecting. We then cut to a shot of three men, Thiat and Kilifeu along with their manager and DJ Gadiaga, who are in the midst of a conversation in an apartment. Kilifeu says, "No one inspired me. Neither Sankara, nor Lumumba."[49] Instead of these monumental figures of Pan-Africanism serving as inspiration for Kilifeu's own activism, he was motivated by local injustices that he witnessed in his own community. Gadiaga agrees, stating rhetorically, "I don't know who Sankara is and I don't care. Sankara and I don't share the same country. Who is he? . . . I only know people who struggled for my nation. I don't know who Sankara is." Although Thiat scolds them, telling his band members that they can't be part of a group like Keur Gui and denounce Sankara, Gadiaga doesn't relent. It isn't that he sees

FIGURE 2.5. Street art portraying Thomas Sankara in Dakar, 2023. Such images are common in the city as many residents adapt the leader's politics and ideology to their own sociopolitical context. Photo by Devin Bryson.

men like Sankara or Lumumba as unimportant or even uninspiring; he simply prefers to look toward familiar, local figures of social activism for inspiration: "I'd rather wear t-shirts with Kilifeu and Thiat's portrait! You are my Sankara! I'm interested in you and the Y'en a Marre! The movement who fought for my homeland!" This scene shows particular limitations to conceptualizations of Pan-African activism due to local and national distinctions. As articulated by Kilifeu and Gadiaga, there is a need for specifically Senegalese revolutionaries and engagement with Senegalese social and political issues. The opening scene of the film posits an important questioning of activist inheritance and mentorship in contemporary Senegal.

This interrogation is then deepened as the film returns to the darkened shot of Sylla. Now, she speaks while looking directly into the camera, her face half-illuminated. Through this staged sequence, Sylla is presented as a narrator writing a letter to her socially conscious artistic descendant Thiat. Sylla refers to him as her "son" as she articulates her own experiences with social engagement and her hopes for Thiat's own protests and activism: "My child, little one, Thiat.... Whenever I see you, I'm deeply moved. My own youth was also illuminated by the flame of rebellion. As you, I loved this People and suffered from its alienation. We were, my revolutionary comrades and I, students at Vanvot high school. We excited the crowd of students as you did on June 23. We organized strikes, marches, sit-ins that were repressed by the police."[50] Like Thiat and the other leaders of the Y'en a Marre movement, Sylla was herself involved in a revolutionary struggle that was opposed by the state. Thiaw has called Sylla "the bridge" in Senegal between the socialist fervor of the 1970s and the activism in the twenty-first century led by Y'en a Marre, as well as between the artists of each time period.[51] *The Revolution Won't Be Televised* articulates this inheritance even further as Thiaw dedicates her film to Sylla, which is incredibly poignant since the latter died of cancer during its production. Doris Posch posits, "Sylla not only becomes Thiat's guiding spirit, she also personifies a lead figure for Thiaw herself."[52] *The Revolution Won't Be Televised* explores the lineage of activism in Senegal, including socially engaged cinema, and the spaces for belonging that such work creates for activists and all Senegalese. Thiaw especially articulates this lineage across the gender binary by linking Sylla, Keur Gui, and Y'en a Marre, emphasizing, as Posch writes, "a transcending of the generational boundaries by expressing solidarity and guidance of this movement through Thiat" but also transcending gender distinctions that are often drawn within activist circles.[53] Posch goes on to say that the scene of Sylla's letter, filmed in the shadows, "not only re-enacts the lead figure by combining activism through the arts, it also positions Sylla as a voice bridging two generations of political struggle," to which we would also add bridging the gender binary of social engagement.[54] Although not as vocal or well known as the rappers of Keur Gui or activists of Y'en a Marre, Khady Sylla is a revolutionary in her own right who attempted to enact political and social change through her films, and Thiaw links her directly to the men in Keur Gui and, by extension, Y'en a Marre. Even though Sylla's scenes in Thiaw's film are minimal, her appearance as a mother figure shows that Senegal has a long and proud lineage of artistic activists who came generations before Y'en a Marre to lead their own rebellions against what they viewed as corruption and injustice and that those lines of inheritance include women as well as men.

Thiat and Kilifeu's activism in 2011 and 2012 that unfurls through the rest of the film is then seen extensively through these opening sequences that, first, push back against the homogenizing dangers of Pan-Africanism that elide national and local distinctions and, second, frame matrilineal inheritance and feminine predecessors within the specific Senegalese lineage of social engagement. As she speaks and writes directly to "her son" Thiat, Sylla, rather than Sankara or Lumumba, stands as the figure who has given birth to Thiat and Kilifeu's social engagement in the opening of the film. Women are active participants in the fight for justice and change as well as in the process of nation building in Senegal. While women are not the Senegalese citizens who typically make the migratory journey to Europe, they are the ones who are left behind to continue to live in and engage with the social circumstances that the migrant men are attempting to flee. While women are not generally the peri-urban residents who enter the arena to compete in wrestling, they are invaluable members of the communities that contribute to and benefit from the revaluation that can occur for individuals and social relations through wrestling. While women might not be proportionately represented within hip-hop, Y'en a Marre, or public representations of activism, they have contributed significantly to the lineage of social engagement in Senegal and continue to contribute to the current urban dynamics of social change. The opening sequence of *The Revolution Won't Be Televised* strongly sets those gendered social realities for the remainder of the film, even as it focuses on two men. If Senegalese men have been rendered socially impotent, they can be reinvigorated not by reifying normative masculine characteristics, values, and practices but instead through inspiration by the cross-gender history and current reality of Senegalese social engagement. The transformation of Senegalese national identity for which Thiat and Kilifeu advocate in their music and activism thus also becomes a reconfiguration of its gendered dimensions due to Thiaw's purposeful framing of their activism through Sylla within the space of the film.

The Revolution Won't Be Televised continually references the complexity, heterogeneity, tensions, contradictions, positionality, and intersectionality embedded within Senegalese responses to social problems, especially along the gendered boundaries of national belonging, even as it primarily documents the actions of Keur Gui and Y'en a Marre in a relatively straightforward manner. After the opening sequence, the film moves to "Chapter 1: In Senegal." The beginning of this section of the film establishes the decision by the Constitutional Court to grant Wade an attempt at a third term and the ensuing protests that included Y'en a Marre. Thiaw provides shots of Thiat, fellow rapper Djily Bagdad, and journalist Fadel Barro speaking at a demonstration in response to the decision. Barro again underlines the question of lineage and inheritance in terms of Senegalese political engagement: "We are grandsons of Mamadou Dia and Cheikh Anta Diop. We are sons of Thomas Sankara. We are not sons of Mobutu or Wade. Y'en a Marre! Together we shall overcome!" While emphasizing their Senegalese and Pan-African predecessors, Barro also disinherits Y'en a Marre from their corrupt father figures in African politics. They are crafting their own community, lineage, and inherited values and practices rather than accepting them from their elders passively and without reconfiguration to their current situation. Although Barro focuses on a national effort and togetherness, he promotes a masculine lineage despite the use of the plural pronoun *we*. Barro highlights the masculine collective—they are sons and grandsons as opposed to children or grandchildren—which limits the process of nation building to men. In an interview, Sarah Nelson asked Barro and Aliou Sané, a journalist and another founding member of Y'en a Marre, about the importance of inclusivity in the movement. Sané indicated that inclusivity was important in the creation and development of Y'en a Marre, although he acknowledges that women have been less visible. He attributes this, at least in part, to the initial violence imposed by the state that led to the deaths of thirteen people: "In that context, it was very difficult for women to be out front."[55] Barro also admits the lack of women participants but argues that change cannot be forced: "We invite women's participation, we're giving them responsibilities, and little by little their participation will increase. It's also worth noting that it takes time and practice to build political and organizing skills."[56] Although Barro promotes the inclusion of women in the movement, it is men who are "giving" the responsibilities and making decisions. Thus, Thiaw's inclusion of Khady Sylla as a woman revolutionary who does not just participate in rebellion but leads it is all the more important in showing women who are front and center rather than marginalized on the sidelines.

This emphasis on the role of women in passing down the revolutionary spirit occurs again a short while later in the film. Thiat tells a story of his mother coming home in 1987 and going straight to her room. When he dared knock on the door and ask what was wrong, she replied that Blaise Compaoré had just killed Thomas Sankara. It was clear to Thiat that this mattered immensely to his mother and so, he says, he learned to appreciate history. Even as this story centers Sankara, his revolutionary fight for the independence of African people, and his continuing inspiration for newer African freedom fighters, it is essential that this news comes to Thiat from his mother. At that point of his life, Thiat did not know who Sankara was but could read his importance through his mother's body and actions. Sankara might be the revered public figure whose face is plastered on numerous murals in Dakar, as shots in the film repeatedly demonstrate, but it is the familial feminine figure of Thiat's mother who provides direct, personalized inspiration to enact social change in his urban community. Thiaw underlines this triangulated lineage that importantly passes through women by following Thiat's words with a return to Sylla in her darkened room, writing her letter to Thiat about her own revolutionary development. She speaks about how Birane Gueye, a colleague of Omar Blondin Diop, both of whom died behind bars after being imprisoned by Senghor in the 1970s, lent her *Das Kapital* by Marx. This led to her participating in mass protests by citizens and workers. Just as Sankara was passed to Thiat by his mother in his personal life, Blondin Diop and Gueye are conveyed to Thiat by Khady Sylla within the cinematic space created by Thiaw. Women are consistently emphasized as necessary predecessors, mentors, and teachers to today's revolutionaries in contemporary Senegal, counteracting the social impotence that can often befall Dakar men.

The Revolution Won't Be Televised also makes important contrasts with dimensions of contemporary masculinity in Dakar portrayed in Sène Absa's *Yoolé*. Due to one of the demonstrations held by Y'en a Marre in the lead-up to the election, Kilifeu is arrested. Thiaw documents members of the movement strategizing about how best to support or free Kilifeu while also sustaining the momentum that they have unleashed among the population for greater transparency, participation, and freedom in Senegalese politics. Eventually Kilifeu is released. The first shot after his release is of him walking along the beach. He says that traditionally the first thing to do after a painful period in an unwanted place is to bathe in the sea in order to purify oneself from the bad energy or evil spirits from that location. We watch as Kilifeu does just that to cleanse himself from his time in jail. He also prays to the sea for peace and serenity in Senegal. Kilifeu's turn to the ocean as a source of purification, unity, peace, and hope, like Nguer's spiritual introduction along the beach in *Boul fallé*, contrasts with the ocean's role in *Yoolé* as a symbol of despair, separation, loss, and death for the migrant men and their families and communities. Kilifeu speaks about how he learned an important lesson about fighting after his father died. Despite his mother's poverty, he decided not to beg or steal but instead to find his way through rap music: "Will you choose the easy way . . . or will you choose the hard one? Make it by yourself in dignity! This is my first awareness, I was thirteen. It helped shape my character." The men who choose to stay and to invest in a better Senegal, like Kilifeu and the other members of Y'en a Marre, as well as the wrestlers and rappers in Thiaw's earlier film resist the globalized attraction of the ocean as a means of escape but also as a source of danger. They are thus able to honor the traditional place that the sea has held in their belief system, even using it as a source of strength for their social engagement. This echo of an important aspect of Sène Absa's film is then intersected by the gender reconfiguration performed by Thiaw in her cinematic work. After his cleansing by the ocean, Kilifeu is further strengthened in his activism by a blessing from his aunt. She speaks to him in the streets of Dakar, telling him that he comes from a long lineage of fighters and that, because of this heritage, Wade has made a big mistake. In this sequence, Thiaw emphasizes that Dakar men can transform the markers of their social impotence and stagnation, such as the ocean as a site of migration, into sources of hope and empowerment through social activism. This transformative process is expanded and reinforced by collaboration and community built across genders and generations, as Kilifeu's aunt and her blessing represent. Kilifeu's and Thiat's stereotypical masculine characteristics expressed through their social engagement—bravery, strength, honesty, courage, leadership—are presented in the film as their inheritance from both women and men but are especially transmitted through feminine figures.

The enlargement of social engagement enacted by Thiat and Kilifeu, as well as by the other members of Y'en a Marre, concerns their fellow contemporary Senegalese citizens, not just their inheritors. This includes the other communities of Senegal, whether peri-urban or rural. The film shows how Y'en a Marre responded through important demonstrations in the streets of Dakar to Wade's announcement to run for a third term and the Constitutional Court's support in that decision. However, it also documents how those demonstrations weren't necessarily accessible to all Senegalese, especially women and older people, due to the violence that ensued. Thiaw's shots of those demonstrations show mainly young men protesting. However, once the campaigns begin and the election approaches, Y'en a Marre switches to a more participatory and inclusive mode of organizing. One of their key strategies in this stage is to ensure that Senegalese citizens are registered to vote and that they in fact go to their polling stations on election day. Thiat says in the film, "It's one of the major weapons we will use against Wade's candidacy." They emphasize the need for all Senegalese to fight apathy or passivity and to be actively engaged in democracy, government, and politics. *The Revolution Won't Be Televised* highlights the inclusivity of this tactic. On election day, Thiat and Kilifeu are in their hometown of Kaolack, a city about 225 kilometers southeast of Dakar. They are in their family homes, surrounded by their familial communities, including women and men. Instead of the young men in the streets from the earlier protests in the film yelling out "Y'en a marre," we now see an older woman shout the same expression to Thiat and Kilifeu as they head to the polls. Y'en a Marre's origins of urban protest have now transformed to participatory democracy in Dakar as well as in other areas and communities of Senegal. The young men of the demonstrations are now joined by women of varying ages. These inclusive dynamics of social engagement expand after election day, as neither Wade nor his primary challenger, Macky Sall, receive a majority of the votes and so must head to a runoff. Y'en a Marre continues their organizing in Mbacké, Kaffrine, and Tambacounda, cities of varying size, in the film. Thiat and Kilifeu call on people to hold up their voting cards and to use them to defeat Wade. They meet with community elders, both men and women, working with them to organize their community members to vote. In one of the shots in Mbacké of Thiat walking the streets and handing out fliers, a woman approaches and speaks to him as well as to the camera: "Women are tired. Elders are not cared for. The household budget went up. Life is painful, especially for women! We don't want Abdoulaye Wade no more! . . . We're fed up!" *The Revolution Won't Be Televised* documents the activism of Thiat, Kilifeu, and the other members of Y'en a Marre that transcends the media-ready images of violent young men in the streets. The film also becomes a site for including and amplifying those voices of regular Senegalese citizens, like the woman in Mbacké, who engage with and contribute to the work of Thiat and Kilifeu. Thiaw's film itself collaborates with the Yenamarristes in expanding their tactics to include all Senegalese, to connect the rural and peri-urban communities to those in the capital, bringing in women and elders, shaping the national body into a purposeful, focused whole.

Similarly to Thiaw's abortive approach to the culminating wrestling match in *Boul fallé*, she does not provide any footage or even clear narration of the results of the runoff election. Again, she displaces the supposed culminating purpose of the actions documented in her film, reorienting her viewers toward the value of the actions themselves for the activists and localized communities. Just as the wrestlers have revalued their lives, identities, and communities by participating in wrestling, whatever the outcomes of the match might be, Keur Gui members have found their destiny of social activism and have energized numerous communities in Senegal toward social and political engagement, whether Wade is defeated or not. At the end of the sequence documenting their engagement with communities outside of Dakar, Thiat and Kilifeu are in Tambacounda at night, attempting to put on a street concert. However, they are unable to perform because their generators die. Thiaw cuts from that frustrated moment to a shot of Keur Gui performing in May 2013, more than one year after that night in Tambacounda. In a pause between songs, Thiat refers to Sall being president and tells the crowd that they can't be content just because he was elected. He encourages audience members to be sure they are registered to vote and participate in their local elections. This is the only moment in which the supposedly culminating point of Keur Gui's activism—the election of Sall and the defeat of Wade—is mentioned. The struggle for a more just Senegalese society continues, and Thiat and Kilifeu's inheritance of social engagement proceeds. Viewers are attuned to the ongoing dimension to this liberatory fight, but Thiaw places greater emphasis on the lineage that Thiat and Kilifeu have fashioned for themselves in order to find a purpose in their lives and communities and on the possibility of other Senegalese being part of that ongoing reconfiguration of Senegalese society. Kilifeu articulates this point again when he says that his dad didn't give him a pen and paper to become a rapper; Kilifeu alone chose his own destiny. Thiaw's elision of Sall's election emphasizes that all Senegalese might make that same choice.

The final section of the film continues and expands these ideas as it documents Thiat and Kilifeu going to Ouagadougou in Burkina Faso for a concert and to collaborate with social activists in that country who have been inspired by Y'en a Marre and are looking to wage their own battle against Blaise Compaoré's undemocratic and never-ending presidency. Thiaw documents the ways that Thiat and Kilifeu bring their experiences, knowledge, and ideas to their colleagues in Ouagadougou but also how they encourage the Burkinabe to find their own specific tactics, approaches, and structures for social and political activism. The network of inheritance that Keur Gui has fashioned can extend across national borders but must also be adapted and personalized, not adopted wholesale. Of course, Thiat and Kilifeu's presence in Burkina Faso also brings the film full circle because they are in Sankara's nation. The film captures them visiting an activist, identified as Le lion, who knew and worked with Sankara. The members of Keur Gui are clearly honored to be in the man's presence. They give him a knit cap that many of the members of Y'en a Marre wear and tell him that they adopted it in recognition of Amilcar Cabral, the Guinean Pan-Africanist and revolutionary leader. Thiat and Kilifeu then visit Sankara's grave, placing rocks on the tomb as a sign of respect. Through this sequence, it seems that the members of Keur Gui have resolved their debate that opened the film; they are indeed the sons of Sankara, having collaborated with activists in his home country, conferred with his collaborator, and visited his resting place. However, Thiaw diversifies the lines of inheritance that can seemingly be drawn linearly. She returns to the shot of Sylla for a final message from her to Thiat: "My child, my little one, Thiat. I would like to finish this letter with a warning.... I would like you to be careful. You are an artist and art is long. You must last. I pray for you, Thiat. May the almighty God protect you, every step you make. And your star, this star so pure keep shining above in the firmament."[57] Sylla enters back into the array of predecessors to Keur Gui, standing alongside Sankara. Most importantly, her words remind Thiat, and the audience, of the inextricable importance of art to his social engagement. Sylla, Thiat, Kilifeu, and Thiaw are artists and social activists. Their art is the foundation for their social change. The film concludes by highlighting this unique aspect of Keur Gui. As the rap group is filmed in a Dakarois studio, Thiat tells the camera that they are working on their new album, which is meant to colonize the world with Wolof. Thiaw's film illustrates how Keur Gui's social engagement has become expansive and inclusive, crossing national, ethnic, and religious borders. Although their lineage of social engagement is diverse, with Sankara and Sylla standing as equally inspirational figures, the film concludes with Thiat and Kilifeu returning to the linguistic, national, and urban origins of their art. They are rooted locally but ready to sow this art and the aspects of their identities that it expresses throughout the world for greater justice and equality. Through Thiaw's film, Thiat and Kilifeu convey an alternative avenue for combating social impotence through social change and global engagement that might be accessible to other men in Dakar.

The residents of the city who board pirogues often do so in the liminal hours of the day, as daylight is overtaken by nightfall or night gives way to sunlight, as they seek out reprieve from the harsh elements of their manual labor or a measure of secrecy for their clandestine activities. However, just as Sène Absa and Thiaw reveal other forms of national cohesion and community, Felwine Sarr reinscribes the meaning of these transitional moments of life in African communities: "As the sun rises over the life of humanity and the forward movement of societies, a new day begins. An uncertain light grows and progressively illuminates the paths of the walkers at daybreak. Throughout the daytime hours, this light will shine brightly over various works in progress and their obstacles. This time of the half-light is also the time of the breakthrough, and those who take part in it need nothing more than a small, weak shimmer of light to embark on the voyage: they are the intermediaries."[58] Instead of boarding the pirogue to cross the dangerous ocean waters to seek out social improvement elsewhere or to eke out a marginal existence through the meager catch from overfished waters, Dakar men, in partnership with Dakar women, can take the diversely populated pirogue of Senegalese society toward the world, offering a just and inclusive model for social change.

3

Community Responses to Peri-urban Water Mismanagement in Joseph Gaï Ramaka's *Plan Jaxaay!* and Abdoul Aziz Cissé's *La brèche*

Due to Dakar's geography as a peninsula, residents of the capital city and its suburbs live closely with water. Besides people's relationship with the ocean, which we explored in chapter 2, water often inundates city dwellers' urban spaces. During the annual rainy season—*nawèt* in Wolof and *hivernage* in French—which extends roughly from June through October, Dakar streets regularly overflow with rain and ocean water. While this is an expected part of life in Dakar, there are times when the rain, the swollen ocean, and the backed-up runoff water converge to cause especially acute and visible problems. Notably, the hivernage of 2022 caused the deaths of several people and submerged the high-end corniche that runs along Dakar's western coast. However, the problems caused by flooding in urban Senegal have historically had a greater impact on the peripheral, vulnerable parts of the capital city.

In August 2005, Dakar witnessed excessive rains, and as a result, the densely populated, often unplanned suburbs of the greater Dakar metro area were significantly affected. Neighborhoods such as Pikine, Guédiawaye, and Thiaroye, all marshes at one time, were flooded. It is estimated that over twenty thousand people were displaced from their homes and forced to find shelter elsewhere.[1] In response to the flooding crisis, President Abdoulaye Wade and urban planning specialists designed a plan they named Jaxaay, roughly translated from Wolof as "the bird which flies the highest." The goals of this policy were twofold: to relocate individuals most affected by the inundations and channel rainwater into catchment basins within the flooded areas. The new housing developments were supposed to feature two- and three-bedroom houses subsidized by the government that the relocated individuals could purchase at reduced cost, provided that they agreed to twenty-year loan repayments.[2] Although Wade promised to pay 52 billion FCFA (US $104 million) to help reconstruct the neighborhood by building cement homes furnished with electricity and running water, he did not follow through. Over a year after this promise, empty fields remained where Jaxaay houses were to be built, and residents were still living in a veritable refugee camp amid filthy water, demolished homes, and mounds of garbage. We visited some of these neighborhoods during the rainy season in 2013 and witnessed the devastation that the floods wrought on these communities. Numerous residents persevered and kept up their daily lives the best they could, even as there were several inches of water

FIGURE 3.1. Residents linger by a catchment basin in Pikine designed to help alleviate flooding but which serves as a dangerous site for children of the neighborhood, 2013. Photo by Molly Krueger Enz.

in their homes and they had to navigate neighborhood streets with the help of improvised stepping stones made out of whatever material was available. A teenage girl proudly showed off her knee-high rubber boots that were necessary for getting around the neighborhood. One resident indicated on the wall of his home how high the water had risen, showing us how his family had to move their belongings up to the second floor. We also visited those who were displaced for the season and had taken up residence in the local high school. Of course, sanitation, cooking equipment, bedding, and privacy were in short supply. The displaced individuals with whom we spoke were hopeful that their plight would be amplified and recognized by those who could help, including the national and local governments. However, they weren't optimistic, given that they had faced this cycle of flooding and displacement for the last eight years.

This environmental management crisis created by flooding and exacerbated by the state is not unique to Dakar. The Senegal River basin, which is located in the north of the country and touches the country's fourth-largest city of Saint-Louis, experienced intense rain and subsequent flooding in the early 2000s. Much of this flooding resulted from natural causes, such as the silting of soil and opening of the Diama Dam to relieve pressure.[3] In 2003, as the floodwaters rose and threatened Saint-Louis, the decision was made by the state to breach the Barbary Strip, an eighteen-mile-long peninsula that serves as a natural topographical barrier between the ocean and the city, in order to allow water from the river to more efficiently drain out into the sea. Despite reservations by some residents of Saint-Louis about potentially dangerous consequences, the state went ahead with the construction of the four-meter breach. In a process that lacked transparency, the breach was constructed overnight and then not discussed afterward.[4] Furthermore, the breach was not adequately bolstered, and it widened over the years, becoming the de facto opening of the Senegal River. While this procedure spared Saint-Louis from having to grapple with urban flooding, it resulted in unintended consequences for nearby fishing and farming communities, including Doune Baba Dieye. Village chief Ahmeth Segne Diagne stated, "This project was carried out without our consent. We're now homeless and unemployed with several problems."[5] Floodwaters were displaced to this area and engulfed the community's houses and buildings, forcing the majority of the residents to leave their generational family homes. Seawater salinized the farmland upon which Doune Baba Dieye relied for sustenance and income. Additionally, fishing became far more dangerous because the breach increased the depth of the water and wave turbulence in areas near the community; observers estimate that around four hundred fishermen have died since 2003 in trying to sustain their long-standing way of life.[6]

In Dakar and Saint-Louis, governmental mismanagement of issues around water has led to environmental and economic devastation. Local communities' strategies of collectively navigating the fallout have underlined the tensions in contemporary Senegal between traditional relationships to the environment, burgeoning needs of urban areas, local agency, and government oversight. In this chapter, we prioritize marginalized, local voices and communities in order to better understand urban environments from those on the ground who are most affected by the government's mishandling of environmental issues such as flooding. The filmmakers we examine, Joseph Gaï Ramaka and Abdoul Aziz Cissé, have turned their lens toward these recent instances of water mismanagement and have highlighted the intersections of the environment, governmental policy and infrastructure, the dynamics between the urban and the peripheral, and local action. Ramaka's *Plan Jaxaay!* and Cissé's *La brèche*, both midlength documentaries from 2007, examine the flooding in the Dakar suburbs and the crisis for Doune Baba Dieye, respectively.[7] Through these two films, Ramaka and Cissé illustrate the interwoven relationship between cinema and politics in twenty-first-century Senegalese cinema. Dovey posits that contemporary African filmmakers are just as political as their predecessors working in the 1960s, which these two films reinforce: "The younger generation simply has new political concerns, and new ways of distributing those concerns. Filmmakers will engage with the particular political issues of their historical moments, with the specific material contexts they inhabit, and with their own, unique experiences of life."[8] In both films, local Senegalese speak for and represent themselves, typically directly facing and addressing the camera with personal examples of how flooding has impacted them, their families, and their communities.

Ramaka stands as one of the earliest examples of a twenty-first-century Senegalese filmmaker who embodies urban social engagement characteristics in his films and his cinematic practices and through his efforts to provide greater access to cinema, which we outlined in chapter 1. In fact, we view Ramaka as a bridge figure whose early filmmaking, especially his 2001 film *Karmen Geï*, represents the more traditional social engagement of globalized Senegalese cinema that dates from Sembène on but with an intense interest in urban contexts. His later work, including *Plan Jaxaay!*, demonstrates qualities of the hyperlocalized, socially engaged cinema of Dakar filmmakers who we focus on in this book. Ramaka engages with local problems in order to improve the everyday quality of life as well as to insist on the necessity of localized knowledge, communal action, and multimodal approaches in dealing with urban and peri-urban issues. He employs the artistic and cultural form of cinema to draw attention to the voices of the marginalized, express disenchantment, and encourage localized urban citizen activism. In reflecting on his role as an artist and filmmaker during a 2009 interview, Ramaka declares, "Things are not right in my country. What can I do as a citizen? If I were a writer, I would write. Cinema is the site from where I can act as a citizen."[9] Through the cultural and artistic medium of film, he provokes citizen agency and ownership over the country's political process, governance, and social problems.

Similarly, Cissé argues that a film is "an instrument of social transformation."[10] He posits that Africans have witnessed a deterioration of their self-worth on the global market that has led them, in turn, to emigrate elsewhere in hopes of discovering a renewed sense of importance. In Cissé's view, cinema has the power to reverse these negative self-perceptions and their social consequences and renew a sense of national pride. He sees culture as the foundation for African societies and argues that cultural artifacts, such as films, are critical for social change. He states that Senegalese cinema, in particular, is experiencing a period of growth. This development is important to "cultural, economic, social, and political sovereignty" because a flourishing cinematic industry improves the Senegalese economy and reinforces the country's cultural position, a process that Cissé is uniquely able to contribute to through his place in the national government's cinematic administration.[11] Beyond cinematic development within official channels, Cissé notes a stance of social engagement especially among up-and-coming filmmakers who are committed to living and working within Senegal, a group in which he includes himself: "We make films to change society.... When young filmmakers point their cameras, they are conscious of the political stakes.... They don't shoot simply to shoot. They shoot for a precise objective."[12] He also points to "the predominance of documentary" among this generation of filmmakers as a marker of their intention to intervene in Senegalese society through their films.[13] In *La brèche*, Cissé clearly shoots his film to critique officials' mismanagement of the flooding situation in the Senegal River basin near Saint-Louis and to document the devastation, but he also shows the resilience of the Doune Baba Dieye community. These aspects are undergirded by Cissé's highlighting throughout the film the hierarchical relationship between urban centers and rural peripheries.

Despite differences in training, approach, and style, both filmmakers depict protagonists living in the margins of the urban cities of Dakar and Saint-Louis and navigating the consequences of environmental crises and their mismanagement by the state. In this way, these films emphasize the necessity of human forms of infrastructure in the face of the failings of official, governmental infrastructure. Mbembe and Nuttall remind us that "urban infrastructure . . . is made up not only of wires, ducts, tunnels, highways, electricity, and automobiles."[14] As governments neglect or underfund those forms of infrastructure, which inevitably falter and deteriorate, urban residents must rely on what AbdouMaliq Simone calls "the notion of *people as infrastructure*, which emphasizes . . . collaboration among residents seemingly marginalized from and immiserated by urban life."[15] Simone continues,

> African cities are characterized by incessantly flexible, mobile, and provisional intersections of residents that operate without clearly delineated notions of how the city is to be inhabited and used. These intersections . . . have depended on the ability of residents to engage complex combinations of objects, spaces, persons, and practices. These conjunctions become an infrastructure—a platform providing for and reproducing life in the city. . . . An experience of regularity capable of anchoring the livelihoods of residents and their transactions with one another is consolidated precisely because the outcomes of residents' reciprocal efforts are radically open, flexible, and provisional.[16]

Simone's articulation of these urban dynamics has been foundational to an ever-growing body of scholarship that centers such interactions in African urban locales between residents and infrastructures within political contestation, citizenship practices, and the negotiation of the social body. Rosalind Fredericks extends the conceptualization of these urban strategies in Dakar to include materiality and labor, arriving at the notion of "vital infrastructures," which "are alive in all sorts of ways with the materials that compose them ... but also, crucially, the human labor through which they take form."[17] Ramaka's *Plan Jaxaay!* and Cissé's *La brèche* document such localized practices and relations among the peri-urban residents of Dakar and Saint-Louis in regard to water while still insisting on the failings of sanctioned, official infrastructures. In their focus on water and on peri-urban residents' improvisational responses to infrastructural water crises, Ramaka and Cissé highlight Senegalese claims to "hydraulic citizenship," to use Nikhil Anand's term, which he elaborates as "a form of belonging to the city enabled by social and material claims made to the city's water infrastructure."[18] We argue that these innovative films deal with themes, populations, and locations that are typically ignored or silenced yet that are as essential to the growth and development of the country as any other social issue, group, or location in Senegal, especially in the way the impacted communities demonstrate the importance of local actors exercising agency over their homes and communities to circumvent and reroute the consequences of governmental disregard and abuse. Ramaka's and Cissé's own cinematic activism corresponds to and amplifies the localized activist strategies undertaken by the peri-urban residents in the face of water crises.

Plan Jaxaay!: Flood Waters Rise

Joseph Gaï Ramaka was born and raised in Saint-Louis, Senegal. After completing his university studies in visual anthropology and cinema in Paris, he established production companies in both Paris and Dakar. Ramaka is best known for his feature film *Karmen Geï*, released in 2001 just one year after Abdoulaye Wade first took office as president of Senegal. Being released at that time, and with its focus on the urban setting of Dakar, the film stands as the cinematic opening of the urban filmmaking that characterizes Senegalese cinema of the twenty-first century. *Karmen Geï* is a provocative rewriting of French author

Prosper Mérimée's 1847 novella, *Carmen*, which portrays the heroine as a bisexual femme fatale who is the object of both male and female gaze and desire. By assigning these socially marginalized gender and sexual identity markers to his protagonist, Ramaka demonstrates his intention to challenge the traditional binaries of male/female, dominator/dominated, and white/Black to underscore the eponymous heroine's quest for freedom. *Karmen Geï* announces a distinct shift to marginalized, excluded identities in twenty-first-century Senegal, and Ramaka specifically views their relevance for an urban context: "Carmen is a myth but what does Carmen represent today? Where do Carmen's love and freedom stand at the onset of the 21st Century? Therein lies my film's intent; a black Carmen, plunged in the magical and chaotic urbanity of an African city."[19] Ramaka's triply othered "black Carmen" is a female, Black, bisexual character portrayed as a "rebellious bird" that "no one can tame." As a heroine who is able to harness the "magical and chaotic" potential of the city, she dominates those around her, including her lovers, police officers, and prison guards. She effectively navigates the urban chaos of Dakar in order to avoid being controlled or dominated by anyone. In doing so, she reflects the change in cinema highlighted by Kenneth Harrow, where women are depicted "as the harbingers for Africa's future."[20] As African urban areas have undergone distinct shifts in recent years, women are often presented as the figures who can navigate these changes in a purposeful way. Phil Powrie posits, "It is not difficult to see how the independent Karmen, organizer of a smuggler group working on the fringes of society, yet at home in social occasions such as the wedding, and at home too in the markets and bars of Dakar, is a supremely urban character who is emblematic of all these changes."[21] Ramaka juxtaposes Senegalese customs and traditions with a society in flux and thus creates a modern version of Carmen who represents the promise but also the challenges of a new twenty-first-century urban Senegal. In *Karmen Geï*, Ramaka announces the urban issues of social change, global connections, marginalization, and agency that dominate the body of films that we study.

Despite the international attention that *Karmen Geï* garnered, Ramaka transitioned to a smaller-scale, localized form of filmmaking with his next film, the 2006 documentary *Et si Latif avait raison!*, a wide-ranging, pointed denunciation of Wade, his presidency, and the deterioration of democracy in Senegal under his leadership. Although the film contains hybrid aspects in its structure, many of Ramaka's other aesthetic choices follow a traditional documentary model, including the numerous talking-head interviews with cultural elites, such as journalists, political figures, activists, and academics, carried out on a soundstage, with the same backdrop for each one. Similarly, the film makes concessions to international cinematic systems, with all of the interviews, the narration, and the reenactment voice-over being in French. While Ramaka's engagement with Wade's corruption and negligence was apparent in this film, his more localized, personal, and community-based cinematic approach to presenting that engagement would develop further in *Plan Jaxaay!*

While *Et si Latif avait raison!* highlights the general way in which Wade betrayed the Senegalese people, Ramaka moved to a focus on one particular instance of Wade's governmental negligence and its consequences for a marginalized peri-urban community. In his 2007 documentary, *Plan Jaxaay!*, Ramaka brings to the screen the local realities of those living in the poorest suburbs of the country's capital in the wake of the 2005 floods and the inadequate population management by the national government. Through his portrayal of individuals living in the margins of the urban capital city, Ramaka expands his audience's understanding of Dakar and its residents, amplifies the voices of the marginalized, and promotes political and environmental transformation within Senegal. The focus in *Plan Jaxaay!* on the Dakar suburbs, namely the departments of Guédiawaye and Pikine, which are situated less than one kilometer from each other, is significant, given both the history of these areas and the role the residents of those communities would soon play in removing Wade from office and sustaining political activism among the wider Dakar population.[22] Guédiawaye was actually once part of Pikine but became its own department in the mid-2000s. These areas were envisioned in 1946 as part of an urban plan following a period of population growth and rural exodus, with the objective to transform Dakar into a "symbol of modernity."[23] The capital was divided into various districts, infrastructure was created, administrative buildings and government complexes were built, and new residential areas were developed to move shantytowns outside of the city center. Rosa Spaliviero asserts that "a displacement of families away from the inner city neighbourhoods was decided by the colonial state: they were truly 'evictions' framed as urban planning projects."[24] As a result, Pikine was founded in 1952 on a former wetland about thirteen kilometers from downtown Dakar. Geographer Marc Vernière labeled Pikine as an area of "pseudo urbanization" that "sprung from nothing" due to the way in which its informal settlements surpassed its planned areas.[25] By the 1970s, Pikine was already the second largest city in Senegal, and today the population is estimated to be around 874,000. Risk of illness, epidemics, malnutrition, and death is high in former shantytowns like Pikine and Guédiawaye due to an overall lack of infrastructure such as water, electricity, medical facilities, and schools. Since their creation, these unplanned areas have been marginalized within the social and political imaginary of the capital city and even the entire country. In *Urban Environments in Africa: A Critical Analysis of Environmental Politics*, Garth Myers posits, "Despite the lively democratic politics of Pikine and Dakar, many people remain disenfranchised or marginalized, particularly those living on the ecological edges. Electoral democracy and peace have not meant that Pikine has anywhere near remotely adequate urban environmental services, for water, sanitation, and solid waste in particular."[26] Ramaka's *Plan Jaxaay!* portrays the lack of essential services and infrastructure that derives from governmental neglect and indifference and the ensuing negative consequences on the health of residents and the local environment in these "ecological edges."

In contrast to *Karmen Geï*, which portrays a protagonist who seamlessly maneuvers the margins of Dakar and represents hope for the future, and to *Et si Latif avait raison!*, which privileges the voices of the political and media elite in Dakar, *Plan Jaxaay!* documents and amplifies the voices of suburban residents who are often subsumed by the chaos of contemporary governance and management of the urban capital space. While Karmen Geï is able to use the "magical" chaos of the city to meet her objectives and the interviewees in *Et si Latif avait raison!* can envision a truly democratic Senegal if Wade were removed, the communities displaced by flooding are victims of former president Wade's and his administration's failure to adequately respond to the urban flooding crisis in Dakar, and they see the only solutions to this negligence as coming from their own abilities and resources. Furthermore, *Plan Jaxaay!* starkly and poignantly shows that when the government doesn't deliver on its promises for change and exploits the potential of the city, more chaos is created. Ramaka shifts his focal point within the urban landscape of Dakar throughout his twenty-first-century filmography. His 2001 feature, *Karmen Geï*, depicts a deft, multifaceted, and independent denizen of the city center; his 2006 documentary, *Et si Latif avait raison!*, centers an educated, politically astute community; his 2007 documentary, *Plan Jaxaay!*, features a community of angry and indomitable yet also confused and distraught residents of the neglected urban periphery. This cinematographic trajectory aptly demonstrates the development of new forms of socially engaged urban cinema within Senegal through the first two decades of the twenty-first century.

This development within Ramaka's filmmaking, as well as within Senegalese cinema overall, is equally exemplified in the filmic techniques used by Ramaka in *Plan Jaxaay!* as he records residents in the Médina Gounass neighborhood of Guédiawaye who poignantly share their personal stories about how they have been negatively affected by the floods and lack of response by the Senegalese government, as well as how they have responded to these effects and the governmental neglect.[27] Ramaka himself is never seen; instead, he prioritizes the voices of those most affected by the crisis, allowing his interviewees to express themselves at length and on a variety of subjects that they see as connected to the original issue of flooding and water management. His interviews concretize the unique, lived experiences of the residents. Yet, simultaneously, Ramaka summons the community as a whole, particularly through interstitial sequences, never allowing his viewers to forget the collective that the personal voices and stories form and that has been as negatively impacted by the environmental problems and governmental negligence as the individuals. Ramaka's film reminds us that a social disaster impacts people and places, with their own unique history, dynamics, and practices. Indeed, all of the interviews in *Plan Jaxaay!* are filmed on the streets of Médina Gounass, capturing the social fabric of this specific place, with its problems and suffering but also its vibrancy and endurance.

The duality of Ramaka's approach is announced in the initial sequence. The film opens with an interview of an unnamed man standing in front of a pool of water, which is intercut with the opening credits. The man's first statement is "We are here in Ama Sow neighborhood," which is then quickly followed by the title card.[28] The viewer is immediately given the specificity of place but is also deprived of the time to become oriented in this place due to the quick intercuts. Even the information conveyed by the interviewee does little to situate the viewer: Where is Ama Sow? In what city is this neighborhood found? In what country? Any viewer approaching the film without adequate background information about the social issue, the filmmaker, the film, or the geography of Dakar would have to become oriented on their own. Ramaka privileges the specificities of the place and its residents from the opening shot, refusing to make his film conform to the perspective, knowledge, or understanding of his audience. Social change in this neighborhood, he implies, will primarily come from the individuals and community depicted in the film, not from the sympathy or generosity of viewers. The man being interviewed then details the problems this neighborhood is facing. He declares that the flooding problems began in 2000: "Since then, we have been living in distress, dirt, and water." Over the course of the film and from other interviewees, we will learn that, as a result of the conditions created by the floods, many residents were forced to evacuate their homes and find lodging elsewhere. Those who stayed suffered from increased health issues such as malaria, cholera, and other gastrointestinal problems. But for the moment, we are only aware of this nameless man, the name of this neighborhood, and the vague problem of flooding. Ramaka opens his film with a disorienting anchoring in a specific location and an emphasis on the collective, and its agency, within the place, even as he documents the personal account of the problems of this neighborhood from one of its residents.

However, just as suddenly as Ramaka plunges his audience into the particularities of the place he is documenting, he subsequently connects these specificities to larger issues. Following the opening testimony, less than a minute into the film, the date February 26, 2007, is displayed on center screen. Although this date is significant because it is one day after the Senegalese presidential election that secured Abdoulaye Wade a second term in office, Ramaka never makes that fact explicit in the film. Again, like the initial mention of the neighborhood's name without contextualization, Ramaka prioritizes local knowledge in his film, and in particular, he depicts a suburban perspective. While disillusionment with Wade and his administration had set in among Senegalese citizens generally by this time due to unfulfilled campaign promises and questionable election practices during the 2007 vote, suburban residents of Dakar had reason to feel particularly betrayed by Wade, as is seen in the frustrations of the flood victims in Médina Gounass. Flooding was a particularly pertinent issue for those living in low-lying Pikine. Myers points out that, at one time, Pikine provided drinking water to Dakar, but today this is no longer the case due to contaminated groundwater. Despite the elevated water table, the water is "unfit for human consumption. Ironically, Pikine is subjected to what has become an annual cycle of flooding."[29] Even residents of central neighborhoods in Dakar may misunderstand, diminish, or ignore the impact of water management on these outlying communities, as flooding is less severe in the city proper. Although Pikine and Guédiawaye are less than ten kilometers from Dakar, the local and underrepresented realities faced by their residents typically go unnoticed. In this way, Ramaka contributes a unique and unheard voice that provides specific contextualization of the generalized complaint of Wade's betrayal and the population's rising frustration.

Following the appearance of the date on-screen, there is a sequence of shots that visually reinforces Ramaka's imbrication of specificity and generality in his treatment of social issues that he introduced through the initial interview and the date on the title card. He shoots an abandoned home, first focusing his camera upward from a low angle toward the dilapidated cement structure and the sky beyond. Then he shoots the flooded floor of the house, including the tires that have been placed in the water to serve as stepping stones, from the same low camera position. The viewer is a resident, even if temporarily, of this house. Ramaka doesn't take an objective, distant view with his camera of the structure and the damage caused by the floods in order to reveal the scope and scale of the problem. Instead, he shoots the house to place his audience in a subjective position of living in these flooded conditions. Ramaka's shots of the damage done to the walls, of the filth of the water that fills the house, and of the precarious navigation through the house over the tires make the challenging conditions almost tangible. This sequence renders the initial interviewees' words about "living in distress, dirt, and water" bracingly real. The life that once occupied the house and that still lingers just outside its walls is recalled as Ramaka pans the camera

FIGURE 3.2. A resident shows his flooded house in Pikine, July 2013. Photo by Devin Bryson.

upward and to the left from his low shot of the tires in the water to reveal a large opening in the structure where a wall once was. Two people walk by the house, surrounded by trash but also by tall grass and vegetation. In the next shot, the camera peers through a glassless window of the house at a man who is sitting against a wall by some water. Again, Ramaka's camera takes up a subjective position; it is almost as if the viewer is peeking out of the home at a neighbor. The man is unselfconscious or unaware of the camera; he is comfortable, seemingly at home, even as his surroundings appear uninhabitable. Life continues within this devastation. The soundtrack that accompanies these visuals reinforces all of this. With slow, deep, and solemn chords of instrumental music in the aural foreground, the viewer sees rippled water filling the home and inundating the neighborhood while residents sit idly next to or carefully walk through the garbage that is evidently everywhere. Such a musical accompaniment is rather standard for a film that documents social ills. However, in Ramaka's film, the viewer simultaneously hears the wind whipping past the camera, the voices of neighborhood residents, and the quiet but steady ripples of the standing water in the aural background. Peri-urban life audibly continues, even as the soundtrack might evoke a standard viewer response of pity. Agency and disaster exist side by side in this location. Ramaka again brings duality, this time aural duality, to his documentation of the flooded, neglected part of Dakar in the early twenty-first century in order to represent the complexity of these issues and of the lived experience of the residents of these areas.

Next is a tracking shot of a woman walking with a bucket and who is accompanied by some children. This shot is overlaid with another tracking shot, this one a long shot, of the neighborhood skyline at sunset, demonstrating the extent of the water and the debris that has piled up due to the flooding. Ramaka finally gives his audience the expected establishing shot, but by laying it over the close tracking shot of the woman walking with the bucket, he reminds his audience of the human component that is always embedded in "the flood crisis" and, by extension, in any social problem. However, the overlay also makes both components of the shot ghostly and ephemeral, evoking Felwine Sarr's description of Dakar as a "palimpsest city" and suggesting that the mismanagement of the water creates a disconnect between people and their neighborhood, between individuals and their environment, between the past and the present. The sequence concludes with three additional shots of different parts of the neighborhood—its life as well as its destruction—adding to the subjectivity and embeddedness that has accumulated throughout. By the end of this sequence, we know this neighborhood, the people who live there, and the conditions in which they live. We come to this knowledge succinctly, without much dialogue, and before we have learned anything about the history or context of the flooding issue beyond its existence and its impact on the lives of neighborhood residents. By the second minute of the twenty-five-minute-long film, Ramaka has masterfully evoked the depth of the critical issue of water mismanagement in the Dakar suburbs by prioritizing the specificity of this problem for the residents of Médina Gounass and presenting it to his audience through multidimensional, at times contradictory images and sound that demand the audience's full engagement rather than simple sympathy.

After this sequence, Ramaka then returns to the interview with the man that began the film, through which we finally learn some of the context to the current situation that the filmmaker has just visually and auditorily represented. However, the man emphasizes a different dimension of the problem than the one we've come to focus on through the opening sequence. He states that since the 1960s, people who were evicted were compensated and given new land. Again, for a certain viewer, this statement is confusing, while for one who has connections to the place of the film, its meaning is clear and powerful. The man continues, "But here in Gounass, since they started evicting us as part of the Jaxaay plan, it appears that it's not about compensation, but rather a sale. Usually, when they tear down your house they should not sell you another one instead. When they tear your house down, they should give you another one." He says that the house that they sell you is much smaller than your original one, leaving your family in disarray. There is no clarification as to who *they* refers to in the man's comments or the name, position, or history of the man speaking, and viewers haven't learned why the flooding has happened or why houses are being taken and demolished. Are the floods that bring destruction and filth to the neighborhood even related to the evictions? Or is the man bringing up a separate issue that plagues Médina Gounass? Ramaka continually circumscribes the information presented in the film so that a locally knowledgeable and engaged audience is most easily able to enter into the community and its problems that are documented. However, one thing that the film does make clear to its audience through the man's words is the significant impact of this disaster and of this plan on the lives of people. Ramaka powerfully articulates the consequences of the problem, even as he leaves the cause and size of the problem obscure to some viewers. *Plan Jaxaay!* does not directly call for social change that will be understood by all audience members. Rather, it artistically and complexly sketches out the ramifications of larger sociopolitical dynamics for a specific Senegalese community and amplifies their own responses to those effects.

The man eventually mentions "the president," but he continues to use the pronoun *they* when referring to the authorities who have enacted the Jaxaay plan. He says that they want to force people out of their neighborhood so they can take over the land. This statement elucidates Ramaka's focus on the people and the community of Médina Gounass. It isn't just land or houses to those who have lived there for their whole lives; it is a location that forms and shapes the communal life and personal existences that develop within it. The interviewee's name is not necessary to report in the film because what matters within the context of documenting the social problems in Médina Gounass is that he is a resident of the neighborhood and can articulate his personal experience, as well as the experiences of his neighbors, living through those social problems. He continues and eventually mentions the president's wife, Viviane, and her trip to the neighborhood that instigated a brief use of the water pumps that could clean out the flooded homes. This is the only reference during his interview to someone with power by name; the other instances are marked with *they*. Through this linguistic gesture, whether conscious or not on the part of the interviewee, the elites are verbally elided and marginalized within the narratives of the film's interviewees. The residents' own voices, their experiences and observations, as well as Ramaka's visuals, which reinforce and expand their comments, are centered in the film. Ramaka chooses not to reify the power hierarchy that has produced this disaster by clearly representing it in his film. During the last part of his time on-screen, the man shows us his home, describing how it was before the floods and the subsequent evictions and how he has had to rebuild it as the flood waters have receded, pointing out the different levels of construction throughout the years in the walls. The nameless interviewee concludes his role in the documentation of the strained life in Médina Gounass by giving a personalized, intimate geography and history of the flooding problem as it is inscribed in the structure of his house. Ramaka's film values and respects the man's account of the social problem that besieges him, his family, and his neighborhood while employing layered, multidimensional visuals and audio to render the narrated experience concrete and meaningful for the audience.

Throughout the rest of the film, images of interviewees are continually juxtaposed with shots of the neighborhood—a passing car or horse cart, residents exiting their homes and walking along the road to complete their daily tasks, and garbage that surrounds it all. The interstitial shots contain beauty and cinematic eloquence—a woman in a strikingly bright-red, flowing dress and head wrap shot in slow motion; the diffuse evening light making a crowded, dirty corner of the neighborhood glow—that contrast with the detritus and squalor but that also pair with them to form an ineluctable binary in this neighborhood. The film shows that life and destruction, beauty and filth, anger and hope exist side by side within Médina Gounass. The style of these interstitial sequences, which alternate between moving tracking shots and stationary shots, also emphasizes the diversity of experiences, needs, desires, and identities in the community. These sequences convey the value of heterogeneity in this urban locale, even as the official governmental plan for the neighborhood is uniform and one size fits all, with everyone being displaced and given a standard new house.

The complexities of this neighborhood, exacerbated by the flooding mismanagement, are navigated with creativity and innovation by the residents, as evidenced in the continuing interviews. Ramaka shoots the residents in their everyday environment, which creates a sense of realism and urgency to resolve this urban flooding crisis. By depicting the residents in their own locale, he also illustrates how official plans have only worked to disenfranchise the residents from their agency, control, and ownership of the neighborhood. In doing so, Ramaka highlights not only the residents' perspectives but also the tragedy of Wade's betrayal of these local spaces and problems. Ramaka shoots an interview with one resident, Kalidu Ndiaye, against the auditory backdrop of children playing and the visual background of people walking through their neighborhood—the daily life of the community. A boy who is interviewed posits that the government is pushing relocation to areas that lack amenities such as electricity, police officers, courthouses, fire stations, district offices, and hospitals. Despite the daily struggles faced in Médina Gounass, he prefers to remain: "We know that we don't live comfortably here, but if they let us stay, we shall develop our neighborhood. We know what life looks like here. That's our problem." Ramaka and the residents again emphasize the importance of localized knowledge and experience in dealing with social problems in the urban periphery of Dakar. The boy's comments acknowledge the importance of official, state-provided infrastructure but also its limitations. He articulates a critique of the state's inequitable distribution of services, especially in the new site for the displaced residents, but he doesn't look exclusively to the state to resolve these inequities. Instead, he privileges localized knowledge and human infrastructure in building and improving his community, which is echoed among all of the residents documented in the film. *Plan Jaxaay!* is anchored in this specific place, its residents, their knowledge of the place, and their history there. Just as it documents a skepticism toward governmental outsiders entering into the community with so-called solutions to its problems, it only permits viewers to engage with the neighborhood if they are ready and able to understand the residents and their concerns from their perspective, history, and knowledge.

Another resident, Kuma Siré, details the logistical, health, and financial problems that the government's mismanagement has created. As she describes these myriad problems, a flute plays lightly in the background, encouraging the viewer to empathize with the resident who poignantly shares her hardships, which she describes as "Armageddon." She compares the murky black color of the tap water to wastewater and declares, "We are tired, we women of Médina Gounass." She describes how these same women staged a demonstration in front of SONES, the Senegalese National Water Company, and wore red scarves to show their anger and frustration.[30] Siré contends, "We are tired of talking." The fact that these women demonstrated to express their discontent shows how Ramaka's film is not simply identifying problems and advocating for abstract change. On the contrary, *Plan Jaxaay!* seeks to achieve Cissé's

Community Responses to Water Mismanagement

goal, which we described earlier in the chapter: to show Africans in general and Senegalese in particular that they can control their own fate, providing them with a sense of agency over their own lives—including the problems they face due to their own government. The fact that *Plan Jaxaay!* is still available to view for free on Vimeo through Ramaka's own account shows that the filmmaker is committed to providing the means for those most affected by these social issues to exercise agency over the problems.[31] Like his urban heroine Karmen Geï, the women of Médina Gounass are presented as societal change makers. The filmmaker shows how Wade and his administration have disenfranchised residents from their homes and neighborhoods, but he also encourages change through his representation of them taking back that power.

Abou Dia is another local resident who is engaged in social change as a member of an organization that was formed in 1998 by residents to help manage the area outside of the purview of local government. He says, "My name is Abou Dia, resident of Médina Gounass," announcing his belonging to this community as a resident first and foremost. His activism comes out of lived, communal experience, not an outside concern for social problems. Dia continues, "We cannot do anything against water flow, but we do what we can." He recognizes his limitations and the

FIGURE 3.3. Residents of Pikine navigate flooded streets, July 2013. Photo by Devin Bryson.

need of the state to intervene, but that doesn't stop him from organizing human infrastructure in the neighborhood to provide for the failings of the state. He points out that since the flooding and the subsequent increase in garbage and waste in the neighborhood, the organization uses the trash to build up a foundation for roads and to provide walkways through the flood waters. Additionally, he demonstrates how they have undertaken home construction projects on top of the abandoned, dilapidated houses. The community uses tactics of repurposing and recycling to carve out their needs within the larger context of destruction and neglect in the neighborhood, just as the filmmaker documents beauty in his film from the dilapidated material in the neighborhood. Ramaka emphasizes this parallel at the conclusion of this sequence with a low, moving shot of the ground covered in garbage, followed by a number of brief shots of the life—people, goats, birds—that persists within this landscape that has been abused and neglected by government officials but reconfigured by local residents.

Even as Ramaka reveals the human infrastructure of the community that has been deployed to productively navigate the flooding crisis and its subsequent mismanagement, the residents who are interviewed describe the neglect they have encountered from those in power. The last three interviews in the film are all with women, and each of them pointedly denounces Wade and his negligence, which, contrasting with the earlier vague references to *them* when speaking of the authorities, reinforces the unique social engagement that Ramaka sees women taking up. The first of these interviewees begins by thanking God that "you" have come to inquire about their living conditions. Since Ramaka is not a presence in the film, either visually or audibly, the *you* she refers to comes to represent the spectator just as much as the filmmaker. While Western or urban Senegalese audiences began the documentary as outsiders to this community, forced to orient themselves without the help of the filmmaker, by this moment of the film they have become participants in the possibility of social change. The viewer's subjectivity has been structured and developed by the film itself. This unnamed woman says that there have been problems in Gounass since 1989, but they have become more poignant since the election of Wade, whom she names for the first time in the film, because of the change he promised: "They said 'Plan Jaxaay' but we have seen nothing yet.... We are tired.... We live in the midst of water, trash, dirt, germs!" These women are critical of the lack of support under Wade, who does not venture to the poor suburb to witness the problems himself. Another woman laments, "As for President Wade, we know nothing about him. He is not helping us because he doesn't know Gounass, our community. When they told him about it, he said he didn't know Gounass. Whereas, we believed in him . . . but he does nothing for us, he does not care for us . . . Wade did nothing in Gounass. We do not exist in his eyes." Throughout the rest of her interview, the woman repeats "He doesn't know Gounass" two more times. Along with the unique shots of the neighborhood, the woman's words emphasize the need for localized knowledge and community engagement to deal with the social problems. However, at the time of the presidential elections, this woman, along with many in Médina Gounass, voted for Wade. When the interviewer almost inaudibly questions why she voted as she did, she claims that she and her fellow citizens were motivated by hope but quickly learned that they had been deceived.

The final interview of the film takes place at dusk, with a fire burning behind the woman who speaks. It leaves a final, bitterly ironic reminder of the turn from hope to anger that has taken place in the neighborhood during Wade's presidency. The woman recounts that after the floods, she was forced to live in a temporary refugee camp, even though she was far along in her pregnancy. While in the camp, a journalist conveyed to her the wishes of Viviane, the first lady, that the woman's soon-to-be-born daughter, the first baby of the camp, be named after her. The woman, holding the now toddler in her arms, admits that she agreed to the first lady's desires, naming her daughter Viviane. However, after this act of respect, Viviane Wade briefly appeared once in the camp to meet her namesake and subsequently never returned to deal with the more pressing issues of the floods, the displacements, and the destruction of homes. As soon as the woman concludes her story, Ramaka freezes the frame and runs the title of the film and the credits over the freeze-frame of the woman, with the fire burning behind her. Ramaka retains the potential for change in the community with the freeze-frame, suspending Médina Gounass at this moment of pointed critique of the Wade family, opening the community up toward further social and political activism to reshape their peri-urban lives. The film is inconclusive about whether the situation in this community will improve, about whether the president will be reelected and continue to ignore the flooding problems, or whether sanctioned political action would even be effective in this situation. Yet it preserves the strategies, articulations, and practices of this community for enacting agency over their own lives.

Ramaka portrays the population's rising frustration with Wade and his administration by allowing residents in Médina Gounass to speak for themselves and to express their discontent. He highlights their voices while emphasizing the images or sounds they see, hear, and face on a daily basis. The quotidian nature of his documentary is reinforced by the temporal trajectory of the film. From its sun-filled opening shots of the initial interviewee and the dilapidated house framed by the bright blue sky through its final interview that occurs at nightfall, *Plan Jaxaay!* seems to take place over a single day. This narrative time frame emphasizes the "day in the life" format of the film and its documentation of the daily reshaping and renegotiation of the Médina Gounass neighborhood by its residents. Through Ramaka's cinema, which illustrates the challenges faced by the most marginalized and their organic, ingenious response to those difficulties, the filmmaker emphasizes the "ways that urban residents contest and confront the governing prerogatives of planners and government officials in their daily negotiations of infrastructure politics."[32] His film also helped to lay the groundwork for a structured opposition to the government that finally arrived with the next election cycle. The problems, issues, and dynamics Ramaka depicts in *Plan Jaxaay!* contributed to the growing opposition to Wade's administration, eventually leading to the creation of the Y'en a Marre social movement, which itself has undertaken campaigns to intervene in urban flooding crises. Ramaka's film, like the others we study in this book, responds passionately in its form and content to the strategies adopted by Senegalese citizens to better manage their own lives within the context of official mismanagement. *Plan Jaxaay!* strives to capture the human infrastructure deployed by the peri-urban residents, which then feeds back into Senegalese society, inspiring other social actors to gather their own human resources to reshape their own local communities.

La brèche: The Diversion of Water

While Ramaka began his career in the 1990s and gained global success with *Karmen Geï* at the turn of the century, Cissé is decidedly a product of twenty-first-century Senegal. His education and cinematic training all occurred within the country. Likewise, his brief filmography has centered on highly localized subjects. Originally from Saint-Louis like Ramaka, Cissé began his filmic development at the Centre de communication Daniel Brottier. This training center has produced a number of participants within Senegal's contemporary film culture, from government administrators to technicians. Cissé's first film, a documentary short entitled *Bët gaal,* debuted in 2001. From this initial work, Cissé's interest in the environment and water in particular is clear, as the documentary looks at the importance of the pirogue, both symbolically and materially, in the lives of fishermen in the Senegal River basin near Saint-Louis. The film won the prize for best documentary at the 2004 edition of the Festival image et vie and was subsequently broadcast on the international francophone channel TV5 and the Senegalese channel RTS. Cissé then collaborated with two other Senegalese filmmakers on a fiction short, *Yacine,* which also won festival awards, both local and international. In 2007, *La brèche* opened a trilogy of midlength documentaries that analyze the ways urban dynamics have reshaped Senegalese traditions, images, cultural production, community engagement, and interpersonal relationships. The trilogy was completed with the release of *Aaru Mbèdd—les murs de Dakar,* which documents street artists, and *Renaissance,* which examines artists' navigation of official infrastructures in the visual arts, both in 2010.

Cissé views the environmental themes that he explores in *Bët gaal* and *La brèche* as foundational to Senegalese experiences and identities, as well as cinema. He believes that African sensitivity to nature comes out of the Charter of Mandé, a document from Mali that dates from the thirteenth century, which states, in Cissé's words, "All life is life. No life is worth more than any other life."[33] This charter established the first African human rights declaration through its focus on equality. In Cissé's view, this statement extends to plant, animal, and geological forms of life. He also insists that environmentalism is inherent to Senegalese cinema, dating back to the work of Sembène and Mambéty, which might have preceded many recognizable forms of environmentalism as a codified social issue but which certainly demonstrated a sensitivity and attention to the relationship between people and their surroundings, especially those natural ones. Cissé states, "Senegalese cinema is genetically environmental.... We can't avoid talking about the environment."[34] The place of the environment in contemporary Senegalese societies and his own cinematic work is complex, as urbanization and development continue apace and spread into areas of the country that have heretofore maintained delicate balances between their needs and nature. He states that one way to navigate these issues is to "place ourselves at the disposition of the elements" and to reflect on the question, "What is the relationship we have with the places in which we live?"[35]

In *La brèche*, Cissé poignantly explores how the residents of the Senegal River basin, including of Saint-Louis and Doune Baba Dieye, have traditionally and recently responded to the question, especially in regard to water, as well as the reshaping of their response that is forced on them by the state's negligence in opening the breach in the Barbary peninsula. He documents the experiences and beliefs of local populations through interviews that emphasize the collective over the individual. In his examination of urban political ecology, a framework which aims to understand urban environmental change, Myers expresses the need to better articulate "the voices of ordinary people in marginalized majority communities in African cities."[36] In *La brèche*, Cissé allows these ordinary people to speak, to share their knowledge about water and flooding, and to lament how their lives have changed for the worse due to the government's negligence. Throughout the film, Cissé visually juxtaposes state-implemented urban infrastructure that attempts to control the area's water, such as bridges and dams, with customs and practices, like fishing and swimming, that have developed in accordance with water. Finally, Cissé structures his film around the local legend of Mame Coumba Bang, who is the Senegalese goddess of the river. He weaves brief fictional representations of this legend throughout his documentation of the contemporary urban milieu of Saint-Louis, reminding his viewers that even as urban centers continue to grow and demand increased use of natural resources, the necessity to live in tune with the environment endures. The goddess is often seen in juxtaposition with the city's urban structures that are remnants of the colonial state in Senegal: a bridge, a dam, and a statue named after or honoring colonial administrators of Saint-Louis. Although Cissé doesn't ever directly mention the city's colonial heritage, it visually contributes to the complexity of the contemporary urban network that has been built up over centuries, very often for the benefit of a select, elite segment of

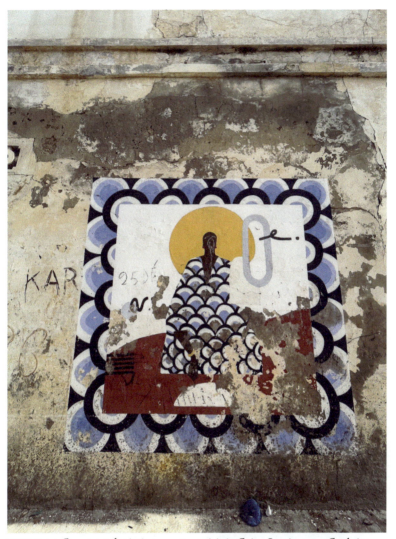

FIGURE 3.4. Street art depicting a water spirit in Saint-Louis, 2023. Such images are found throughout the city, which is the supposed home of Senegalese water goddess Mame Coumba Bang. Photo by Molly Krueger Enz.

the population. Throughout *La brèche*, Mame Coumba Bang stands in firm but silent visual opposition to the inequities and disempowerment of this deeply entrenched urban landscape. Myers argues, "Spiritual and supernatural conceptions of urban environments are crucial, often hidden, dimensions of the produced ecosystems in Africa."[37] Our analysis of *La brèche* is in line with Myers's argument as we emphasize Cissé's strategies for highlighting the importance of this river goddess in the lives of the residents of the peri-urban area of Saint-Louis and the role of the supernatural in understanding the complexities of urban environments.

Whereas Ramaka focuses on the political contestation that the community of Médina Gounass enacts through its discursive and practical engagement with water infrastructure in the wake of Wade's mismanagement, Cissé emphasizes the long-standing local customs and practices within the Senegal River basin that have been centered on water and which the breach disrupted, perhaps irreparably. *La brèche* opens with a form of localized knowledge that is arguably even more deeply anchored in the site and community than those highlighted in *Plan Jaxaay!*, plunging its audience into systems of knowledge that are little known outside of the area. The sound of flowing water plays over the opening credits until Cissé gives his audience an opening close-up shot of the currents in a body of water. We then hear the voices of children speaking to each other about what "she" is going to do them and where "she" is going. They say, "She is going to hit you. No, she tortures you first before eating you."[38] For an extended portion of this opening sequence, the filmmaker provides no referent for this pronoun, and contextual clues are slow to arrive as well. Eventually the kids say, "We can encounter her but she is invisible." They state that she returned from the market to eat, dressed in white. The metaphysical, mythical qualities of this figure start to come into view. A man's voice intervenes for the first time and asks questions to the boys about the figure. To appease the children's fears, he reassures them that they are just talking about her and not doing anything wrong. Finally, he says that he thought she was a good spirit, to which most of the boys respond with incredulity. The film then cuts to a shot of the people whose voices we've been hearing: the boys on the bank of a body of water, crowded around the knees of a man just in the frame. Their conversation continues for a bit longer, discussing the temperament of this spirit who is still unnamed. Cissé cuts to a sequence of shots of running

Community Responses to Water Mismanagement

FIGURE 3.5. The Senegal River occupies a prominent place in the city of Saint-Louis and in the lives of its residents, 2023. Photo by Molly Krueger Enz.

water. A man's voice-over comes in on the third shot and explains the belief of starting one's day by looking out at the river and sea first thing in the morning, as they are "filled with good vibrations, with good influences." There are then several shots of people by the water: boys playing on a docked fishing boat, people walking along the shore, a boy balanced on a bridge over water. Then Cissé cuts to a close-up of the man who provided the voice-over about the relationship between water and good luck at the start of a person's day. The director does not provide the man's name or credentials with a title card, disregarding the common approach to interviews in standard documentary films. Through this technique, Cissé emphasizes that the importance of the local legend comes from the long-standing beliefs and practices of the area's residents rather than the educational or professional credentials of this so-called expert. The interviewee continues on to explain that Mame Coumba Bang is a water spirit who can serve as a protector but who can also take vengeance at times. She appears in different forms and settings despite originally having been a human being. We are finally given details of the metaphysical being that the boys were discussing at the opening of the film.

This man also mentions their location of Saint-Louis, the first time that we've been provided geographical orientation in the film. Sitting on a bench alongside the river, he mentions the particular setting of the interview as the living room of Mame Coumba Bang and warns the viewer not to confuse it with "big bang." He clarifies that *bang* is the Wolof word for *banc*, or "bench," and according to the popular legend, Mame Coumba Bang often sits on a bench in the evening when it's chilly outside and the sea breeze envelops the island and city. Cissé seems to keep the references to Mame Coumba Bang intentionally mysterious and elusive. Only those who are anchored in local lore may understand, which demonstrates how the film emphasizes the tensions between local beliefs and urban infrastructure around water. At the end of the man's interview about Mame Coumba Bang, the film cuts to a low shot of the water from the shoreline. A pair of human legs dissolves into the shot, with a white gown falling over part of them, recalling the boys' belief that the water spirit appears at times dressed in white. The legs walk out of the water onto the shore, and the film fades to black. Cissé's film seeks to valorize African indigenous knowledge of the supernatural, which was downplayed by European colonizers and Eurocentric scholars. Through the continual appearance of the river spirit Mame Coumba Bang in the film, Cissé prioritizes indigenous thought and perspective as a counter-narrative to that of inevitable, perpetual urban development.

Just as viewers of *Plan Jaxaay!* who aren't intimately familiar with the local dynamics, history, geography, and beliefs of Médina Gounass might be disoriented at the beginning of the film, those audiences of *La brèche* who are not Senegalese or who are not originally from the Saint-Louis area might be initially distanced from the subject of the film. Cissé surpasses concrete, codified knowledge like geography and political policies in the film's opening to express the long-held traditional beliefs that undergird the environmental issues and their social consequences that will be subsequently depicted in the film. These beliefs are far more than just stories told by boys, as the shots of local residents living in accordance with the water in the opening sequences remind us. These communities' daily practices and livelihoods are still determined in many ways by the myth of a water spirit that has endured in their culture for centuries. Cissé returns to the image of Mame Coumba Bang throughout *La brèche*, reminding his viewers of the continuing necessity of living in harmony with water for local residents, but his incorporation of her into the film is consistently mysterious and elusive. He doesn't return to the talking head to expound the spirit's significance from an academic perspective nor does he ask local residents to explicate her importance for their lived experience. Instead, Cissé includes her subtly, at times obliquely, in shots of Saint-Louis and even without specifically naming or identifying her beyond a recurring visual motif. As Cissé concludes the opening section of the film by rendering Mame Coumba Bang visible, tangible, and real, he emphasizes the centrality of water, its power, its dangers, and its support of life, to the communities in the region. As the boys at the beginning of the film recount, it is necessary to be thoughtful and attentive to water in the Senegal River basin.

Of course, as we know, governmental officials who cut the breach in the Barbary peninsula were not attuned to water dynamics in the area nor did they listen to the residents who attempted to share their localized, indigenous knowledge of those dynamics. The state chose to prioritize the needs of the urban residents of Saint-Louis to the detriment of the rural inhabitants of Doune Baba Dieye and Mouït Gandiol, the two villages documented in the film. *La brèche* therefore resists "simplistic binaries that separate the rural and the urban by showing precisely how the two are interpenetrated in all sorts of complex ways."[39] The film also demonstrates that "custom is alive and well in many projects to define the contours of civility today" and suggests that "the tensions and implications of colliding sovereignties implied by citizenship that is defined by custom are, perhaps, most powerfully illuminated where the urban and the rural literally intersect."[40] The film begins with the customs around Mame Coumba Bang and then carries out the implications of the breach for those beliefs. The second sequence in *La brèche* is a still photo of the peninsula before the breach, then a title card that describes the circumstances of the breach, followed by another still photo of the peninsula but this one after the trench has been dug. This sequence is auditorily accompanied by the sounds of ocean waves. The title card states that on September 3–4, 2003, the Senegalese authorities decided to dig a canal on the Barbary peninsula to reroute the water from the river into the ocean and to fight the recurrent floods in Saint-Louis caused, in part, by the water discharged from the Diama Dam. The note claims that the initial canal width of eight meters quickly turned into a breach of eight hundred meters, which is evidenced by the still photo of the peninsula after the breach. Cissé begins his film by plunging his viewers firmly in local beliefs and traditions and only then opens up the documentary to the wider political and infrastructural context. He prioritizes the values, practices, and experiences of local residents over the official narrative of the breach and its aftermath.

After introducing the documented details of the situation, Cissé returns to the importance of local customs around water for all of the residents in the Senegal River basin, including the inhabitants of Saint-Louis. Even though they might have been the primary beneficiaries of the breach because it alleviated their flooding, they are not immune to the negative consequences of the project since they are as beholden to the delicate balance between water and human existence as any other residents of the area. The next sequence visually reinforces that this incident has played out within the tensions and negotiations between the urban and the rural, particularly regarding water. Three teenage boys empty water out of a small boat and reel in a fishing net while we continue to hear the sounds of the ocean waves as well as the splash of the water due to the boys' work. A woman in white enters the shot from the left and passes on the shore in the background. It is easy to overlook her since our attention is initially focused on the teenagers in the boat. We might also simply see her as a common pedestrian, like the man who hurries by in the foreground of the shot. However, if we are attuned to her presence, we can understand that Mame Coumba Bang lingers in the contemporary urban context, even as some individuals might ignore her influence. The sequence continues with a long shot of fishing boats in the water with the city in the background as we continue to hear the sounds of water. Next is a shot that moves closer into the city. A pirogue rests in the water in the foreground while we see buildings and a bridge extending over the water in the background. The soundtrack in the shot reinforces the film's approach to the city as the sounds of the water now intermingle with the sounds of the city, such as car horns and crowds of people. Finally, the film cuts to a shot from within the heart of the city. The lingering sounds of the water have now been fully replaced by the clamor of the city. Cissé shoots the entrance to one of the few bridges that connects the peninsula, the island, and the mainland of the urban Saint-Louis area as vehicles and crowds of pedestrians pass over it. Once again, a woman dressed completely in white enters the shot, this time from the right. She crosses the street to the pedestrian pathway of the bridge, joining the crowd and continuing away from the camera. In this shot, from the center of Saint-Louis, the woman is even more difficult to identify than in the previous shot of the teenagers in the fishing boat. Her image lingers as a constant reminder of how important it is to consider local perspectives and traditions when making decisions that impact the lives of local residents, which was not done in the construction of the canal. Cissé's shots of the city's structures—its skyline, waterfront, streets, and bridges—with Mame Coumba Bang embedded within them, remind us that "delineations of citizenship are codified and contested in the built form of the city."[41] The river goddess is all but lost within the urban milieu except to the most attentive viewer. Cissé leaves it up to the spectator to seek her out—she may be mysterious and hidden, but she is nevertheless very much present. Her critical role in understanding the environment has perhaps been hidden by European colonizers and the Senegalese state who attempted to suppress indigenous knowledge and perspectives, but Cissé magnifies and valorizes her importance.

As the woman walks away, the camera pans to a statue of a white patrician gentleman that looms over the busy street. The plaque below the statue states that it is dedicated "to its governor L. Faidherbe."[42] Until the nineteenth century, access to the island of Saint-Louis was restricted to boats, but the colonial governor of Senegal, Louis Faidherbe, decided to construct the now famous, eponymous bridge to connect the island with the African mainland. According to Munyaradzi Mawere, "With the advent of colonialism in Africa, the African cultures and indigenous knowledges were *unjustifiably* and *unfairly* despised and relegated as superstitious, primitive, illegitimate, irrational and unscientific."[43] The inclusion in this sequence of the statue honoring Faidherbe and a work of infrastructure that traverses the water, allowing urban expansion, reminds viewers of Saint-Louis's colonial past and harm to the country and city by outsiders and those associated with the state. The images of the statue and bridge are accompanied by bustling activity, as opposed to the peace and tranquility of the river basin represented in various parts of the film by fishermen in their pirogues, quiet flowing water, and mangroves. The emphasis on urban growth and globalization has often been to the detriment of the local population, especially those in the peri-urban area of Saint-Louis.

Traditions and customs of the area have long sought an equilibrium with the water that surrounds residential areas, providing the population sustenance and income while still protecting the water. "Hydraulic citizenship," to return to Anand's concept, for the rural residents of the Senegal River basin has not been an issue of advocating for the state to adequately control the water that threatens their material life and the consequences it has created, as it has been for the inhabitants of Médina Gounass portrayed in Ramaka's film. Instead, rural communities of the area have long-standing forms of hydraulic citizenship that they have shaped in careful relation to the water that is an essential part of their surroundings and their way of life. The criteria for their hydraulic citizenship transcend or predate colonial power and state structures and authority. They build from environmental and traditional systems of knowledge and beliefs. These values and practices, symbolized by the fictional representation of Mame Coumba Bang in *La brèche*, endure into the present day, even into urban settings. They intermix with the colonial past and the globalized present, forming a complex intersection of various values, practices, and infrastructural forms that local residents must continually negotiate. As Cissé shows, many residents, especially those villagers who live outside of but remain connected to the city, have successfully accomplished this difficult feat. The film warns that it is when governmental and infrastructural administrators disregard the role of local customs that dire consequences ensue, particularly for those on the urban margins. In this way, the film emphasizes "the hybrid and ambiguous character of peri-urban space" in which "traditional authorities and state agents vie for power, access to resources and legitimacy in an unending negotiation process."[44] It points to the inequitable outcomes of that process for the villagers in the Senegal River basin.

Cissé begins to catalog those consequences in the next sequence, which is composed of additional shots of the imbrication of human life and water in the region. We see two men along with a younger boy in a fishing boat and can hear the water's waves and see the mangroves. Over a close-up of one of the men, the other speaks about how, at one time, there were many species of fish that inhabited the marsh. After a shot of many people washing clothes or playing in the shallow water, we hear a louder electronic noise and then see the dam. Over a shot of the water with a dead fish floating in it, which also reflects the infrastructure of

Community Responses to Water Mismanagement   131

the dam, the voice of the man from the fishing boat says that, today, those species of fish have disappeared: "There was a type of fish that sold for 75–100 euros. That allowed us to live free from need. And even more serious, its disappearance coincided with the release of the water of the breach. It was the period of reproduction and they were decimated by polluted water." As he speaks, Cissé provides additional shots of dead fish floating at the surface of the water, and we hear the hum of the dam intermingled with the soft flow of the waves. The opening of the breach led to people who had previously relied on fishing for their livelihood to experience a significant reduction in income. The entire community was forced into financial distress. Once again, subsequent shots of the city, including of the bridge, tie these consequences for rural, water-based communities back to the urban focal point. Cissé visually reinforces the reality for the residents of the Senegal River basin that "infrastructure comes to mediate a diversity of competing ethical projects, political disagreements, and subterranean conflicts that often concern central political questions of civic virtue, basic needs, and the rights and obligations of citizenship. . . . Infrastructure itself becomes *a political terrain* on which such questions are negotiated and contested."[45] In the next shot, the water crashes out loudly from what is assumed to be the dam, and then the Faidherbe Bridge is shot from afar (fig. 3.6). The camera

FIGURE 3.6. The landmark Faidherbe Bridge in Saint-Louis, 2023. Photo by Devin Bryson.

moves in more closely on the pedestrians crossing the bridge and closer still to a pan of their feet moving. The camera comes to the feet of a woman in white who isn't walking but is instead standing on the bridge, looking out at the water. While residents of Saint-Louis are occupied by their contemporary urban tasks, the traditions and customs of the area continue to focus on water and its necessary preservation.

The camera pans up her body and continues up into the upper parts of the bridge and then into the sky before the shot dissolves to white. In this sequence, Cissé illustrates that urban centers like Saint-Louis require infrastructural management of water, as evidenced by the dam and the bridge, to sustain and protect life for its residents. However, the film asks, What are the unforeseen costs of such urban infrastructure? What knowledge and experiences are disregarded in our contemporary rush to privilege the urban? What values and beliefs are ignored in urban processes of infrastructural development and natural resources management? Theodore Trefon writes, "It is nonetheless clear today that city and village, from both conceptual and utilitarian perspectives, are inseparable—notably by the people most concerned."[46] As this sequence of *La brèche* emphasizes, rural residents of the Senegal River basin have preserved the balance between the environment and development, yet they have also been the ones who have primarily borne the consequences of infrastructural urban projects. The final shot of the sequence insists that the local customs of water, represented by Mame Coumba Bang, endure within the city of Saint-Louis, even as the urban residents may not notice her or focus on her importance to the larger Senegal River basin area.

The residents of Doune Baba Dieye and Mouït Gandiol, in contrast, are acutely aware of Mame Coumba Bang and her symbolism of the importance of water in the region. Their knowledge, however, was disregarded by Wade's administration in the breach project. Although Wade himself is not named, the plural *they* is repeated to refer more broadly to the state and to Wade's administration, just as the residents of Médina Gounass did in Ramaka's *Plan Jaxaay!* A fisherman speaks about what "they" said about flooding and the need for the breach. He states clearly that he didn't agree with them, that he knew that the natural makeup of the peninsula would have alleviated flooding. Residents of Saint-Louis and of the larger region possess localized, indigenous knowledge about the relationship between fishing and human life. However, the breach did not only impact the ways fishing has sustained life in the area, and many of these practices and quotidian actions are specific to rural communities. For example, some men pour water from jerricans into bowls for cattle in a noticeably rural setting. Obviously, raising livestock is another essential component of life in this area that is sustained by access to water and that was impacted by the national government's breach project.

Next, Cissé underlines the collectivity and unity of the rural communities, between the various members and between the environment and the people. Five men face the camera, with the water at their backs. Two of the men's individual faces are shot in close-up, emphasizing the relationship between individuals and the community. Then a group of women is gathered together under a tree. Neither the men nor the women speak yet. Cissé initially establishes their physical connection to their environments, to the land that sustains them, and to one another. Before they are speaking subjects in the film, they are members of a community that lives in relation to the water and land. When the men and women do begin to speak, Cissé, like Ramaka in *Plan Jaxaay!*, emphasizes the communal voice of these people. While he includes the individual articulations of various people, he rarely provides their names. Instead, the unity and collective experiences of these individuals are of the utmost importance, as the wordless establishing shots of the groups emphasize.

Once the subjects begin to talk, they powerfully articulate the extensive impacts from the breach on their lives, their well-being, and their way of life. The men explain how the flooding of the river brought silt to their fields, which contributed to good harvests. In their region, flooding was actually beneficial. One of the men states, "This breach is gnawing at our island. If nothing is done, the village will disappear in less than three years. Considering the erosion's progression, we are under no illusion." The next shot is of large waves crashing along the shore and the mangroves. The interspersing of the residents' interviews with shots of the water and environment shows how the breach has impacted both human and marine life, particularly in terms of food and water security and access to healthcare facilities. Several of the women describe the impact the breach has had on their families, especially their children, who now cry because of hunger. They have to pay twice as much to fish, and they must now rely on fish from Saint-Louis: "The most worrisome for us is the plight of our families. How to bear spending an entire day without having anything to feed the children? And all of this, due to people from who knows where." This woman's comments emphasize the line between local agency and administrative control. Despite the fact that their community is surrounded by water, they lack clean drinking water and therefore must also find it in Saint-Louis: "We continue sometimes several days without water. We must go around the village to collect a kettle of water and give something to drink to the children. The others must wait." Another woman laments that the lack of water also impacts how they clean themselves, their homes, and their clothes: "How can one wash his or her child before bringing them to school, do the laundry, the housework and the washing? The water brought back from Saint-Louis is too expensive." The women describe the disastrous impact of the lack of potable water caused by the breach but also the opposite problem of too much water caused by the floods. Saint-Louis remains inaccessible except by pirogues, which often break down. A woman complains, "At night, in an emergency, there are so many difficulties bringing a sick person to the hospital. Sometimes, pregnant and terrified women give birth in the pirogue. It is impossible to take another way. When we arrive at the hospital, the doctors accuse us of negligence." As these frustrated women tell their stories, we hear waves in the background and see in the last scene a close-up shot of crabs walking slowly along the beach.

It is clear that these villagers are disadvantaged by the urban structures, including the governmental decision coming out of Dakar and the divide between Saint-Louis and the villages. Cissé evokes the idea of "multiple elsewheres," referred to by Mbembe, Nuttall, Diouf, and Fredericks, and the ways these places are inequitably connected. Cissé transitions to a collective interview with a third group of villagers, during which one of the men underlines the tragedy of the villages' vulnerability when he states, "They forget that this city exists because of us, because of the agricultural production of this entire region." Another man from that same group states that the fruit their region produced had always been found in all of the Saint-Louis markets, but this is no longer the case. An additional man insists that this interpenetration of the urban and the rural, and the consequences of privileging the urban in this area with respect to water, will extend all the way to Dakar: as the agricultural, fishing, and livestock production of the region declines due to the breach "it is only a question of time, but [the issue] will reach all the way to the Dakar region. It will attain incommensurable proportions." It is clear that there are dire economic and human consequences resulting from the breach. Another man states, "This breach has caused the death of 57 people. Among these victims, there were 32 fathers. It destroyed 37 pirogues, each at a value of 40,000 euros." These comments echo Trefon's findings that "linkages between city and hinterland take various tangible forms. City dwellers have a vital dependence on peri-urban agricultural produce and small livestock."[47] Beyond these tangible linkages, Trefon finds that there also exist "intangible forms" of connection between the city and the village, namely that "peri-urban spaces are geographies of psychological transition, 'hinging' village to a neighbouring city and sometimes beyond."[48] These psychological linkages are readily and easily articulated by the residents of the villages. They recognize how much urban identities and existences depend on rural practices, even as they are able to critique the actions of urban political elites who disregarded their cultural conceptualizations. One final man from the community even makes the conceptual linkage to the "beyond," extending the implications of the breach and its aftermath to global connections. He points out that, with fewer economic opportunities in the region, the communities' young people will attempt to cross the ocean in pirogues to migrate, an attempt that will increasingly lead to their deaths due to the rougher waters caused by the breach. While the urban planners did not adequately account for or strategize in accordance with rural knowledge and practices, village dwellers are shown by Cissé to be uniquely situated to think flexibly and interconnectedly about the city, the villages, and their relationship to global elsewheres. The provisionality, even precarity of their existence, balanced delicately between the sustenance and the destruction of water, has cultivated these positionalities among them.

After archiving the various locally, nationally, and globally connected consequences of the breach from the perspective of villagers, Cissé ends the film by returning to Saint-Louis, with shots of pirogues docked on the city's shores. He then returns to the interview with the man from the beginning of the film who outlined the importance of Mame Coumba Bang. This time, the man emphasizes the way that officials, for the project of cutting the breach, disregarded the importance of the belief in Mame Coumba Bang. He says that local rural communities should have been consulted and their beliefs and myths respected: "They have things to say, which are important." In particular, "the collective imaginary sometimes has solutions, sometimes has answers to questions because they are the result of lived experience that has endured for centuries or millennia. The population knows very well the work of water and the relationship to have with water as a source of life, which it has understood and codified through oral tradition." The film then concludes with a final reminder of the role of Mame Coumba Bang and customary beliefs and practices in this negotiation between the urban and the rural in contemporary Senegal in regard to water.

A young boy walks in shallow water, holding a fishing line in his hands, echoing the boys from the beginning of the film who first told the viewers about the river goddess. Despite the problems in the Saint-Louis area brought on by the breach project, traditions and beliefs around water, such as fishing and Mame Coumba Bang, endure in these communities. Next, in a long shot, a man stands at the water's edge, pouring something into the river. In the next close-up, the viewer sees a white substance cascade into the water. Mame Coumba Bang walks away from the camera along a paved street lined with palm trees as the sound of the falling liquid continues. We watch the bowl that held the liquid empty completely, followed by shots of the faces of the villagers who spoke earlier in the film. Once again, Cissé does not situate his audience within this highly localized ritual that would be readily recognizable to local residents. Those who wish to gain Mame Coumba Bang's favor must give her offerings, which must be white, reflecting her clothing, and which are often composed of millet and curdled milk. Cissé ends his film by asking for Mame Coumba Bang's blessing and protection for the residents of the rural Senegal River delta communities. The last shot of the film is of the offering dispersing in the water. In this final sequence, no one speaks, and we hear waves and birdsong, with the occasional rumble of a car or infrastructural component being moved. As the camera pans out and the screen becomes black, we are left with the sound of the waves and gentle water. Neither Cissé nor his film nor the villagers themselves can reverse the staggering amount of damage caused by cutting the breach in the Barbary peninsula. However, all three can depict the disastrous consequences of disregarding rural perspectives in favor of urban experiences and knowledge. Like the offering to Mame Coumba Bang, these depictions have the power to positively alter their relationships to their environments once circulated out into the world.

In their respective documentaries, both Ramaka and Cissé project their cinematic gaze outside of urban centers to focus their films on those who live on the urban periphery. Through this focus, they highlight the dynamics within the relationship between the urban and the periphery that privilege urban spaces, issues, and existences and that subsequently tip peripheral lives and communities into tenuousness and precarity. While Sène Absa and Thiaw consider the implications and causes of the connections between Senegalese cities and global sites in their films, Ramaka and Cissé show that the import of the interrelatedness of Senegalese urban space also exists more locally, bringing the urban to bear on the peripheral, and vice versa, through the thematic of the simplest yet oft-contested source of life—water.

4

Urban Precarity, Voice, and Contingent Communities in Adams Sie's *Voix silencieuses* and Khady Sylla's *Le monologue de la muette*

The residents of urban Senegal deploy a variety of resistant and creative strategies to build community, publicly express themselves, intervene in social and political processes, and combat marginalization in favor of inclusion and equity, continuously remaking their urban environments. Contemporary Senegalese filmmakers have undertaken aesthetic approaches that mirror, reinforce, and amplify the tactics of urban dwellers, and the films we study in this book are complementary sites of urban reconfiguration. Like the four filmmakers we have highlighted thus far, Adams Sie and Khady Sylla advocate for greater social justice and inclusion through a cinematic depiction of the lived experiences of those who negotiate Senegalese urban spaces and power dynamics. In their work, Sie and Sylla document the marginalization and inequities that exist within the city due to power disparities, as well as the strategies for survival, resistance, integration, sustainability, and reconfiguration that these urban subjects enact.

In this chapter, we analyze Sie's *Voix silencieuses* (2005) and Sylla's *Le monologue de la muette* (2008), which reveal new understandings of the intersections of cinema and the urban in contemporary Senegal.[1] Both of these films push the cinematic representation of the contemporary Senegalese city into the extreme ends of urban precarity and the tactics of survival that arise within those spaces. They document segments of urban communities that are the most vulnerable, the most marginalized, and the most disempowered due to their intersectional identities and social positionalities. Sie's midlength film *Voix silencieuses* follows the experiences of a small band of street boys in Dakar, a portion of the urban population that is well known to those who live and move within the city. As one walks the streets of Dakar, any number of young boys might approach to ask for donations to help them eat and survive. While they are often piteous sights, given their dirty bodies, poor clothing, and dilapidated shoes, their prevalence in Dakar can produce indifference from passersby as they come to be seen as an ordinary part of the city. Another response could be to ignore their pleas due to the fact that giving money or food will not solve the root causes of the problem. Many aid organizations in the city have documented the reality that the young beggars are the puppets of corrupt marabouts looking to profit from the boys' derelict state. This knowledge can leave people in Dakar wary of contributing to the exploitation but also uncertain of how exactly to help. Sie's film plunges into the lived experiences, personal histories, and community dynamics of these figures, moving beyond the superficial and homogenizing urban responses to their presence. The boys in the film come from various backgrounds and regions in Senegal, but they all share educational disruption and economic vulnerability as they struggle to survive in these extreme urban conditions. Sylla's *Le monologue de la muette* documents the feminine counterpart to Sie's street boys, the urban maid. Most middle- and upper-class families in Dakar include a feminine figure who does the majority of the housework, cleaning, errands, and domestic duties. The urban social role of maids serves as an essential component of the informal economy in Dakar, and the women's employers may view and include them as members of the family. However, there can also be a clear and rigid hierarchy within the families that sets unbending expectations and strictures on comportment for the maids. In these cases, while maids are the cornerstones of the proper functioning of the home and family, they can also be positioned as generally retiring, even submissive presences in the home, fading into the background of urban family life. Like the boys in Sie's documentary who have been abandoned to Dakar's streets due to unstable family and parental situations, the maids of Sylla's film often leave their rural villages in order to earn money for their families back home, rendering them totally reliant on the financial support of the families who employ them.

In many ways, the street boys and urban maids in Sie's and Sylla's films align with the migrants, wrestlers, hip-hop activists, and peri-urban communities in the films we have previously studied. These individuals all face significant obstacles in carrying out fulfilled, empowered lives within contemporary urban Senegal. However, the subjects in Sie's and Sylla's films are facing extreme urban precarity that perpetually fluctuates between social visibility and invisibility. The members of these communities are decidedly not hidden within Senegalese urban space, as impoverished children persistently occupy the streets in Dakar in noticeable numbers and maids are present in most middle-class urban homes. Nevertheless, the subjectivity of these populations—how they came to be on the streets or in these homes, how they live and survive, how they articulate their existences, the communities they form, and what they envision for their futures—remains obscure to observers, even as the subjects themselves are in plain sight. These figures mark the limits of social knowledge, understanding, and empathy for socially marginalized populations. The documentaries of Sène Absa, Thiaw, Ramaka, and Cissé all build from the potential for social change in telling the stories of urban injustices and urban social engagement. In contrast, the films of Sie and Sylla highlight the forms of liminal existence within urban spaces for those individuals who are simultaneously hypervisible and socially illegible in the urban extremes and the articulation of self that is produced from such contexts yet with no sure possibility for social change.

In these films, Sie and Sylla generally eschew systemic or structural examinations in order to focus on their subjects' own understandings and articulations of their plight. Similarly, they avoid making straightforward calls for social action. Films that undertake macrolevel analysis of social problems can often lose sight of the personal lived experiences within tenuous circumstances. This can then reproduce the quotidian, on-the-streets experience of viewers who see but don't understand those urban figures of the street kids and the maids. In contrast, Sie and Sylla convey the thoughts and emotions of those in extremely precarious situations in Dakar so that the viewer gains an intimate understanding of the subjectivity, and its ongoing articulation, within this social position.

As we show in this chapter, Sie and Sylla engage with these urban positions from a decidedly subjective position. The filmmakers themselves are clearly involved and implicated in the lives of their subjects. The films enter into the restricted experiences and triumphant persistence of their socially disenfranchised yet personally empowered subjects from the personal perspective of the filmmakers. This approach underlines *les déchets humains*, or "the trashed lives," in Senegalese cities that have been produced by the sociohistorical dynamics of colonizing and imperialistic countries but that also touch on the lived, daily experiences of all those in urban Senegal.[2] While the West has been "the site of appropriation," Africa, on the other hand, serves as the site "of expenditure . . . where the excretion or waste of that consumerism has been dumped."[3] Sie and Sylla represent these trashed or expendable lives in order to circumvent the forces of power that have discarded them, emphasizing the agency and subjectivity on the part of their subjects who oppose those forces: "There is more here than loss; more than decay and a descent. In fact, the descent is here only because of the belief that the depiction of it will serve to enable a change, an ascent, to become possible."[4] These two films are aesthetic interventions in the extreme ends of urban marginalization, depicting the way in which "trash is hidden in the unspoken words" but making it apparent even when silenced or muted.[5]

These films unveil the extent of creativity and resistance within the subjects' strategies for urban persistence and fulfilled lives. Despite their often difficult social circumstances, the subjects of *Voix silencieuses* and *Le monologue de la muette* have found tactics for surviving in and provisionally overcoming their marginal urban contexts and the globalized and local forces that have helped shape them. While the subjects of films we have studied in earlier chapters face significant difficulties in navigating urban life, the films themselves document the problems and then emphasize the strength of the residents in facing those problems, even if they do not decidedly overcome those obstacles. Sie's and Sylla's subjects are depicted living within their precarity, overcoming some things, struggling with others, and muddling their way through life in urban Dakar. One of their common strategies articulated in the films is the formation of contingent communities in these sites of extreme urban precarity. *Voix silencieuses* and *Le monologue de la muette* articulate the strength and empathy necessary among the individuals within these spaces to forge bonds of friendship and cooperation in order to survive on the urban margins. Yet they also show the tenuous and fraught nature of these relationships. While this interpersonal and communal flexibility is necessary for survival in these conditions, it means that no community is permanent, that perhaps all relationships are transactional.

In this way, these films interrogate the potential for reconfiguring the city and also cinema's role within that reconfiguration. Among the various marginalized urban communities—the young men who are out of work, the fishing communities threatened by water mismanagement, urban maids—some members have more agency to reshape their lives and their relations to the city. Sie and Sylla recognize and cinematically document these intersectional limitations on strategies for urban living. They emphasize that survival, as opposed to resistance, is often the best that can be achieved. Relationships and communities formed within extremely precarious circumstances are often contingent and temporary, unlike the collective strength forged in other marginalized urban spaces. To this extent, the films of Sie and Sylla "grapple with often ambivalent and contradictory new spaces that are not easily classified within a lens of domination or resistance ... [but] through which people dynamically negotiate incremental change while also recognizing the circumscriptions and challenges implied by these new spaces."[6] The films' depictions of contingent communities on the extreme urban margins demonstrate the limitations of any relationship and community within urban space, whether on the margins or not, but also offer possibilities of reconceptualizing communal life outside of the neoliberal model.

This includes the cinematic relationships that are formed and portrayed on-screen between a documentarian and their subjects. These cinematic subjects did not gain subjectivity when the camera was finally turned toward them; they had tenuously crafted their strategies for agency from their extreme lived experiences. The films self-consciously express and convey the already existent subjectivities that were formed within the crux of social forces, acknowledging the tensions that exist within their subjects' social positions but also cinema's relation to such subjects. We take on the complexity and contradictions of the films and their subjects in our own analysis, striving "to elaborate a perspective from 'below,' from the trash heap, where *déchets* are lost and then restored as *humains*—not as an oxymoron but as a transvaluation."[7] We argue that these films work aesthetically to instigate social change toward their subjects by contracting the cultural and aesthetic distance between observer and those on the urban extremes. The films settle into the social spaces and positions of the boys on the streets and the maids in the recessed corners of urban homes, adopting aesthetic approaches from those sites. Furthermore, the subject formations that are represented in the films cannot be disentangled from the urban contexts in which they take place. Sie and Sylla emphasize "the city as a field of intervention for solving an array of problems associated with modern life . . . as a sphere of action is called into question, and a set of difficulties are transformed into problems to which diverse solutions are possible."[8] More directly, the filmmakers emphasize the complexity of these urban interventions within social and cultural institutions—economics, employment, families, friendships, the national social body. These films insist that even impoverished urban youth and maids in Dakar are all worldly citizens who draw from and contribute to the ongoing re-creation of social, cultural, and economic life in the city. Even as their access to such strategies and interventions might be severely limited and tenuous, these individuals are centered as essential urban actors.

The titles of both *Voix silencieuses* and *Le monologue de la muette* convey these relational and community building urban dynamics, as well as the representational stakes in those dynamics, through the shared trope of voice. The films then proceed to express and articulate, amplify and strengthen the voices of their subjects, privileging the subjective expression of urban precarity and the necessary strategies for survival rather than employing the objective remove of the standard documentarian. From this personalized view, anchored in the lived urban experience of their subjects, the films of Sie and Sylla that we study in this chapter raise essential questions about the tensions and limits of strategies for reconfiguring urban life and spaces. These films do not amplify and direct the pointed critique of Senegalese urban dwellers toward the governmental policies of the state nor do they present unequivocal collective strength and resistance of urban subjects, as we have seen in films by Ramaka, Cissé, Sène Absa, and Thiaw analyzed in prior chapters. Instead, we watch as the subjects of Sie's and Sylla's films conceptualize and deploy their tactics for urban existence on-screen, succeeding at times, struggling at others. Their working and reworking of the Senegalese city is tenuous and fraught, vulnerable to the extreme precarity of their actual lives. The films of Sie and Sylla therefore, we argue, provoke self-reflection about the efficacy and equity of those urban processes of creation and reconfiguration that all of our filmmakers represent and that we have been centering in our book. Sie's and Sylla's films are not skeptical of the necessity and potential of such creative reimagining of the city by its residents. However, they are direct in their questioning of how the most precarious segments of the urban community might contribute to those processes: How are the city in Senegal and its communities constructed to elide and dissipate these imaginative energies even as they are produced? Who struggles to access modes of resistance and creativity within the city?

Furthermore, within the films themselves, Sie and Sylla lay bare their own cinematic relationship to the street boys and urban maids, as well as their subjects' social contexts and urban creativity for survival on the margins. Each filmmaker is noticeably present in *Voix silencieuses* and *Le monologue de la muette*, respectively, drawing the viewer's attention to the social stakes of such representations on-screen. These films evoke the urban interplay between recognition and invisibility, between subjectivity and otherness. They highlight the potentially exploitative cinematic dynamics that can reify and entrench urban hierarchies of agency and power. *Voix silencieuses* and *Le monologue de la muette* reflexively pose the following questions: What are the boundaries of or even dangers in cinematic documentation of these urban dynamics? How might cinema simultaneously or alternately contribute to but also counteract currents of inclusion and equity in the Senegalese city of the twenty-first century? Who has the right to the city, its expressions, and its possibilities? The filmmakers themselves are visibly and aesthetically interacting with the extreme ends of urban vulnerability in their films, grappling with how to understand and depict their subjects while preserving their subjects' agency. This, in turn, may provoke viewers to no longer view street children or indentured housemaids as inevitable components of the urban landscape, visible even as they are not full subjects. Yet, that questioning is also turned toward themselves as filmmakers. Sie and Sylla make explicit the various practices that illustrate the potential dangers inherent to contemporary documentary filmmaking in

Senegal of exploiting filmic subjects for professional cinematic benefit. They highlight and question the power dynamics inherent to the action of a filmmaker turning their camera toward such socially excluded individuals. Even as they film the pain and exclusion—as well as the joys—of their subjects, they simultaneously offer up themselves and their cinematic practices for critical appraisal in relation to that pain and exclusion. In regard to Sylla's 2005 documentary, *Une fenêtre ouverte*, Bronwen Pugsley writes, "Sylla's positioning as subject and observer disrupts the dualism at play in many documentaries where the film-maker and viewer are positioned as the standard against which the Other—the object of documentary investigation—is to be compared and judged.... As Sylla moves back and forth between her various roles as film-maker, narrator, camera operator, subject and object, however, she bridges the gaps between Self and Other."[9] *Voix silencieuses* and *Le monologue de la muette* undertake similarly disruptive documentary practices, centering the ways cinema can contribute to the marginalization of the socially vulnerable within the questionably ethical history and dynamics of documentary filmmaking, especially within West Africa.[10] The aesthetic articulation of self-reflexivity is coterminous with Sie's and Sylla's focus on the extremes of urban life in Senegal, bringing the city, its creative potential, and its cinematic representations under question. Our critical attention in this chapter to this interrogative mode of urban filmmaking expands and enriches our study of contemporary Senegalese cinema.

Voix silencieuses: Boys Living on the Streets

Born in Sierra Leone, Adams Sie was sent by his Senegalese father to live with his family in Senegal when he was fifteen. There, Sie lived with and was educated by the Caliph-General of the Tijaniyya, one of the largest Sufi Muslim brotherhoods in the country. Despite these years immersed in devotional life and training, Sie was encouraged by his family to pursue higher education at a secular institution, Cheikh Anta Diop University in Dakar. Sie has credited this unique upbringing, divided between the religious and the secular, in leading him to cinema and visual culture.[11] Living with the Caliph-General, he observed Tidiane followers supplicate the Caliph for help and guidance with their intimate problems, and then he studied the social causes and results of those issues once he was a university student.

Experiencing these two approaches to social problems, Sie eventually saw filmmaking as a unique way for him to both personally and socially engage with problems in his community and culture. After graduation from Cheikh Anta Diop University, he enrolled at the now-defunct Media Center of Dakar to train as a filmmaker. The Media Center was, according to Sie, a place of practical, on-the-ground training. He states that such instruction has been difficult to find in Senegal in recent years since the only other avenue open to this kind of apprenticeship is through industry internships, which are few and far between. Along with providing its students with a wide range of technical skills—editing, sound, directing—the Media Center gave people, in Sie's words, "entrepreneurship" and encouraged "young people to tell their stories and to make films, to overcome poverty and be self-employed."[12] This social engagement was then inculcated in the students. Speaking of his community of filmmaker graduates of the Media Center who have cinematic opportunities abroad, Sie says, "All of us who go to festivals come back because we know we have a job to do [in improving the country]."[13] His cinematic education gave him a sense of responsibility to use his films for social betterment and change, which we see carried out in Sie's filmography.

Once his training at the Media Center was complete, Sie began his career right at the height of "the crisis" of Senegalese cinema in the early twenty-first century. Faced with limited opportunities for funding, production, and distribution of his films within Senegal, Sie has used these restrictions to rethink cinematic practices in the country. Collaborating with television production companies, NGOs, and governmental agencies, both Senegalese and international, Sie has been able to produce a sizable and diverse body of work in a relatively short period of time, with a number of personal festival-vetted documentary shorts, numerous industry films, a television reality series, and one feature, *Le cheval blanc*, from 2015. Certainly, this sort of hybrid career in which a filmmaker works across television and film, receives funding from independent and established sources, and mixes personal, auteurist techniques within mainstream industry productions has become increasingly common, admired, and profitable in the film industries in the Global North. However, Sie and other contemporary filmmakers in Senegal have not had the luxury to independently choose this hybrid career path and then to reap the financial and critical rewards. Speaking of his community of filmmakers who have worked in this multimodal way and their relationship at the beginning of their careers to the group of established cineastes, Sie laments, "We were not considered as cinematographers, but videographers. If we wanted to become a member of their association we had to direct, produce, film, or work on two feature length films on 35mm."[14] Instead of being able to strategically choose digital filmmaking, streaming platforms, industry films, and television productions to advance their careers, these filmmakers have adapted to the limited opportunities within the Senegalese film industry. They have forged careers that might be disregarded by some but that ultimately stand as examples of new possibilities through an innovative synthesis of the current economic and industrial realities of Senegalese cinema, the heritage of social engagement through culture in the country, and the potential for transnational connections and exchanges. Just as Sie's own career has been situated between various value positions within the contemporary Senegalese film industry, his films themselves focus on the tensions and potential within the subject positions and formations of the socially disenfranchised. He highlights the social power that structures and exploits urban subjectivities, as well as the strategies deployed by those subjects in the creation and re-creation of their marginalized lives within urban space.

The title of Sie's film *Voix silencieuses*, which means "silent voices" in English, designates the possibility of speech, of expression, on the part of the street boys. Importantly, however, their voices are silent but not silenced, implying that they can choose to speak. The film then becomes a site in which they may enact that choice and the viewers may choose to listen and to understand. The title announces the tensions and contingency inherent to its subjects, their enactment of agency, and cinema's intervention in and expression of those processes. The film offers clear, sobering depictions of the realities of living on the streets of Dakar as a young boy and the strategies that such subjects enact to survive in these conditions. The boys in the film were once able to form a community among themselves that offered support, protection, and resources, yet the film emphasizes how that community was temporary and is now lost in the cinematic present. Sie himself is shown to be a contingent member of that community in the film. In this regard, *Voix silencieuses* is also a sharply thoughtful exploration of what it means to cinematically represent such vulnerable subjects in their full humanity, consistent with their voices rather than by adopting or, even worse, exploiting them.

In his filmography, Sie consistently questions and plays with the myth of the all-knowing, exemplary artist through his process, his techniques, and his subjects, rendering his own position as director unstable and nonauthoritative. Perhaps the apotheosis of this approach in his filmmaking comes in his 2006 film, *Oumy et moi*. At one point in the personal documentary of Sie's relationship with Oumy, his girlfriend who has albinism, Sie comes to her home and finds her studying. When he, speaking from behind the camera, tells her that she studies a lot, Oumy replies that she wants to have a lot of diplomas like he does. Sie retorts, "I'm a director, I don't have any diplomas. I don't know anything." Whether true or not, Sie's auto-portrait in the film is of someone attempting to learn something about the people around him as well as about himself. At another point, Oumy questions Sie as to why he is always filming her, and she suggests that he give her the camera so that the roles can be reversed. He turns it over to her for only a moment or two, but from that point of the film on Sie relinquishes his role as cameraman and becomes a subject of the camera's gaze, engaging fully in this world that he had heretofore only been observing, working to articulate his own subjectivity within it, prompting his viewers to do the same. Of his filmmaking process, Sie says, "I stay with people and let them tell their own stories. I just follow them and from that, eventually there is a complicity between me and them. But, also, I'm a presence with the camera and how it moves, so you know someone is there and there is a specific view."[15] Sie's filmmaking is a continual process of learning and discovery instead of a masterly unveiling of knowledge and authority, and his most poignant use of this cinematic approach toward urban precarity is found in *Voix silencieuses*.

The film catalogs many of the material realities of life for the boys on the street, making clear this social problem and its consequences for the boys personally but also for Senegalese society. It is difficult to accurately estimate the number of street children in Dakar. Some organizations that work in the city with street children populations place the figure near seven thousand.[16] Most of the public discourse on street children focuses on *talibés*, the children who have been sent by their families to be educated and live at a *darra*, or Qur'anic school, but who are forced to beg on the street by the teacher for his personal financial benefit. The impact of this street life on children has been clearly documented: nutritional disorders, injuries, infectious diseases, violence and sexual abuse, substance abuse, and mental health problems.[17] Throughout *Voix silencieuses*, the boys speak openly of the difficulties they face in their street existence, and the film captures images of that precarity. We see the boys sleeping on the ground with nothing more than a piece of cardboard as a bed, as other urban residents pass them by without much of a glance. The boys must procure potable water so they can wash, eat, and drink. One boy, Babacar, talks to another street child about how people refuse to give them food when they ask for it, even when the food is being discarded as trash. We then watch as they fish in the ocean and prepare and eat whatever small catch they have. The boys discuss their health risks, social ostracization, and uncertain, bleak futures. Another boy, Kema, speaks about the difficulty of fighting for survival, seeking out whatever food and water they can get, and how other urban residents see them as violent, criminals, and drug addicts due to their precarious sustenance. The boys of *Voix silencieuses* clearly live on the extreme edge of urban precarity in contemporary Dakar.

They come from various backgrounds and have ended up living on the streets for various reasons; the film implies that it is possible for almost any child to slip into such conditions, that even more stable, secure existences are precarious and uncertain. Kema speaks of having problems with his family: his mother died and his father remarried. Since he didn't get along with his dad's new wife, he decided to leave Casamance to try to earn money in Dakar. He eventually joined the army in the hope that his technical training from the military would help him find employment, but it hasn't. Babacar says that he was in school, but then his dad stopped paying the fees and so he was forced to leave school against his will. In contrast, Elhadji says that he didn't like school but that his parents were forcing him to stay, so he chose to run away from home and live on the streets. The fourth member of their group, who is never clearly named in the film, mentions that some people might find purpose in school and education, but others will find it through work and employment. Sie emphasizes that there is not one downward path into precarity on the streets for Senegal's children and that it threatens many children in the country. These various avenues into precarity that can loom over any child in Senegal are highlighted in a number of evocations of the specific national context. One shot begins with a close-up of the Senegalese flag flying atop the presidential palace and then zooms out to a wide shot that includes the boys passing in front of the building from some distance. Their social marginalization is distinct in this zoom shot that emphasizes the distance between their life on the street and normative society marked by the flag. The diversity in the origins of the small group's street existence, contextualized within the national and urban social body, is significant in how it contrasts with the dominant narrative of talibés as representative of Dakar street children. Sie displaces corrupt darra and marabouts, and even the government's failures to regulate those entities, as the publicly recognized sources of the city's street children and instead centers on the range of social but also familial and personal factors that contribute to making street existence a possibility for children in Dakar. While the boys' precarious lives on the streets are extreme in the ways they lack access to resources and the strategies they must undertake for survival, the forces leading them to live on the streets are not presented in *Voix silencieuses* as distant impossibilities but instead as distinct outcomes of contemporary urban life.

While Senegalese society and political leaders recognize the social problem of having so many of its urban children living in such extreme conditions, social institutions and political structures have struggled to adequately intervene. In many ways, street children are the indelible but ignored problem of contemporary Dakar: ever-present, easy targets for social programs, ready objects of political rhetoric, but never adequately, comprehensively understood, supported, or protected. *Voix silencieuses* directly engages with the subjects' social position, the inequitable outcomes produced by this position, and the possibility of reshaping it cinematically. Sie does not just film the street boys in Dakar from afar but personally interacts with them to show their struggles and to detail the community they have formed among themselves. He personalizes and individuates his subjects while also documenting their contingent community in order to overcome their social invisibility, to move their representation out of a place of rhetorical and imaginative construction to one of intimate subjectivity and communal, if precarious, struggle. He works visibly in the film to make the boys' silent voices heard.

Sie's documentation of the street boys' difficulties is always complex and rooted in the autonomy of the boys and their community. The film establishes and sustains an equitable relationship between filmmaker and subjects while prioritizing the subjectivity of the street boys. We hear a boy quietly singing as the first shot of the sun above the Dakar skyline appears. The simple, repeating lyrics of the song indicate the subject of the proceeding film: "I am going to teach you about the life of the street children. It's a life full of wonder."[18] Besides reorienting our expectations for the subsequent documentation of the life of children living on the street from one of tragedy to one of wonder, the lyrics also center the agency of the street boys in telling their own story. One of the street boys is the singer, the one who proclaims that he will tell us, the audience, about street life. This voice that accompanies the first image is present and active in the film and returns periodically. *Voix silencieuses* privileges the boys' own agency and control over their own subjective experiences, refusing to subjugate their voices to the visual authority of the documentarian. After this opening shot, a sequence begins with a handheld camera moving shakily through a park until it stops on a boy in a shaded, wooded area. The singing about the wonders of the street boy's life continues over the beginning of this sequence. Once the camera comes to rest on the boy, the singing stops, and from behind the camera, Sie greets the boy, warmly using his name, Babacar. The boy responds by calling Sie by his first name. The filmmaker asks Babacar a few questions, and the boy answers readily. It is clear that the two individuals know each other and have established a friendly relationship. The filmmaker demonstrates obvious familiarity with these socially isolated boys and the community of street kids through his opening greetings and his questions, but he also remains hidden behind the camera throughout the sequence. While he is a documentarian observer, Sie is careful to abdicate any objectivity toward or distance from his subjects. Instead, the film is a subjective, partial view into the lives of these children based on personal relationships. Through his easy navigation of the boys' marginal social space and his personalized exchange with Babacar, Sie clearly conveys that he is implicated in the lives of the boys and that he has breached the gulf of social marginalization. However, with his position behind the camera and his questions that allow the boys to speak for themselves, Sie equally signals that knowledge about the boys is not his to pass along. The viewers will have to come to know the street kids just as Sie himself did, by adopting a subjective position of social exclusion.

Besides establishing Sie's personalized documentation of the boys' street life, the film's opening sequence also articulates the relationships formed between the boys themselves. After their greetings, the filmmaker asks Babacar, "Where are the others?" The boy responds, "It's been a long time since I've seen them." Sie then asks specifically about Kema's location, and Babacar says he's gone home to Casamance. As the film proceeds, we see how this small band of boys was an actual community. They share in the duties of resource gathering, of cooking what little provisions they have, and of keeping one another as safe as possible. They recount the stories of their lives to one another and empathize with the others' struggles and sadness and pain. They assist one another in finding whatever transcendence is possible, whether that is through dreaming about the future, staring out at the ocean, sharing a laugh, or breathing in toxic fumes to get high. The community formed by the boys is necessary, and it functions effectively to compensate for the lack of resources they face in their precarious existence. However, as the opening sequence makes clear, this community has dissipated in the interim between the initial filming of the boys' life on the streets and the shooting of the sequence in the park. The boys have lost touch with one another, not even knowing the others' locations. The precariousness of their urban realities forces these communal ties into contingent dynamics. The opening sequence emphasizes the deleterious impact of social forces on community by presenting the group of street kids as already dispersed and lost to one another. The film begins with the dissolution of this community, indicating the tenuousness of the boys' social position and the strategies they employ to sustain themselves and one another but also the contingency of all subjectivities within the field of social power. The possibility of having one's voice heard is increased when that voice is joined by others in community, but often the potential for collective strength is foreclosed due to one's extreme precarity in urban space.

The rest of the film is structured between alternating sequences from that lost communal past and from present-day interviews with the only two remaining boys, Babacar and Elhadji. This structure continually sets the stark precarity of the boys' existence in relation to the strategies of community building and resource sharing that the boys develop for survival, which are narratively shadowed by the understanding that this community is no more. Nevertheless, this contingent community was real and necessary. In one sequence, Sie shoots the boys huffing as they sit on the beach. While Kema resisted the street boys being stereotyped as drug addicts in an earlier interview, it is evident that they do indeed engage in a form of substance abuse in order to manage their precarious existence. However, this sequence does not serve to flatly contradict Kema's earlier rebuttal of society's view of him and the other street boys. Instead, the scene opens up into a portrait of the diversity of this community of street boys. Babacar vocally critiques the others for choosing to huff, saying, "I heard that huffing kills.... Stop huffing, it isn't good. You have to stop." While two of the boys might somewhat fall into the social view of street boys with their huffing, Sie documents the difference of opinion among the group and the sole critic's desire to stay safe and for his friends to protect themselves also. Furthermore, Sie reveals the negotiation taking place of the community's values, cohesion, and personal identities. The boy who has most demonstrably defended his huffing from criticism says that he goes home every night, trying to show that he doesn't huff out of living on the margins of society but out of personal choice. Babacar finds this foolish, retorting that they are all the same, all in the same social position, with the only difference being that he is not a *guinzeur*, or a sniffer. His friend responds, "It's full of feeling," again moving to justify his substance abuse through personal agency. Their situation is indeed precarious, with very uncertain opportunities for change or improvement, yet even in the midst of their precarity, the boys find complex layers of belonging and individuation within their temporary community.

In another scene, the group is relaxing and smoking cigarettes on the rocky shore. Babacar asks Elhadji whether he has ever had sex, and when the response is affirmative, he responds, "Are you aware of what is happening today in this country?" Elhadji responds, "Of course, there are illnesses such as AIDS, cholera." Babacar follows up, asking what his friend does before having sex, to which Elhadji answers that he buys condoms. Babacar wonders about the price of condoms and then is surprised by the answer. Finally, the inquisitive boy asks what Elhadji does before having sex with a prostitute, to which the boy answers that he treats himself. The boys engage in mutual education and care in dealing with the very real health threats they face in being sexually active. As Elhadji then breaks into a whistled rendition of Senegal's national anthem, Sie briefly inserts the previous close-up shot of the Senegalese flag before returning to the boys on the beach. There is still stark distance between the boys' precarious life on the shore and the bastions of national power, which has abandoned them to their own sex education, their own healthcare, their own forms of safe sex. However, in this sequence, the boys have some autonomy over their relationship to the national social body, as exemplified by the boy's whistling of the national anthem. The boy's singing introduction to the "wonders" of street life at the film's opening establishes the preeminence of their subjective voices in the film's documentation. Here, this boy's whistling of the national anthem reasserts the trope of voices as an expression of the boy's agency. They might be spatially and infrastructurally situated in the extreme ends of social life in Dakar, yet they are cinematically evoked as full members of the national community, able to insert their voices within national social discourse. The tactics employed by the boys for survival, including the tenuous community that they form, are direct products of contemporary urban Senegal; the city creates these street children, both in their precarity and their strategies for navigation of that precarity.

Yet even those survival strategies are temporary. Between the sequences that document the full community's life—fishing in the ocean, cooking and sharing their catch on the beach, huffing, smoking, discussing sex—Sie sets brief interstitial interviews or shots of dialogue between the two remaining boys, Babacar and Elhadji. In one of these early interviews, Babacar states clearly how important the group was to him and the ways it functioned and was structured: "We went to eat at the university and then we'd spend the night together on the beach. We were close. . . . We lived in peace and Kema was the head of the group. But since he left, the group fell apart." Later, Babacar and Elhadji talk of their desires for the future. When Elhadji asks Babacar what he wants to be when he grows up, he says simply, "I want to be a respectable person." He says this might mean being an imam or, at the very least, something pleasing to God. Elhadji responds to these tentative projections into the future with sobering responses about the present, especially their lost community: "Here, everyday isn't great. We're sometimes happy, sometimes unhappy. The others like Boy Poulo, Yaya, Bernard and Kema are all gone. Babacar and I are the only remaining ones. We feel abandoned now." The film returns often to this idea and these images of a lost community. Even though the boys have always lived precariously on the streets, those difficulties were easier to overcome when they had a community of support. The film ends with one last articulation of the necessity, but also contingency, of this street-based community. After a final interview with Babacar and Elhadji speaking of the challenges of street life, the film closes with small, in-screen shots of the boys playing with one another and swimming, documenting the joys, the "wonders," of their existence. Title cards appear alongside the images, intermingling those tender memories with the sober realities of the present, which, while not completely hopeless, do leave the group divided: "I went to see the boys in May 2005. Since then, Kema started a small business in Casamance, his native region. Babacar and Elhadji still live on the streets of Dakar. They hope to, one day, realize their dreams." While the film depicts the difficulties of such a life on the streets and evokes the ways that urban society marginalizes some of its members into extreme precarity, even those who are studying or have families or are trying to improve their social standing, it also conveys the possibilities and limits of forming temporary community in such conditions. The boys have real camaraderie, support, and friendship. However, these dynamics cannot and do not last. The film suggests that community on the extreme margins can only ever be provisional, even as it is essential during the period it exists. Similarly, the cinematic relationship between filmmaker and subject in the documentation of such precarious lives is equally fraught and temporary. However, *Voix silencieuses* shows that communities created with thoughtfulness and intention matter, even when they are temporary due to extreme urban precarity. Likewise, Sie's film models the documentary filmmaking strategies, such as transparency, personalization, collaboration, and self-reflexivity, that can potentially render the cinematic representation of precarious urban subjects as equitable and transformative.

Le monologue de la muette: Girls Working in Homes

Khady Sylla was born on March 27, 1963, in Dakar. Little is known about her early life, but her mother worked as a secretary for renowned

Beninese Senegalese film director and scholar Paulin Soumanou Vieyra. Sylla completed her elementary and high school studies in Dakar and then went to Paris, initially to pursue a degree in business. However, after just a week of classes, she decided to change academic directions and ended up studying philosophy at the École normale supérieure. She stated that she was always drawn to writing and started the day she learned, while living in Paris, of her grandmother's passing: "I thought that by writing about her I would be able to survive, ... that I would be able to save her from what was, for me, a devastation."[19] Sylla states that although she had lived many years in France, her native Dakar served as a "mythical city" and her inspiration during her "exile."[20] Sylla worked as an assistant for illiterate immigrant workers and also at a smaller publishing house, and then she began to write screenplays and helped others to write them as well.[21] She published her first novel, *Le jeu de la mer*, in 1992 and then followed a few years later in 1996 with her first film, a fiction short entitled *Les bijoux*. While this film is different in form from her later documentaries, *Les bijoux* clearly announces Sylla's enduring interest in centering women's experiences and identities in cinema. As one of the daughters in a poor family of four girls prepares for a date with a rich businessman, the personal dynamics between the daughters and their mother come to the surface of their family life.

It is with her next film, *Colobane Express* (1999), that Sylla's filmmaking shifts to the form and techniques, as well as a decidedly urban focus, that would solidify her position in the community of rising Senegalese filmmakers of the early twenty-first century. Sylla created *Colobane Express*, identified by critics as a docudrama or a docufiction, by collaborating with nonactors who were playing roles in the film that they held in their actual lives—market vendor, bus driver, mechanic, et cetera—to recount a day in the life of the driver, conductor, and passengers of a *car rapide*, the colorful, small buses that residents of Dakar often rely on for public transportation. During shooting, Sylla encouraged these nonactors to invent dialogue on the spot, adding urban authenticity, creativity, and spontaneity to the film. She indicates that this is a process she learned from her mentor, acclaimed French filmmaker Jean Rouch.[22] In her depiction of daily life in Dakar, Sylla literally traverses the city as she follows the car rapide throughout its day, picking up and dropping off a wide range of urban dwellers along its route (fig. 4.1). This collaborative

Urban Precarity, Voice, and Contingent Communities

FIGURE 4.1. Passengers board a car rapide in Dakar, 2013. Photo by Molly Krueger Enz.

and socially anchored filmmaking process produces a film that allows viewers a glimpse into the chaotic yet quotidian urbanity of Dakar. Françoise Pfaff explains the film's title as "borrowed from a drawing by the Senegalese cartoonist Moïse, whose satirical renditions of Dakar life are sold as postcards. It is also a homage to director Djibril Diop Mambéty, who grew up in Colobane and filmed his lively neighborhood."[23] In *Colobane Express*, Sylla embraces the documentary form and then adapts it to her own purposes. For example, she refuses to clearly demarcate the line between authorial creation and documentary subject. This approach proved to be a hallmark of her subsequent films, which we highlight in our own analysis. *Colobane Express* also stands as the first entry in Sylla's cinematic work in which she reflects on the particular intersections of urbanity and gender as she films the challenges, lives, and courage of everyday women in Dakar. This thematic and social interest is subsequently prevalent throughout her filmography, and Sylla consistently depicts urban women who have fraught relationships with their community and mainstream culture. While *Colobane Express* portrays the diversity and community of contemporary urban life in Senegal, the film brings particular attention to women within that urban journey. The opening and closing scenes of *Colobane Express* both highlight women, showing their essential role in Dakar's economy and society. In her following films, Sylla entirely prioritizes female voices and experiences—including her own—in order to instill a sense of authenticity and raise awareness about the experiences of Senegalese women, especially the ways in which they face exclusion from their urban communities. In doing so, she inspires political and social change by bringing visibility to gendered topics that are typically marginalized or silenced.

Like *Voix silencieuses*, *Le monologue de la muette*, through unique documentary techniques, enacts a similarly complex portrait of community, autonomy, and self-expression on the edges of urban existence, yet Sylla's film also specifically genders urban precarity, emphasizing the unique deprivations that women face on the urban extremes, as well as the potential for change that they may draw from that space. Like the street boys, the primary maid whose life is documented in the film, Amy, is a socially silenced figure, as emphasized by the title of the film, which could be translated directly as "the mute's monologue."[24] Again, as with Sie's film, the trope of voices is essential to the dynamics evoked in the film between social precarity, subjectivity, community, and representation. The literal translation of the title encourages the viewer to consider the paradox of how one might get a mute individual to speak or enunciate a monologue. Perhaps the most evident resolution to that paradox is that the monologue is not vocalized but is instead an interior monologue. The film is not a direct expression of urban maids' voices but rather an exploration of their interiority, their subjectivity, which joins their potential voices to those of other urban women fighting for gender equity. Sylla's response to this problem is not simply to let Amy speak on camera but to make the film a site for her experiences to be articulated, her expressions to be tried out, and her voice to be amplified and joined with others'. Through her work, Sylla indicates that it isn't enough to simply record or document Amy's voice in order for it to be heard; rather, it is necessary to imbue it with poetry, artistry, collective strength, and communal support through cinematic rendering. Sylla is personally touched by the exclusion and marginalization of these urban women, and her films become a site in which marginalized Senegalese women may find their collective voice and use it to express their experiences to the wider Senegalese society.

Urban Precarity, Voice, and Contingent Communities

Nicolas Azalbert describes Sylla's films in the following way: "Cinema, for Khady Sylla, consists of telling the invisible, of attempting to reconnect a link between what has been separated, between what is and what is not or no longer there: small Senegalese villages and the capital, youth and adulthood, ancestral practices and liberal economics, madness and normality."[25] In *Le monologue de la muette*, Sylla amplifies the voices of people who have been silenced and makes visible those who reside in the recesses of society, especially those who suffer from such marginalization due to their gender, including Sylla herself.

Sylla renders the urban quotidian fraught with power dynamics and social hierarchies by drawing her viewers' attention to the overlooked, marginalized components of the urban milieu. The film opens with shots of women and maids sweeping in front of houses in the early-morning twilight of Dakar. These crepuscular figures go about their

FIGURE 4.2. The sun sets over city streets in the neighborhood of Point E in Dakar, 2023. Photo by Devin Bryson.

chores in the landscape of the city before many residents of Dakar have even arisen and begun their days. By the time the city roars into full life, the maids have retired to the confines of the houses in which they labor. In this opening sequence, Sylla's film visually centers our urban perspective on these essential yet marginalized members of the Dakar community, which is then reinforced through a voice-over that expresses solidarity with Amy and articulates her social position as common to that of other urban maids: "We are minorities. We are marginalized. The world does not go around for us."[26] They remain liminal individuals within the city, as the opening shots of the transition from night to day emphasize, perpetually just out of sight of the population, even as they leave an indelible mark on the urban landscape.

Sylla's camera then enters the home where Amy works, and it documents the reality of Amy's life there. Constant orders are given to Amy throughout the film, and we see her running around the home to take care of household tasks while her employer sits or watches: "Bring the bread. Put it on the platter. Put the tea down in front. Push the platter over. Where's the sugar, Amy? Go get it." Amy always does what she is asked, and as she works the woman yells from across the home to do things like grab a chair and bottle of water. Despite the title's promise of a silent central figure, we do in fact hear Amy, in voice-over, describe this place as a prison due to her endless tasks: "I do the laundry in a small tub in the courtyard. I sweep the courtyard, the sidewalk, the street." Amy talks about doing the same tasks over and over again, which makes the monotony of her life oppressive. She lives in a small, mosquito-infested, dark, and gloomy room with five other girls. As we see shots of these living conditions, Amy repeats, "My spirit is in my mother's hut." She continually dreams of her childhood home, although she realizes that a return to her village and childhood isn't possible: "Over there is my childhood. Here is my wretched youth." The combination of Amy's voice-over with the shots of her difficult life in Dakar and the evocation of her cherished native village provide a powerful documentation of the precarious existence of urban maids, trapped between the financial obligations of their families back home and their economic dependence on the urban families employing them, between their emotional connections to their mothers and their duties to the domineering women who supervise their work.

While international migration captures national and global attention, with mediatized images of capsized pirogues, rescues at sea, and groups of men arriving on European shores, internal migration is more hidden, personalized, and feminine, with Dakar serving as the essential urban hub for these internal trajectories of economic displacement.[27] Yet Sylla also turns her camera on life in Amy's village, reflecting the call to understand migration patterns in Senegal "by exploring the local options and *in situ* opportunities that are open to the inhabitants of differently situated rural communities. A better understanding of village conditions facilitates linking the rural to the urban. And a proper construction of the continuum between countryside and city provides the necessary perspective."[28] Linkages between the rural and the urban, and the gendered dynamics of internal migration, are readily apparent in *Le monologue de la muette* as Sylla delves into that less visible form of migration in urban Senegal, beginning with a close focus on the singular maid but then expanding her film to reveal the full scope of Amy's precarious existence in Dakar.

As the film progresses, we see that Sylla crafts a work that is rich with women's voices expressing their various experiences, even though the title promises just a monologue. The film does indeed open with one single voice that we hear in voice-over over the shots of women and maids sweeping in front of houses in early-morning Dakar. This initial voice remains central throughout the film, and it introduces us in this first scene to the collective female strength that the film will portray: "The sun and the moon don't shed their light for us. Well, this Spring will be ours. The bougainvillea will bloom for us. Trees will bud and butterflies will take wing. Time is our ally. It flows like a lazy river. We can't throw in the towel. We must dry our tears. Our star will soon rise. The black star of our Spring will shine forth. For you, Amy. For us." While the shots of the maids and women are observational and from an outsider's perspective (one maid even looks directly at the camera with an inquisitive look on her face, suggesting that she may have been shot without her knowledge or at least making the audience recognize our social distance from her, that we are being voyeurs toward her), the voice-over is directed toward fellow maids, maybe even Senegalese women writ large, as evidenced by the use of *we, our,* and *ours*. This voice-over isn't for the outside observer. It isn't a warning to them but rather a conspiratorial call to arms for the minority, marginalized community, delivered in a whisper that only some will or should hear. The juxtaposition of the present and future tenses in the aforementioned quotation shows that although the maids may currently be marginalized, there is hope on the horizon that their conditions will be improved and that their muted voices will finally be heard. The possible community that the maids could be a part of is not yet fully realized, but its latent potential lies within urban Senegalese society and relationships with other women and is brought to the fore by women's creativity and Sylla's cinematic expressions.

The film continually enlarges this expression of community as it articulates the communal experiences of maids in Dakar, rather than just Amy's own trajectory, and adds various female voices to those that have already spoken in the film. After the sequence demonstrating the direness of Amy's work conditions and expressing her longing for her native village, the film cuts to a shot of a woman facing the camera against a black backdrop. She says in Wolof, "If I'm so pretty, why don't you hire me? Why do you prefer me black, ugly, short, one-eyed and toothless. You haggle when you hire me as if I were an object for sale. Why? Why?" At this point the woman's voice rises, and she becomes even more angry and aggressive in her statements, coming out from the shaded spot where she was being shot into the bright sunlight, moving toward the camera, crowding the frame. She continues her denunciation of her exploitation: "You don't feed me yet you eat your fill thanks to me. Yes, thanks to me. If something's lost, it's my fault. It's always my fault. But I keep your house clean. I slave away while you relax. I do everything." This sequence gives voice—angry, full voice—to Amy's quiet grievances through the poetic utterances of Senegalese slam artist Fatim Poulo Sy. If Amy is not able to fully express herself, Sylla's film can permit other women to raise their voices to join Amy's muted or inwardly turned articulations. Sy returns later in the film, no longer covering her head or resting in the shadows. She is in the city streets and has evidently liberated herself from the situation in which we previously found her since she doesn't speak of *me* or *us* or *you* this time. Instead, she speaks of *they* and *them*, both about maids and employers. Now, she can be more of a voice of warning and a model of future possibilities for maids like Amy who are still trapped in exploitative conditions. Her voice is still just as aggressive, as angry, as denunciatory as before, but it now serves as a guiding call to freedom rather than just as a cry of pain. Sy's own abilities to artistically create, and the cinematic space Sylla offers for her to voice those creations, serve as ballast to Amy's precarious identity and silenced voice. For women on the urban extremes in *Le monologue de la muette*, one way to fashion community is through creative expression and artistic independence.

In one striking sequence of the communal power of artistic creation in the film, we are fully immersed in the private space of the urban maids. We are in the neighborhood where the maids live, and there is a large group of girls, female teenagers, and women. They are smiling at times, being loud, more relaxed than when they are at work. The sun shines on them brightly, and a few of them shield their eyes. One woman says, "She hit me and threw me out without feeding me," but she recounts these horrors in her full voice, without fear of reprisals, among sympathetic, supportive listeners. We see other maids listening, asking questions, telling the abused woman that they will go with her to talk to her employer. No longer are the maids' experiences and frustrations projected through the artistry of Sylla as a filmmaker or Sy as a slam artist. The maids can now convey their subjective experiences through their own artistic creation. The angry group of maids proceeds to the employer's home, but they are clearly still in the same impoverished neighborhood. The house they come to is obviously not one that would employ a maid. We begin to sense a form of recreation or theatricality in this sequence. The maids denounce the employer and ultimately steal her pots as recompense for the money she owes the maid she fired. There is a brief fight, and the police come to sort things out. At this point the women start smiling and laughing, breaking character. It all seems to be playacting. We don't know if Sylla asked them to do it, if it was their own form of entertainment, or if they were using theater to educate each other about the exploitation they often face at the hands of their employers. However, we do see that this community of poor urban women use art and creativity to work through the precariousness of their social conditions. They strengthen their communal bonds with joy and humor through their own artistic rendering of their economic precarity. Again, Sylla's film interpolates a variety of creative forms and women's voices to emphasize the maids' urban precarity but also to convey the means of community building and personal expression that these women undertake to reshape their social circumstances.

Amy's voice is present in the film through voice-over as she details the travails of her existence as an urban maid, the reasons that she does this work, and her hopes for her future. However, the unique power of Sylla's film as an act of artistic engagement comes from the collective construction of Amy's voice-over and the way it presages the polyphony of female voices that the film brings together. Noticeably, Amy's voice-over isn't entirely her own but most likely written by Sylla and voiced by an actor of Sylla's choosing. Nevertheless, this does not vacate the meaning for Amy's identity and experiences. While questions of power, representation, and agency could be raised about a traditional documentary in which the director provides the voice for his subject, *Le monologue de la muette* resolves such issues by embracing them fully and adapting them to ends of justice, equity, and community. Sylla appropriates these contradictions and tensions, turning them into empowering tools for the young Dakar maid and those women like her. Along with the content of the initial collective voice-over and the continuing representation of female solidarity and collaboration in the film, we can conclude that Amy's voice-over is another opportunity for female collective action. Sylla provides the articulations and turns of phrases that Amy might lack but that still effectively represent her experiences and render her voice audible to an audience that would be disinclined to listen to Amy in other contexts. In fact, Sylla describes to Pfaff how such maids live in the darkness and margins; they are, in fact, invisible: "When you enter into a home, you see everyone but no one looks at the maid.... She is part of the furniture! It is a terrible social violence that is being done to these women!"[29] Through the creative form of Amy's voice-over, Sylla strikes against this social violence and demonstrates that these maids can be part of a social body, one that is decidedly female and that takes its power from that female identity. Sylla continually adds diverse women's voices and experiences to her portrayal of urban maids in the film. Collectively, they form a heterogeneous yet unified representation of this ignored segment of the population in Dakar. In this way, the film does follow through on its promise and becomes a monologue: a cohesive, purposeful articulation of the emotions, experiences, and thoughts of a marginalized gendered community, even if that community is materially

Urban Precarity, Voice, and Contingent Communities

disparate, hidden, and socially excluded. Its cinematic articulation by Sylla emphasizes its potential strength and transformative power.

While defining the existences of the maids, Sylla is just as invested in relating them to other gendered social roles and responsibilities. Again to Pfaff, Sylla explains the importance of these domestic workers who are caged in the houses where they work: "It is something rather extraordinary, these women who are in houses, who assume all of the most difficult domestic tasks and who actually allow Senegalese women to emancipate themselves. . . . I owe my own emancipation to the maids!"[30] Having established female solidarity and community in the film, Sylla is not afraid to then interrogate and critique that gendered unity. Her shots of Amy at work reveal the woman of the house to be Amy's primary antagonist, barking orders as she sits idly by, criticizing Amy, and at one point even accusing her of stealing. While men are occasionally raised as threats, especially sexual ones, to the maids in the film, it is generally fellow women who carry out the quotidian exploitation and dehumanization of the young women coming to Dakar from rural villages in the hope of supporting their family back home. Sylla even goes so far as to identify the privileges that many urban-dwelling girls obtain due to the girls from the villages doing the housework in their families. As she shoots teenage girls coming out of school, an authoritative, relatively neutral voice-over—the closest to a narrator that this multivocal film has—says: "Without the young maids, many of these girls would be home cleaning. . . . Why does the emancipation of some result in the servitude of others? What are the ranks of these girls who slave to feed their families in the villages? They'll never have the chance to learn how to read, write, or count, or a real trade. They've no real future. They'll end up sitting idle back home or begging in the city streets. How many are they? Some 150,000 in Dakar alone." Sylla creates a connected community among the female maids and other women through the multiplicity in the voice-over and the variety of subjects she portrays on-screen. However, Sylla also introduces a new dimension to the female community: the fact that urban women are profiting from the exploitation of these rural women. Sylla could have identified patriarchal society as the culprit, but she chooses to make this social issue more complex with provocative questions about the various players in this national system of exploitation and few easy answers. She emphasizes the gendered privilege that many urban women retain at the expense of more precarious rural women in Senegal.

Sylla's questioning of solidarity and community extends to national and global relations. Amy's voice-over states that even though this film is set in Dakar, it could occur anywhere because the plight of these maids is representative of women's and the rural poor's general social vulnerability to economic and social exploitation: "Anyone could end up being a maid. The woman who pays me is a sort of maid herself. Everyone's working for someone." Amy earns just thirty euros, has to pay eight euros for rent and then food, and the rest is sent home to her village. Sylla transitions to a shot of men filling up water cans from a river and of rows of produce that need to be watered. The narrator's voice-over returns to say that this garden is on the outskirts of Dakar and that these day laborers were once farmers in rural Senegal, like the maids. Children from the village are also sent to the city to earn money. Sylla cuts to shots of male teenagers selling products to the drivers and passengers of the cars on the streets. She references how some will go far away to provide for those they left behind. Next, the voice-over says that maids may hope to be washerwomen one day; this statement is followed by shots of washerwomen doing their work in a communal washing area. Sylla includes their voices in the communal female voice of the film as she documents their complaints of the difficulty of the work, of not being paid, and of working hard but not earning much. Thus, Sylla connects the specific conditions of rural maids in Dakar to the larger economic conditions of contemporary Senegal and beyond, overcoming the contingency of any possible material community of maids with the imaginative construction of an expansive international community of women.

Near the end of the film, as Sylla shows shots of rural life, we hear Amy's voice-over declare that she will never go back to her village. The maids from villages sacrifice everything in order to support their families—they are worked to the bone physically and even sexually abused by the men in the homes. Despite the fact that these maids long for their childhood villages, they no longer fit there either. Amy is nostalgic, but she also knows that there are no opportunities in her village and that she would become like everyone else, waiting out the dry season for the rainy season: "No, I must return to Dakar." Through

Amy, Sylla shows the harsh realities of life for rural women and the inability for them to find gainful employment or to support their families except by moving to the city to earn a living. Their conditions are compounded by the globalized economic realities of developing countries like Senegal. The liberated, aggressive slam poet Sy returns to ask, "It makes no sense, but there it is . . . 5% economic growth in Senegal since 2000. More than France, Europe, the USA. So why is there more and more poverty?" The narrator's voice-over then returns to state, "It's too easy to rely on the NGOs with their stopgap measures. . . . We need to question the rules that govern the global economy. The few exploit the masses and profit greatly from it. They ruthlessly exploit an exploitable workforce of oppressed, submissive, expendable human beings. Maybe the maids don't have it so bad. They're not really enslaved. They're free to go elsewhere." Sylla connects the specific conditions of rural maids in Dakar to the larger economic conditions of the country and of all people exploited through globalized economic relations that prioritize the urban and, ultimately, the Global North. She is able to toggle seamlessly and coherently between the micro and the macro, between the maids and the globalized forces that are shaping them, to ultimately create a coherent portrait of the travails and the strengths of contemporary Senegal and the unique role the city plays in those dynamics.

Odile Cazenave describes how Sylla's depiction of the suffering of women becomes collective through stories like that of Amy: "In choosing to let us hear Amy's inner monologue, she becomes emblematic of a plural temporality and a genealogy. . . . Such voice and vision become Khady Sylla's aesthetic signature, that is, to *tell* suffering, have us experience the pain of these women, through the individual and personalization of the collective."[31] Near the end of *Le monologue de la muette*, in a sequence in which Amy imagines her life if she were to return to her village, a woman comes into the fields where Amy has been working, addressing Amy as she stares into the camera: "Your voice joined with ours and those of our sisterhood, what a storm it'll unleash! Our Spring will triumph. We'll free ourselves from the gloom of the past. For you, Amy. For me and our sisters. We'll desert the modern slavery ship. We'll pull down the ramparts of exploitation." Sylla shows how women, in a unified though distanced and heterogeneous community, have the power to break the chains that have enslaved them for centuries. She calls them—and all of her viewers—to action in order to make long-lasting change that will have a positive impact not just on the maids but Senegalese society as a whole. In *Le monologue de la muette* and *Voix silencieuses*, Sylla and Sie illustrate that while urban space in Senegal can be a site of precarious existences, it also gives rise to strategies of survival that deploy artistic creation, reimagine the shape of community, and amplify the voices of the most vulnerable.

5

Intersectionality, Complexity, and Contradictions of Senegalese Women's Experiences in Khardiata Pouye's *Cette couleur qui me dérange* and Angèle Diabang's *Sénégalaises et Islam*

As we show in our analysis in chapter 2 of Rama Thiaw's attentiveness to urban forms of personal and social reinvestment and change and in chapter 4 of Khady Sylla's documentation of urban maids, Senegalese female filmmakers of the twenty-first century work alongside their male counterparts to reshape urban landscapes by shedding light on a wide variety of social issues that often affect marginalized populations. However, as we equally emphasize in our analysis of *Boul fallé*, *The Revolution Won't Be Televised*, and *Le monologue de la muette* and aim to highlight in this chapter, women filmmakers consistently center gender dynamics in their works so that their films become unique sites for audiences to identify and to engage with the intersections between gender and other aspects of contemporary urban life in Dakar. In this chapter, we demonstrate that women filmmakers of urban Senegal craft uniquely intersectional cinematic expressions by incorporating a multiplicity of voices and the perspectives of numerous women, all of whose positionalities are clearly distinct and varied in the films. The female cineastes bring these different articulations of gendered experiences into dialogue with one another, emphasizing the diversity, contrasts, and even contradictions that are part of women's experiences in twenty-first-century urban Senegal. They document the ways that women "dynamically negotiate incremental change while also recognizing the circumscriptions and challenges implied by these new spaces."[1] We argue that the dialogic construction of these films gives full expression to the localized realities of women's lives in the country and simultaneously offers points of exchange with globalized constructions of African feminine identities.

Our analysis of women filmmakers' articulation of gender, women's issues, and feminized experiences in the contemporary African city contributes to the significant work that the cineastes themselves are undertaking outside of their films to draw attention to gender inequities in African cinema and society. In the foreword to Beti Ellerson's *Sisters of the Screen*, Mbye Cham posits that "scholarship, criticism and general commentaries on African cinema and video have focused disproportionately on the films made by men and, among other topics, the various roles, images and portraitures of women in these works."[2] Cham goes on to note that few scholars "have actually made it a task and a priority to *look for* these female filmmakers and videographers, as well as other modes of female presence and practice in the arena of African cinema and visual media."[3] In our book, and specifically in this chapter, we intentionally select films by Senegalese women directors who have been marginalized in scholarship and who are working on the continent. As Ellerson argues, "Boundaries are blurring, borders are extending, and ... there must be differences made between African women working in and out of Africa."[4] We attempt to draw out and analyze what makes these contemporary Senegalese women filmmakers unique and the innovative strategies they employ to reflect on their daily realities and current society.

The issue of gender was paramount in the para-cinematic events and discourse at the 2019 Festival panafricain du cinéma et de la télévision de Ouagadougou (FESPACO). Well-known filmmaker, visual artist, and writer Fatou Kandé Senghor released a statement and a video through social media before the commencement of the festival that drew attention to the underrepresentation of African women filmmakers at FESPACO and their difficulties in securing resources from the cinema industries across Africa. The statement cited the unbalanced numbers of the festival's selections and awards: of the twenty features in competition that year, only four were directed by women; and in the fifty years of the festival, a woman has never received the top prize for filmmaking, l'Étalon d'or de Yennenga. It continued on to emphasize the importance of cinema and the importance of women having access to the tools of filmmaking: "[Cinema] is a large, open window to our world, through which our children can watch the imaginary and the ideology of all other types of people pass by. Access to cinema, to us, means access to the means of production, of distribution, of screenings for our imagination, our emotions, our perspective on the world. Access to cinema also means a role in the decision-making processes of our profession and its continuance. And in this struggle to exist in the world, we must have equity, of course."[5] Kandé Senghor retook the image of the warrior princess Yennenga of Burkina Faso from the Étalon d'or to launch the hashtag #WeAreYennenga and planned, in collaboration with UNESCO, an open forum at the festival entitled "Assembly of the Yennengas: Where Are the Women Directors?" The poster describes the event held on February 24, 2019, as a "think-tank workshop" and poses the question "What can we change and how?" It was at this venue that women filmmakers and their allies could discuss, organize, and plan for combating the gender inequality in African cinema.

In an interview with journalist Fatimata Wane from France 24 English during FESPACO, Kandé Senghor elaborated on why the #WeAreYennenga movement was created and her goals for the future:

> We just noticed that all over the world, no great gratification was given to a woman. There's no Oscar, there's no César.... The women in film that have been honored are always actresses and editors.... Nobody ever held this huge stallion up in the sky and was a woman. And you know that stallion is named Étalon de Yennenga because there is this princess riding the back of that horse. So it's time that we focused on the princess riding the horse rather than the horse.... Why aren't they there? And it's not because they're not good. It's because nobody's taking them there. Nobody's selecting them.... We need to fix this.... Where are the decisions being made and are there women sitting there?[6]

Kandé Senghor points out that if women are at the table, then hopefully greater representation will follow. As Lizelle Bisschoff and

Stefanie Van de Peer contend in *Women in African Cinema: Beyond the Body Politic*, "Cinematic representations of women have primarily been created by male filmmakers. Many filmmakers and historians argue that these representations will always be flawed, partial and incomplete, and need to be complemented by women making films. . . . The fact that women have directed far fewer films than men results in an imbalanced representation of socio-cultural complexities, and disproportionate representations of individual and collective subjectivities and identities."[7] It is clear in the images that circulated on social media during FESPACO that Kandé Senghor's characterization of the gender divide in cinema resonated with many in the film industry. Subsequently, they rallied behind her call to action. UNESCO Dakar tweeted an infographic entitled "Did you know?" which revealed the lack of women filmmakers who have won awards for best director at major ceremonies and festivals such as the Oscars, Cannes, Venice, and Berlin.[8] While Bisschoff and Van de Peer argue, as cited in chapter 1, that African cinema and film festivals are marginalized by the Global North, there is nevertheless the commonality of the underrepresentation of women in all global cinematic sites. Prominent filmmakers posed for photos in front of a large art exhibit at the headquarters of FESPACO that featured individual black chalkboards, each including just two lines written in chalk: a woman filmmaker's name and her country below in parentheses. Each slate was outlined by a bright border in colors such as yellow, red, green, and purple. Women filmmakers were also active at the 2019 FESPACO in calling out their mistreatment, including sexual assault, by men during productions, launching another hashtag, #MemePasPeur, holding emotional press conferences at which they denounced abusers, and starting a petition against the distribution of abusers' films.[9]

In the same vein as the open forum and other events at FESPACO to raise awareness about the role of women in cinema, Thiaw curated an initiative promoting equality for African women called Sabbar artistiques—les ateliers réflexives féminins de Dakar in March 2019. The title, *sabbar*, refers to the traditional Senegalese dance, typically performed by women, that is accompanied by drumming and a community celebration. These diverse workshops took the form of conferences, expositions, film screenings, dance performances, and debates organized around two primary themes: the role of Africans after the 1968 global revolutions and the place for African women, Afro-descendants, and Black women fifty years after these events. The brochure features a quote from Angela Davis's 1981 book, *Women, Race and Class:* "The success or failure of a revolution can almost always be gauged by the degree to which the status of women is altered in a radical, progressive direction."[10] The workshops invited reflection on how Davis's definition of race and its intersection with feminism can apply to the African continent: "But on the African continent, what does it mean for these resurgences of feminism and theories that hope to rethink the Black African woman, Arab-African woman, Tuareg-African woman, Berber-African woman, White-African woman? How does Angela Davis's quote resonate on a young continent on the edge of the 50th anniversary of the 1968 revolutions?"[11] The flyer indicates that African women are not just triply marginalized as poor, Black, and African, but, in fact, they are quadruply othered because they are African *women* in addition.[12] The Sabbar artistiques sought to give voice to African women from the continent and diaspora through these artistic and reflective workshops that included writers, artists, lawyers, and intellectuals from all sociocultural and political backgrounds. The goal of this inaugural event was to create a "feminine laboratory ... in a spirit of inclusivity."[13] Like Kandé Senghor, Thiaw has used her position as a cultural creator and her community of fellow artist-activists to launch a globally intersectional project for the empowerment of African women.

The rallying together in the promotion of equality continues to serve as an important tool for women filmmakers, and those in Senegal, in particular, are attuned to the importance of support and community between women not only in their films but also in their own lives and work. The activist and awareness-raising interventions of Kandé Senghor and Thiaw emphasized dialogue among women, even if that could lead to conflicting or contradictory expressions. These gestures were important in creating space for all women's voices to be heard and acknowledged and then for thoughtful processes of change to be shaped from the multiplicity of the voices raised. This collaborative, complex, intersectional approach to gendered identities within filmmaking and the cinematic community in Senegal and Africa is likewise deployed in the documentaries of Khardiata Pouye and Angèle Diabang. In this chapter, we profile each of these filmmakers and analyze one of their documentaries that highlights the construction of femininity in urban Senegal. Pouye and Diabang highlight diversity, contradiction, debate, complexity, and difference in their depictions of Senegalese women. They respond to gender inequalities in Senegalese cinema and urban life by showing the heterogeneity of the category of Senegalese women. In her 2012 film, *Cette couleur qui me dérange*, Pouye documents the personal, social, and political contexts that contribute to the practice of skin lightening in contemporary Senegal, while in *Sénégalaises et Islam* from 2007, Diabang surveys women's relationships to the predominant religion in Senegal.[14] Pouye and Diabang are not themselves members of the femininized communities they portray; Pouye has not lightened her own skin and Diabang is Catholic. In their filmmaking practices for these documentaries, they approach the women who are part of these groups, observe, and carefully listen. These two films thus highlight women's voices without inserting the filmmakers' personal perspectives or judgments. In this radical gesture of listening, Pouye and Diabang bring to light private, domestic, and interiorized dimensions of feminine identities and experiences, namely beauty practices and dynamics of faith, that are often sublimated in sociopolitical conceptualizations of women. This is especially significant for gender issues, as the two filmmakers are taught by these diverse women who have the personal experience themselves and make particular choices, and such "innovative daily experiments usher forth new configurations of sociopolitical community entailing new patterns and built spaces of exclusion and inclusion."[15] We posit that Pouye and Diabang uniquely deploy the transformative power of listening and intersectional analysis of women's voices in these two works for the social standing of Senegalese women's lives, within both the local urban context and gendered global networks.

Senegalese Women Filmmakers: Community Building and Social Engagement

Any cinephile would only have to turn to the issue of *Senciné* described in chapter 1 for a clear demonstration that there are many women filmmakers working creatively and proficiently in Senegal today. However, despite the myriad of women filmmakers undertaking important work in the country, their films and contributions have generally been marginalized within the Senegalese film industry and criticism on Senegalese cinema, which is indicative of the experiences of women cineastes throughout the continent. Bisschoff and Van de Peer articulately highlight this tension between the creative, ongoing presence of African women filmmakers and the persistent disregard for them within cinematic communities and scholarship: "As is the case for female film practitioners everywhere, women are underrepresented in the male-dominated African film industries as well as the male-dominated scholarly work on African cinema. And yet, even a cursory glance at the landscape of African cinema rapidly reveals that an ever-increasing number of women are using the audio-visual medium as a way to tell stories, reveal important issues, express identities and subjectivities, and reflect on traditions, histories, and cultures."[16] In order to help rectify this situation and amplify the voices of these important filmmakers and the stories they tell, we highlight a few cineastes who produce socially engaged urban films, particularly in regard to gender and women's issues, in this section. Moreover, these female film practitioners advocate for more attention and resources for women filmmakers, including through supportive collaborations with one another.[17] We provide this overview to reinforce our claim of the prominence of women in contemporary urban Senegalese cinema, despite critics' and scholars' consistent disregard for women filmmakers in considerations of African cinema generally. Also, this survey serves to distinguish Pouye and Diabang as directors who uniquely contribute to a diverse, creative, and collaborative community of urban Senegalese women filmmakers. While many female filmmakers in Senegal create socially conscious films, Pouye and Diabang are noteworthy in their inclusive depictions of complex intersectional feminine identities and experiences.

Although Khady Sylla might be the most recognized member of this community, her sister Mariama Sylla has also worked in the documentary format on socially conscious topics and personalized feminine stories. The latter's debut film, *Derrière le silence* (2005), explores the suffering that HIV-positive individuals in Dakar endure due to social marginalization, familial denouncement, and religious and cultural superstitions. While Mariama Sylla documents women and men who face this social stigma, the women subjects in particular become active, independent agents in the film, making it a tool for their urban social engagement, not just a documentation of it. They provide voice-overs that state directly that they are "participating" in the film to "send a call to society" and to come out of the shadows. One of the women, Anta, directly addresses the viewers, saying that as much as HIV-positive people need to be visible in society and to make their voices heard, they will nevertheless face familial and societal consequences for doing so. Therefore, she says, people must change their views of HIV-positive individuals, making society more hospitable to those who are tentatively revealing themselves as living with the disease. As the women move toward being more visible and vocal in urban society by participating in the film, Mariama Sylla and her collaborators call the viewers to approach these marginalized figures, both through the medium of the film and in social relations. In doing so, the audience members confront social taboos and hopefully overcome their prejudice. Mariama also worked on Khady's final film, a documentary collaboration between the two Sylla sisters entitled *Une simple parole* (2013), which portrays their grandmother's influence on their artistic lives. They show how women, especially those in rural communities, have been the protectors and progenitors of communal cultural values through oral traditions. The film ultimately makes the claim that cinema is a continuation of this traditional feminine practice, making the urban Sylla sisters, for all of their revolutionary activism and creation, inheritors of their grandmother's social role in their rural home village.

Along with being an activist for women's rights and equality within cinema, Fatou Kandé Senghor is also a well-known documentarian. She has made numerous documentary shorts, including *Diola tigi* (2007), which examines the initiation ceremonies of the Diola ethnic group from Senegambia and Guinea Bissau in the face of modernization and globalization. Additionally, *L'autre en moi* (2012) examines the complex intersections of identity, community, and belonging for Senegal's diaspora through the story of Léopold Sédar Senghor's grandsons returning to Senegal from the United States.[18] Her documentary *Donner naissance* (2015) highlights the story of Senegalese ceramist Seni Awa Camara, who was married at the age of fourteen and then struggled to bear children despite becoming pregnant several times, and how her personal journey is reflected in her work. The film follows Camara's creative process through the artist's own words and centers her as an important figure not only in the Global South but also women's art making in Senegal. Kandé Senghor's artistic and cinematic interests are wide ranging, including the television adaptation of her 2015 book *Walabok: Une histoire orale du hip hop au Sénégal*. This series emphasizes the specific challenges that young urban Senegalese, especially women, confront in realizing their dreams and improving their lives. Her work demonstrates a keen perception of Senegalese society, its particularities, and its unique challenges.

Women filmmakers, while prominent in the documentary format, have also produced socially engaged fiction films. Senegalese Martinican director Marie Kâ made the short *L'autre femme* in 2013 as part of the anthology *African Metropolis*, which brought together seven short films, each one set in a different African capital. Kâ's contribution shows the growing intimacy between two cowives, the first in her fifties and the second twenty years younger. While Kâ's film explores the feminine dynamics that can be created within a polygamous family, Fatou Touré Ndiaye's *La promesse* from 2016 examines the beginning of such a family, the possible renegotiation of the marriage, and the transformation of the wife's feminine identity that can come from polygamy. Sophie, the protagonist of Touré Ndiaye's short, has given up her career as a midwife to enter happily into a life in which she orbits around her husband and their two children. When her husband abruptly announces that he has taken a second wife, Sophie grapples with the revelation, looking for ways to reconcile her previous relationship with her husband and the possibilities of this new matrimonial alignment. She ultimately decides to reject this arrangement and to exercise ownership and agency over her future. These fiction shorts by Kâ and Touré Ndiaye about the potentialities and limitations of polygamy reveal the enduring social engagement of contemporary Senegalese cinema made by women but also the diversity of perspectives and techniques that are employed to tackle social issues in this cinema.

Similar to Kâ and Touré Ndiaye, Khadidiatou Sow has gained recognition for her filmmaking primarily through fiction films. Her 2017 short, *Une place dans l'avion*, won second place in the category of fiction short films at the 2019 FESPACO festival. It depicts the comedic aftermath of a random announcement that a plane will leave the airport in Dakar for the United States in a few hours and all passengers aboard will be able to enter the country without the need for a visa. A mad dash to the airport through the Dakar cityscape ensues, as the hungry ambition of urban residents to abandon their lives in their home country for the idealized vision of the American dream is laid bare. While Sow has made two previous documentaries about immigration in Senegal and France respectively, *Une place dans l'avion* explores this topical subject by introducing the heretofore underused genre of comedy to women's filmmaking in the country. Similarly, Iman Djionne's 2016 fiction short, *La boxeuse*, shows a fantastical escapade across the city as a young woman dons a pair of boxing gloves by happenstance. The film debuted with other shorts at the Grand National Theater in Dakar before being shown internationally at a number of film festivals. Even as all of the previously mentioned female filmmakers demonstrate the variety, innovation, and insightfulness of Senegalese feminine filmmaking in its social engagement, Sow and Djionne reveal the potential of this cinema to further develop into new genres and fictional forms.

As this overview of contemporary women filmmakers in Senegal demonstrates, a number of female cineastes practice social engagement in their work, especially within urban contexts, remain attentive to gender and to women's experiences in those contexts, and deploy unique cinematic strategies. Community and collaboration are essential practices in the artistic productions and social engagement by these women cineastes. Many of them consistently collaborate on their films, which helps to develop a stronger community of filmmakers, produce more works by women, and model community building and social engagement in their cinematic creation. Along with the example of Thiaw including Khady Sylla in *The Revolution Won't Be Televised*, we note that the script for Kâ's *L'autre femme* was written by Angèle Diabang, Khadidiatou Sow was the head costume designer on Kâ's film as well as on Touré Ndiaye's *La promesse*, and the script for Sow's *Une place dans l'avion* was written by Touré Ndiaye. Furthermore, Khady Sylla's *Le monologue de la muette* was produced by Diabang's company, Karoninka, and Diabang's *Sénégalaises et Islam* includes interviews with Khady Sylla and Kâ.[19] Women filmmakers in twenty-first-century Senegal have formed a diverse, collaborative, and innovative community in their cinematic practices, their social engagement both on-screen and off, and their films. We presently examine how Pouye and Diabang exemplify these characteristics but also how they distinctly deploy the strategies of difference, dialogue, and collaboration in their use of documentary cinema to treat intersectional urban social issues that impact women in particular but that are often silenced or ignored in society and on-screen. Like Sylla showed with the maids, Pouye and Diabang prioritize a complex range of personalized female voices and experiences in order to instill a sense of gendered authenticity and urgency, raise awareness about the variety of experiences of Senegalese women, and ultimately inspire social change among their viewers.

Cette couleur qui me dérange: Navigating Global Networks with Local Strategies

Khardiata Pouye's work distinctly exemplifies the widespread value and practice of collaboration found among female filmmakers as she undertakes collaborative documentary projects with her subjects for the purpose of provoking social change in Senegal. Pouye was born in 1977 in the Thiès region, specifically the village of Diass, where she grew up and attended high school. She completed her university studies in Dakar with a degree in modern languages from Cheikh Anta Diop University. She then studied at the Media Center in Dakar, benefited from the mentorship of several filmmakers, most notably Samba Félix Ndiaye, and completed various internships in Japan, Benin, Egypt, and Norway. In addition to directing her own films, she was a script supervisor for Alain Gomis's *Tey* (2012). Along with her work in cinema, Pouye is an in-house director and producer for RTS, the national television channel of Senegal. The multiplicity and variability of Pouye's training and career trajectory reflect that of Adams Sie, which is unsurprising given the similarities in their age, training at Dakar's Media Center, and career stages. Likewise, many of Pouye's documentaries focus on marginalized populations, and all of them examine cultural and social issues prevalent in Senegal. Pouye depicts everyday Senegalese citizens who work to better their local communities in whatever small ways possible. In a 2021 interview with us, she described why she prefers the documentary form, indicating that it is "practically reality" and that she enjoys "sharing true reality and the people who live this.... We enter into their intimacy."[20]

In a 2018 interview, we inquired about her experiences as a female filmmaker and her representations of women in her films. She stated that she doesn't define herself as a feminist and has never even asked herself the question "Am I a feminist?" Instead, she prefers to think of herself first and foremost as a cinema professional who "wants to say something" in her work.[21] Nevertheless, in surveying Pouye's extensive filmography, it is clear that many of the themes and issues portrayed in her films concern female identity, expression, and lived experiences. Along with *Cette couleur qui me dérange*, which deals with the specifically feminine issue of skin lightening, and her current work *Élan brisé*, which documents the social causes and implications of rape in Senegal, Pouye has shown a particular interest in documenting female artistic creation.[22] From her portrait of fashion designer Oumou Sy in her eponymous short from 2013, to her depiction of an artistic cruise down the Senegal River organized by Senegalese female author Sokhna Benga in *La croisière des arts* (2014), to her short on francophone literary scholar Lilyan Kesteloot, subtitled *Pionnière de la littérature africaine* (2016), women artists loom large in Pouye's socially conscious filmmaking. This demonstrates how Pouye is a product of the specific intersections of gender, culture, and cinema that arise in Dakar, especially for women filmmakers, even as she undertakes her own distinct approach to these issues. While some female cineastes, such as Khady Sylla, directly engage with gender in their films and are unabashed in speaking explicitly about their female-centric filmmaking practices and conceptualizations, Pouye demonstrates an alternative yet similarly effective approach to rendering gender more visible on-screen and in Senegalese society. She contextualizes and integrates female subjects in expansive social settings that allow for issues of gender to rise organically and more subtly to the surface of her films and to the fore of her viewers' reactions. For example, in her depictions of Sy, Benga, and Kesteloot, Pouye never diminishes the role that the feminine identities of these important women have played in their art, their social engagement, and the challenges and successes they have had. Furthermore, she foregrounds the act of creation and artistic communities, allowing gender to be a theme that viewers can tease out from her films as they choose. Her cinematic social engagement is richly intersectional, relating gender to other social factors. In her work, Pouye brings to screen the experiences of everyday Senegalese citizens, and often women, who may not be featured in news headlines but who, nevertheless, are helping to construct a stronger citizenry and local community, including in terms of gender.

Pouye made her first film, *L'école espoir*, in 2004 after discovering École de la rue, a school in "the heart of Plateau," the historical colonial center of Dakar, that serves children and adults who do not have access to the formal educational system.[23] Pouye said that she created this film to show the hope given to the students by the school's director, Amoul Yakar Mbaye.[24] The school educates people of all ages living in Dakar, including talibé children, women who work as maids, and disabled or unemployed adults who beg on the streets. Mbaye explains that all of these students, regardless of their background, learn to read and write in French and English so that they have skills needed to succeed, such as bartering, writing down the names of clients, maintaining bills, or communicating in foreign languages. Pouye's film emphasizes the urban strategies that Mbaye and his students have fashioned to persevere and to overcome the educational inequities in social life in Dakar through collaborative, innovative teaching and learning.

Although the film does not center around women, it does show how an education can provide girls with a career that extends beyond working as a maid. Pouye follows a young woman named Amy as she works as a maid during the day and attends the École de la rue in the evenings. Her friends gently tease her for always being so concerned with school; however, Amy tells the viewer she is the only one who is educated in her entire friend group. She says that she knows all of her friends' secrets: "They give me mail to read or write. Sometimes, after work, I teach them the basics of the alphabet." Amy believes that the school helps the entire neighborhood by giving its students a chance to pursue their dreams, even later in life. In *L'école espoir*, Pouye emphasizes the importance of urban community building by everyday Senegalese citizens who do not rely on outsiders or on outsiders' value systems to build and strengthen their communities but rather combine their own knowledge and expertise to serve their fellow urban residents in finding personalized standards of hope and success.

Pouye continued her focus on educational strategies for marginalized communities in her 2008 film, *Obscure, clair-voyance*, which highlights the creativity, intelligence, and capability of blind children enrolled at the El Hadji Malick Sy High School in Thiès. In an interview in the film, one of the philosophy teachers, Monsieur Diene, argues that these young students are just as capable as their full-sighted peers since they use all of their senses to learn: "We note that they are more clear-sighted.... I would even say more resourceful." Just as Pouye documents the improvisational, organic strategies for education among the urban poor and disenfranchised of Dakar in *L'école espoir*, in this film she reveals the unique ways that blind students in another of Senegal's urban areas undertake learning, community building, and social engagement. She depicts a school that serves a specific, delineated community, but she does so by meeting that population on its own terms and emboldening its own knowledge and abilities rather than imposing exterior hierarchies. By showing these bright and motivated students, she helps to break stereotypes about people with physical disabilities, which will hopefully lead to a more inclusive society.

Pouye applies these forms of urban self-empowerment and community building to women in her most socially pointed film to date, *Cette couleur qui me dérange*, which highlights the widespread practice of skin lightening among women in Senegal. The film first ran on Senegalese state-funded television station RTS and has since been recognized and shown internationally. Pouye stages a narrative of women seeking out the best products to lighten their skin in Dakar and interviews individuals implicated in this consumer market, including vendors, consumers, a scarred former user, dermatologists, and even a customs official. This hybrid form, mixing fiction with documentary, allows Pouye to evoke the full complexity of skin lightening. In her historical study of skin lighteners in South Africa, Lynn M. Thomas emphasizes the critical need when studying the practice of skin lightening to take into account "intersecting political and affective formations of class, gender, and sexuality, . . . a variety of transregional and multisited processes, . . . institutions of slavery, colonialism, and segregation as well as the collateral development of consumer capitalism, visual media, techno-medical innovations, and protest politics."[25] She argues that to effectively understand why people practice skin lightening, observers must bring "an openness to the multiplicity, ambiguity, and opacity of meaning" because these practices reveal "the importance of both surface appearances and the layers that lie beneath them."[26] *Cette couleur qui me dérange* deftly exemplifies such an approach toward skin lightening in Senegal. In twenty-six minutes, Pouye powerfully evokes the scope of this practice, called khessal in Wolof, showing how it functions within domestic, private space in the city, as well as the way it continues due to international economic relations and global standards of beauty. Pouye insightfully represents the interiorized, personal dynamics of this social issue while also contextualizing it within wider dynamics.

In this way, Pouye's documentation of skin lightening among urban Senegalese women resists "the maintenance of an aesthetic order in the city that keeps people in their proper place."[27] D. Asher Ghertner characterizes such practices as "rule by aesthetics, a mode of governing space on the basis of codes of appearance" that draws lines of belonging and marginalization across cityscapes.[28] Pouye's film shows that such strategies can also be extended to the aestheticized contours and surfaces of the bodies of those excluded and included individuals who inhabit the city. As Ghertner argues, these aesthetic practices then not only shape the systems of belonging within the city but also the modes of seeing. For Ghertner, these visions are particularly trained toward the dwellings and infrastructural developments of the city, while Pouye shows in *Cette couleur qui me dérange* that the "aesthetic governmentality" of urban centers can equally discipline the ways of seeing one's own physical self.[29] Feminized bodies, of course, are the foremost physical sites for such exchanges and contestation, and "few beauty practices have been the site of more struggle than skin lightening."[30] Pouye herself states that the idea for *Cette couleur qui me dérange* first came to her as she noticed women on television with light skin: "On television, the majority of the entertainers or hostesses practice skin lightening and are on programs that broadcast at peak periods."[31] She points to the women government officials who lighten their skin, to the camera operators on talk shows who spontaneously prioritize crowd shots centered on women who have lightened skin, and to internet culture that virally spreads these images of female beauty standards. Pouye reiterated the troubling reality of young people who view these images and are attracted by "ephemeral and abstract beauty."[32] Such aestheticized physical projections shape the sociopolitical realities of who may fully participate in urban life. Pouye's film unveils the private thoughts, actions, and consequences of these cultural aesthetic dynamics for Senegalese urban women while also accounting for the wider structures that bolster these individuated experiences of beauty practices. Pouye states that her goal in making the documentary was "to shock people" and to reveal the reality of the situation in Senegal.[33]

The film opens with a shot of a black-and-white photo that is placed on a mirror and that features a woman with light skin, and in front of this photo within the shot is a plastic tub of white cream. We see a hand take some out of the container, and then the camera moves to the face of this woman applying the facial cream, and we see that she is in a bedroom. The camera then cuts to a seemingly older woman who has leathery, blotchy, scarred skin and who claims that "if you have darker skin, you do not count."[34] This brief interview is only six seconds, and then the camera cuts back to the woman from the opening scene who speaks directly into the camera and explains that she "loves to lighten her skin." She states that when she meets a woman with lighter skin, she asks her what products she uses. Pouye intersperses shots of women's hands and feet that have been scarred due to skin-lightening products with interviews of women articulating the powerful social value placed on those who have successfully lightened their skin. In this opening sequence, Pouye raises the same questions of value systems and the social construction of self-worth that she documented through the schools and students in *L'école espoir* and *Obscure, clair-voyance*. The beginning of *Cette couleur qui me dérange* pushes us to ask how these women can believe and adhere to such beauty standards when the result, as the shots of the hands and feet demonstrate, is unintended self-mutilation. After a close-up of these mutilated body parts, a physician stresses the importance of allowing skin to remain its natural color. In this brief but telling statement, Pouye proposes an initial answer to the question she has provoked in her audience by cutting from this sequence directly to the title card.

The next cut is to a shot of a television commercial for a skin-lightening cream and two women watching the commercial who wonder if that product could give them skin as light and beautiful as that of the model in the advertisement. The younger woman, later identified as Fanta Sow, is curious about the product and asks the older woman, who we later learn is named Néné Sow and is the younger woman's sister, whether she will ever have light skin like the woman on the commercial. Néné responds that the product's name will likely be mentioned in the ad. She then makes a call to a man she refers to as the Expert and indicates that she received his name from a friend. She explains on the phone that lately she feels "very black" and asks the man to make her "a mix." Pouye has transitioned her audience into the staged portion of her film; the transition is somewhat jarring upon an initial viewing since in the opening sequence Pouye uses a conventional documentary style of talking-head interviews and shots taken from life as it happens. It is unclear from just viewing the film whether the staged sequences are reenactments of moments from the subjects' lives or fictional scenes created by Pouye. In a 2021 interview with us, Pouye explained that she originally intended for the primary interview subjects of the film to be a governmental minister and a leader of an NGO on women's issues. However, she came to know Fanta on the set of another film where she learned that Fanta lightened her skin and was beginning to have health concerns about the practice. Pouye encouraged her to be involved in the film because "it was the moment to speak about it."[35] Fanta mentioned her involvement with the project to her sister, and subsequently, both of them came to be the protagonists of the film. In collaboration with Fanta and Néné, Pouye recreates their daily skin care routines, their trips to the market to purchase the products, and their expressions of, in the case of Fanta, worry toward skin lightening and, for Néné, her full valorization of it. Pouye insists that the women are not playing roles and that she collaborated with them to make those recreations as accurate as possible to their real lives. Nevertheless, the staged portions of the film prove to be powerful reminders of the artificiality of the standards of beauty that propagate this problem. Néné and Fanta are two of the women interviewed in the beginning sequence and who extol the worth of light-skinned women in Senegalese society. Pouye has gotten these women to openly articulate on camera their views of feminine beauty, and she now takes her viewers into the constructed state of trying to live up to those standards within an urban context. The shift between documentary and fiction cinema in *Cette couleur qui me dérange* reflects the relationship between the social construction of female beauty that occurs through social narratives and the significant consequences of such narratives for women's physical, emotional, and economic realities.

Fanta proceeds to go to the market for skin-lightening products and Pouye interviews the market vendor, Baba Traoré, who explains and demonstrates how he makes his products. Most are made with different fruits, but "all the soaps are lighteners, even regular soaps." He explains that women scrub on the soap for five to ten minutes before getting in the shower, and this helps to lighten their skin. He says that some of the ingredients that seem to help lighten the skin include palm

FIGURE 5.1. A cosmetics shop in the Tilène Market of Dakar, 2023. Photo by Devin Bryson.

oil and honey, and he also adds cosmetic products to the mix. After Traoré describes the components of the concoction, Fanta selects a bag and finalizes her purchase. Throughout their conversation, he mentions the various ingredients in the soaps, which are all different colors and combinations, as well as their prices. Pouye shows that skin-lightening products create a profitable business in Dakar for soap producers and market vendors alike. Of course, these profits extend beyond Dakar, as Thomas points out that "skin lighteners are a booming global business," with projected sales to reach $31.2 billion by 2024.[36] Even as Pouye emphasizes how much women are forced to confront the implications of skin lightening for their bodies and feminine identities, she does not portray those who choose to lighten their skin as helpless victims or unthinking dupes. Instead, she contextualizes their personal navigation of female beauty standards in urban Senegal within the networks of commerce, government, and healthcare that sustain the practice of skin lightening.

Another component of this network is elucidated in the next sequence. After the market scene, we are back in Néné's home, where the

Intersectionality, Complexity, and Contradictions

Expert makes a home visit to sell his own skin-lightening products in another seemingly staged sequence. In our 2021 interview, Pouye stated that Néné put her in touch with the Expert and that he is not playing a role but that this is his real job, just as the women are depicting their true everyday routines and practices: "It is reality. There is no fiction."[37] He brings with him a satisfied customer named Kadia who has successfully lightened her skin. Néné asks the following question: "Expert, one day will I have a complexion like hers?" Kadia responds positively, encouraging Néné, "But of course! I am very proud of the Expert!" There is a close-up of the Expert, who we later learn is named Idrissa Diop, mixing some sort of cream in a plastic tub. As he mixes, he discusses his special recipe. Then, the film cuts to a shot of Néné, who looks from the Expert over to Kadia. Next, we see Kadia's lightened face as she watches the Expert do his work, seemingly unaware of Néné's gaze. The camera pans down to Kadia's equally lightened arms and hands that rest folded in her lap. Pouye cuts back to Néné looking Kadia up and down; Néné assesses the effectiveness of the Expert's products, desiring lightened skin like Kadia's for herself. There is an overhead close-up of the Expert's products being mixed and then a medium shot of him finishing up, over which Néné says, "You came with your model who you perfectly whitened. You are a real pro." The Expert then explains to Néné the five soaps she will be using, giving directions for when and how to use them. Pouye brings out the ways that, once female beauty standards are inculcated through media and commerce, female relationships and community become the ground in which those profiting from the industry sow the desire for their products. This is emphasized in a later interview with Fanta as she talks about how an older sister who successfully lightened her skin when Fanta was younger really influenced her to want to have lightened skin herself. Vendors like the Expert exploit women's connections and intimacy in order to increase demand for their products by expanding the imposed beauty standard of lightened skin among women themselves. Pouye portrays women negotiating their personal female identities within a patriarchal society that can exploit female relationships for masculinist power and market profit. In this sequence, Pouye convincingly shows what the Expert—and, by extension, the entire skin-lightening industry—is doing when Néné calls him "a real pro" for bringing Kadia with him, suggesting to the viewer that she is onto his game of setting women in relation to each other within hierarchal beauty standards, even as she purchases the skin-lightening cream. Although Néné is aware of his exploitation, she simultaneously desires and consumes his product. While that statement could potentially pass by viewers unremarkably because it comes within the staged sequence, the blending of fiction and documentary forms allows Pouye's audience to understand the various levels of meaning, including critique, that is embedded in what Néné says.

After the interview with the Expert, Pouye transitions to interviews with Néné and Fanta. The women are finally named and allowed to more fully describe their own experiences to the camera, without the intermediary of the filmmaker's staged enactments. We learn that Néné is a businesswoman. She recounts how she came to start lightening her skin fifteen years ago, before she was married, and details the effectiveness of the various products she has used during this time period. She says that people consistently tell her how beautiful she is when her skin is lightened and that she also feels better about herself, like a "queen" who "dictates laws at my discretion. I have a lot of fans, everyone asks me which products I use." In contrast, whenever she allows her skin to return to its natural, darker shade, her friends and family members scold her, and she feels like "a trash can." Next, Pouye interviews Fanta, an actress. Fanta discusses the influence that her older sister had on her regarding skin lightening. It's significant that both Néné and Fanta work in visible, upper-class, urban professions, where the societal expectations for female physical appearance are demanding and unbending. Pouye demonstrates how peer pressure, societal standards, and female friendship in the city all contribute to this social trend while she also centers women's expressions of their personal relationships to the larger context.

The potential ramifications of these influences and the act of skin lightening are made explicit in the next sequence as Pouye interviews an older woman, Soda Diouf, identified by a title card as a "master of ceremonies." Like Fanta and Néné, as demonstrated in both of their interviews and the staged sequences, Diouf's desire for lighter skin can be traced back to beauty standards that were inculcated through a confluence of female relationships and public visibility. She says that the first time she tried to lighten her skin was after being invited to a radio session to perform with other women. When she noticed that she was the only one among the group who had not lightened her skin, she felt awful and immediately spent 12,000 FCFA (US $20) on items to make a lightening product at home. Although during the rest of her interview she only talks about how she prepared the harsh chemical ingredients into a cream that she applied to her skin, the long-term consequences of her actions are evident in each shot. Pouye begins shooting the interview with a medium shot of Diouf seated. She then intercuts with a shot of Diouf's hands, which are visibly marked with scars. To conclude the interview sequence, Pouye cuts to a close-up shot of Diouf's face, which reveals the full extent of her skin lightening: her facial skin is now two different shades and significantly wrinkled and worn. The film then cuts to Néné and Fanta Sow grating bars of soap that they will mix up into a skin-lightening cream, during which Néné mentions, with admiration, a woman who has so dramatically lightened her skin that she would pass for a white woman. While Pouye draws out the roles that market forces, constructed beauty standards, and feminine peer pressure all play in the practice of skin lightening in urban Senegal, she clearly demonstrates that the full implications of the skin-lightening industry come to bear uniquely on women's bodies and health. She gives space to Fanta's and Néné's articulations for why they desire lightened skin, and she respects their agency and self-worth. She even cinematically collaborates with them to recreate their actual daily practices for achieving their ideal beauty standards. Yet Pouye equally points to the contributing social factors that construct this personal desire and the individual, gendered consequences of carrying out the practice of skin lightening. Her filmic gaze on the skin-lightening industry and those who participate in it, both as profiteers and customers, is multifaceted and intersectional. Pouye offers a better understanding of the practice while simultaneously criticizing it, especially through her interviews with medical professionals and the close-ups of damaged skin. Despite her condemnation of the practice of skin lightening, she does not condemn the women who are taken up by its allure. Rather, she illustrates how easy it is for them to buy into the practice as a result of societal pressures, availability of the lightening products, and the lack of information surrounding this detrimental practice. She allows a variety of women to express their personal opinions about skin lightening in the film, including by bringing in Fanta and Néné as collaborators for the staged sequences, leading to a multivalent documentary. Pouye centers women's agency and self-expression, even as she critiques the social area in which they are implicated. Thus, the interviews with medical professionals interspersed throughout the film are critical in terms of raising awareness about the grave medical consequences that can ensue after repeated use of skin-lightening creams. Pouye indicated to us that the medical professionals featured are well-known figures in Senegal, and therefore she was hopeful that viewers would believe their warnings about the dangers of skin lightening.[38] Yet this cinematic gesture of activism is balanced in the film with the privileging of women's complexity and diversity.

The film returns to the staged portion as Fanta visits a medical clinic. She reports to the doctor that she has spots on her hands and feet and that they have made it difficult for her to appear in public. Again, public perception plays a significant role in every facet of how Pouye depicts skin lightening. The doctor proceeds to explain to Fanta that the dark marks are due to some of the products she has used and urges Fanta that she must stop lightening her skin immediately and must begin a prescribed treatment. She hypothesizes that perhaps with time the spots will fade, though this is not guaranteed and will not happen quickly. While Fanta's situation sounds and appears dire, Pouye illustrates that it could be even worse. Fanta asks the doctor if some of the images that she has in her office portray skin issues that are caused by skin lightening. The doctor answers that this is indeed the case and that the longer someone uses products to lighten their skin the greater the risk is for severe dermatological conditions like skin cancer. Pouye then turns the camera on those same images, directly demonstrating the life-threatening potentialities of skin lightening. A brief interview with the dermatologist who Fanta has visited is followed by an interview with a different medical professional. Both of them speak about the significant number of cases they see that are due to skin lightening and the health consequences and emotional fallout for these women who become permanently disfigured. These health concerns are not new, limited to Senegal, or simply anecdotal. Thomas describes an in-depth study undertaken between 1969 and 1975 by two dermatologists at the University of Natal in South Africa, analyzing the biomedical concerns surrounding the practice of skin lighteners. The researchers concluded that the continued use of creams containing the chemical hydroquinone was "a trigger for the condition" of exogenous ochronosis, which is characterized by "faces marred by patches of bluish-black hyperpigmentation and caviar-like clusters of darkened papules."[39] They date this "exogenous ochronosis epidemic" in South Africa to the year 1966, which was when "a number of manufacturers increased concentrations of hydroquinone from 3 percent to upward of 8 percent. By the mid-1970s, nearly 30 percent of African patients seeking treatment at dermatology clinics did so for exogenous ochronosis."[40] This important study in South Africa had global repercussions because the US Food and Drug Administration began to more carefully regulate concentrations of hydroquinone in skin products and require labels with detailed warnings about the link between exogenous ochronosis and exposure to ultraviolet radiation. The final sequences in Pouye's film, which turn toward medical professionals and government officials, evoke a similar dynamic in skin lightening between the local Senegalese context and globalized systems of health, finance, trade, and beauty.

Although the medical professionals interviewed throughout the film play an important role in raising awareness about the negative effects of skin lightening, Pouye does not privilege their authority over the personal experiences of individual women with skin lightening in daily life. She continues to foreground the voices of these women, even as she uses the medical perspective to make the health ramifications of skin lightening undeniable to her viewers. After the two short interviews with the dermatologists, Pouye returns to Soda Diouf, who explains that she was never selected as a featured performer in ceremonies when she had dark skin, and it was this neglect that led her to skin lightening. However, now that she has badly discolored and marked skin, her only objective is to "do everything to stop young people from lightening their skin. Skin lightening always ends up betraying you." After Diouf's statements, Pouye cuts back to the doctors, but it is the older woman's personal experiences with gendered social pressure and her turn to social engagement and activism that most significantly demonstrate the social construction of female beauty standards on which skin lightening depends and the potential for the social valuation of light skin to change due to the efforts of women like Diouf and Pouye. Pouye takes an expansive view on skin lightening in her film, as evidenced by the final sequence, which cuts from the second doctor decrying the fact that there aren't any governmental regulations on importing the most nefarious skin-lightening products to an interview with a customs official who explains that there is no way for him to distinguish between various cosmetic products that enter Senegal and to determine which ones should be banned. The insertion of the interview with the customs official demonstrates that skin lightening is a global issue extending far beyond the borders of Senegal. Beti Ellerson argues that more African films addressing the perceived beauty associated with lighter skin are being produced, which she links with this growing global practice and trend: "The globalization of a normative beauty based on a constructed white female body (which is also challenged by white feminists) without doubt contributes to this appeal. Another influence may well be the translocal circulation of ideas, styles, and attitudes, especially through global cultural media exchanges."[41] In our 2021 interview, Pouye expressed doubt about how much the government could regulate or limit the spread of skin lightening in Senegal given the unceasing power of beauty standards that encompass the globe and that are propagated through all forms of entertainment and media, most powerfully online. While Pouye concludes *Cette couleur qui me dérange* by gesturing to the global market forces that support the skin-lightening industry, she does not extend her analysis or critique into that full global context. The ending structure reiterates that the film's power to provoke social change comes primarily from its depiction of urban female daily life and its attendant social expectations and from its amplification of the full range of voices of women implicated in these contexts.

Pouye begins the film in personal space, with the individual desires of women, expressed to one another, for lighter skin. Only after allowing the trajectories of these women to play out within urban space does Pouye introduce authoritative medical voices that condemn the practice for health reasons and draw attention to the lack of national and international regulation of skin-lightening products. Pouye documents the stories of these women to understand their plights and to identify the social factors that have so significantly influenced them to equate beauty with light skin. Within the social and global contextualization of skin lightening, Pouye privileges Senegalese women's voices and experiences in quotidian living, bringing them honestly to the screen in all of their complexity.

Intersectionality, Complexity, and Contradictions 193

FIGURE 5.2. An anti-skin-lightening ad in front of a pharmacy in the neighborhood of Mermoz in Dakar, 2023. Photo by Molly Krueger Enz.

Sénégalaises et Islam: Women's Religious Solidarity and Diversity

Angèle Diabang does not play with the formal conventions of the documentary format in the same way that Pouye mixes aspects of fiction and documentary styles in *Cette couleur qui me dérange*. However, like Pouye, Diabang does create a site in her work where the multiplicity of women's voices and experiences can be witnessed. Diabang has worked in various roles within the cinema industry, including as a camera operator, script writer, editor, producer, director, and head of her own production company, Karoninka, which she founded in 2006. Born in Dakar in 1979 to a Catholic family with origins in the Casamance region, she began her cinematic training as a university student when she posed for a photographer who was also a filmmaker. She agreed to serve as a model if he would teach her about cinema, and she quickly became interested in editing.[42] Diabang completed an internship in film editing with Pape Goura Seck on Moustapha Ndoye's film *Sénégal salsa* in 2000 and then expanded her filmmaking knowledge into additional areas at the Media Center of Dakar, which she began in 2003. Like Pouye, Diabang pursued additional education and training abroad in France, Germany, and the Netherlands following her graduation from the Media Center. It seems important to note that both Pouye and Diabang experienced extensive training and education in cinema in other countries, which has seemingly allowed them to return to Senegal with the ability to cast a sharpened cinematic eye on their native culture. Contemporary Senegalese filmmakers' engagement with the world empowers them to more fully film and document their own societies in Senegal.

In an interview with Françoise Pfaff, Diabang notes her personal desires in filmmaking and the importance of Africans in depicting their own continent, culture, and history: "For the moment, I want to speak about Africa and African women, about my immediate environment.... The history of Africa needs to be told by Africans. Others have always been coming to Africa and describing it as they see it. I think that now it's up to us to describe our Africa."[43] This harkens back to Felwine Sarr's work *Afrotopia*, which promotes the idea of self-reinvention by and for Africans. Diabang is a versatile filmmaker who tells diverse stories of African men and women in documentary and fiction shorts as well as in feature-length documentaries. Many of her films have been shown at international film festivals, and she has become one of the most widely recognized woman filmmakers from Senegal in the twenty-first century.

Diabang began directing her own films modestly, with a five-minute documentary short, *Mon beau sourire* (2005). Despite the film's short running time, it contains the kernels of her continuing themes and approaches in filmmaking. Like Pouye's *Cette couleur qui me dérange*,

Diabang's film examines a specifically African beauty practice for women: gum tattooing. She stated that learning about and filming this ritual was an important step in her life that made her proud of her African heritage.[44] Also similar to Pouye's work, this short demonstrates Diabang's ongoing engagement with women's issues in her filmmaking, which focuses on the particularities of female experiences but draws those particularities from an inquisitive gaze on daily life in Senegal and a desire to render African culture accurately visible on a global scale. When asked whether her intent was to break stereotypes in creating this short, she responded that she wanted to show "realities in the process of developing."[45] She explains that, in the past, women tattooed their gums because it constituted a ritual marking the passage into adulthood. Today, the reasons for this practice have changed, and it has become more of a beauty choice to highlight the contrast between the white teeth and dark gums. Diabang stresses that gum tattooing is a choice that involves suffering but also leads to a sense of pride and accomplishment.[46] In this way, *Mon beau sourire* documents the complexities of Senegalese women's lives, connecting beauty practices to issues of tradition, family, and gendered social roles.

In our interview with Diabang, we commented that many of her cinematic topics seem to focus on women and asked her how she selects her subjects. She responded, "I cover a subject that is close to me and that often stops me from sleeping for a while. But I am conscious of the fact that having made films up until now about women positions me as a feminist.... I am just an artist who looks out over my surroundings and who wishes to share with the entire world the culture and the true history of my continent from an insider's perspective."[47] Diabang's emphasis on her artistic perspective on daily life and African culture, rather than her feminist activism, echoes Pouye's conceptualization of her own filmmaking practices and their relationship to the representation of feminine identity, community, and experiences. Much like Sylla and Pouye, Diabang uses hybrid approaches in her films to depict Senegalese or African specificities to a global audience while advocating for the recognition of women's unique experiences and importance within Senegalese or African societies. These filmmakers refuse to shunt women, their experiences, their relations, and their cinema into a circumscribed section of Senegal. While they consistently include women in their work, they just as often contextualize them within the full range of social dynamics and community exchanges. In privileging the inclusion of the voices of African women, Diabang works to fill the gap described by Bisschoff and Van de Peer: "Women need to get the opportunities to tell their own stories, from perspectives and in forms, styles and ways that offer alternatives to men's films."[48]

After two collaborative shorts on the personal and social value of visual art—*L'homme est le remède de l'homme* (2006), about psychiatric therapy through visual art in Dakar, and *Le revers de l'exil* (2007), about Haitian artists exiled in Senegal—Diabang returned to Senegalese women for her next solely directed documentary, *Sénégalaises et Islam*. Following that film, Diabang directed a fifty-two-minute documentary entitled *Yandé Codou: La griotte de Senghor* (2008). The film profiles the titular subject, a renowned female griot (an oral and musical storyteller) from the Serer ethnic group. She was President Senghor's official griot and a musical influence on a number of Senegalese music stars, including Youssou N'Dour. Although the film may seem like a departure from Diabang's focus on social engagement in her previous work, it retains her abiding interest in women subjects and aspects of the feminine experience in Senegal. Similar to Pouye's shorts on the work of Sy, Benga, and Kesteloot, Diabang's film especially highlights female creativity and self-expression and their social value. It also contributes to the lineage of women artists that the community of women filmmakers in Senegal has archived in their filmography. In addition to producing her own musical creations, Yandé Codou also participated in socially engaged cinema in Senegal through her appearances in Safi Faye's *Mossane* (1996) and Joseph Gaï Ramaka's *Karmen Geï* (2001). Diabang, like many of her fellow women filmmakers in Senegal, recognizes her female predecessors in socially engaged cinema and presents her own work as the contemporary continuation of that heritage.

After having released these short and midlength documentaries, Diabang directed her debut documentary feature in 2014 with *Congo, un médecin pour sauver les femmes*. The film documents the work of the 2018 Nobel Peace Prize winner, Denis Mukwege, a gynecological surgeon who founded Panzi Hospital in the Democratic Republic of the Congo. After founding the hospital in 1999, Mukwege quickly realized that the clinic would need to be more than a facility for general female healthcare due to the increase in sexual violence that many women in the eastern part of the country were facing because of civil war, separatist violence, and human displacement. Mukwege and his staff made the hospital a site for survivors of sexual assault and rape to receive medical and emotional care as well as legal assistance. Diabang's film is not the only documentary on Mukwege and the hospital staff, but hers is noteworthy within her own filmography for its continuation of her efforts to document African women's unique experiences and to provoke social change for women's social ills.[49] In a lecture presented at the West African Research Center for a group of American university students, Diabang spoke about her desire to show more than the pain and suffering endured by these women. They are dignified, proud, and strong, which is the image that she wants to share about her continent.[50] Her shift from Senegal to the Democratic Republic of the Congo speaks to Diabang's ability to retain a focus on the specificities of African women while still looking broadly for subjects that can convey African women's stories to the wider world.

Although Diabang is better known for her documentaries and has more experience with this genre, she garnered international success for two fiction shorts, which were featured at festivals in February 2019. *Un air de kora* was nominated for the Berlinale International Film Festival in Berlin, Germany, and the FESPACO festival in Ouagadougou, Burkina Faso. Diabang won awards at FESPACO for this film, including the Poulain de bronze for best fiction short and the Economic Community of West African States (ECOWAS) award for best director. *Ma coépouse bien aimée* was selected to be shown at the International Short Film Festival in Clermont-Ferrand, France, the largest international film festival dedicated to short films. Both of these forays into fiction filmmaking are significant for drawing international attention and recognition to Diabang's work as well as for demonstrating her potential to retain her cinematic engagement on women's social issues outside of the documentary format. In this regard, *Ma coépouse bien aimée* is especially important as it reflects the thematic concern of polygamy that is at the heart of Diabang's in-production adaptation of Mariama Bâ's 1979 novel, *Une si longue lettre*.

When we asked Diabang about her interest in adapting Bâ's novel and the story's pertinence to Senegalese women in the twenty-first century, she emphasized the interior life of Ramatoulaye, the narrator-protagonist who felt betrayed by her husband years ago when he took a second wife. Ramatoulaye decided to stay with him but continues to deal with the emotional ramifications of that choice now that he has passed away, an event that occurs at the outset of the novel: "It's that unconditional love of a woman for her husband that will give the film its universal character. Beyond polygamy, *Une si longue lettre* relates the position of a woman in relation to her family, to love, and that concerns all women in the world. For me, there's no difference between Western women and African women—there's just women! And the necessity for solidarity between women!"[51] Alongside this universal quality to Bâ's story, Diabang does recognize it as a clear, profound representation of the specificities of Senegalese life and society: "Through this novel, Mariama Bâ evokes Senegalese society with rigor, severity, and tenderness without ever pronouncing moral judgement. So I tried to follow that wisdom in my own writing, even when I know that certain of my heroine's reactions will be disconcerting for Western audiences."[52] Given Diabang's previous films, which intersectionally and complexly document the realities of Senegalese female existence while conveying universal connections, it is unsurprising that she is approaching the adaptation of *Une si longue lettre* in a similar manner. Equally understandable given her filmmaking history, Diabang sees her film version of Bâ's novel as a social tool for provoking discussion and a reconceptualization of polygamy but, more widely, of women's social standing. In our interview, she says:

> Adapting this book in modern Senegal will restart the debate on polygamy and its sociocultural demands that are sometimes too constraining and ineffective for social cohesion as much as for individual freedom. Although they are conscious of their progress and their emancipation, women are still prisoners of stereotypes that are obstacles to the realization of their inner rebellion. The societal "We" dominates over the individual "I." . . . I would like my film to go beyond a simple statement against polygamy; it's a more general interrogation of the place of women in Senegalese and African society today. In an Africa that includes both modernity and tradition, which mutually interact with one another, this novel retains its pertinence and strength because its themes and details are still contemporary.[53]

Diabang's adaptation of Mariama Bâ's trailblazing novel further connects the contemporary cinematic inheritors of socially engaged cultural productions on women's lives in Senegal to their forebearers. Diabang links twenty-first-century Senegalese urban cinema to literature and further enlarges the community of filmmakers and their tools for provoking social change in urban Senegal.

Diabang's practice of intersectional documentation of women's issues, experiences, and voices is on full display in *Sénégalaises et Islam*. The diversity of women's perspectives contained in the film is especially poignant given its topic of Islam and the masculinist dimension of Islam in Senegal, as well as the religion's authority in influencing political and social life. Lucy Creevey writes, "The role of Islam in shaping the position of women in Senegal is curious and complicated."[54] Diabang explains the reasons she took on this project: "It seemed important to me to hear women's voices on the question of Islam. These voices that, in Senegal, are rarely raised on this topic. Also, it was innovative to show the relationship of a Muslim woman with her religion. Senegal is a country where Islam is led by the brotherhoods; it was interesting to have a diversity of women coming from different brotherhoods."[55] Indeed, the film goes a long way in breaking stereotypes of Muslim women as a homogenous, monolithic entity. Diabang interviews six women of varying ages who live with and practice their religion in a variety of ways: some are devout but secular; others are nonpracticing but maintain a belief in Islam's doctrine; some are veiled, some aren't at all, while others wear burqas. The women are interviewed in various urban locations—including a home, a library, an office, and outside sitting on a bench—which documents the daily and lived reality of Islam for these women. Between the interviews, Diabang intercuts footage of the streets of urban Senegal that depicts everyday citizens who walk throughout the city on their daily routines. Within these shots of quotidian Senegalese, we view women who are veiled, who are wearing tank tops and jeans, and who are wearing traditional dresses. Although the film does not provide extensive coverage of any one woman's life since there are so many women included in a film with a short running time, the footage of daily urban life in its cumulative effect portrays the diversity of experiences and the ways that religion fits into those experiences.

FIGURE 5.3. A woman walks along a street in Pikine, 2013. Photo by Molly Krueger Enz.

In addition to the visual representation of the multiplicity of Muslim women in urban Senegal, Diabang portrays the diversity of thought and feeling among these women toward the intersections of religious and social issues. During her interviews with them, the filmmaker asks about veiling, the intersection of beauty, desirability, and modesty, gender equality, Islam's influence on politics and social relations, Islamic extremism and Sharia law, and the possibility of understanding between the West and predominantly Muslim countries or Islamic states. Diabang interviews two young women, Aïssatou and Maïmouna, who appear to be around the same age. Maïmouna is featured in a pink, traditional dress along with a pink veil, which she wears as "a way of making myself pure."[56] Despite her personal choice, she posits, "One shouldn't even differentiate between those that are veiled and those that aren't. We are all Muslims. The veil is only one of the divine recommendations. Wearing the veil doesn't make me better than a woman who doesn't wear it." Aïssatou, who is shown in the first scene of the film putting on hand cream and rings, claims that she lives her religion "in a fairly relaxed manner. I respect the hours of prayer and I fast when you have to fast." Despite these practices, she also lives her life like others her age: "I go to the beach, I go clubbing." She does not wear a veil but says that perhaps she will when she is older. A few minutes later into the film, Aïssatou gets ready for a party wearing a tight green fashion T-shirt and fitted green pants. As she speaks, we see shots of women walking on the street with a market, taxis, and other vehicles in the background. She argues, "People who think that African women should stay at home are not living in the real world, or they don't see that the world is changing.... We take on elements of other cultures and they do the same." Diabang's next shot is of Aïssatou and other young women dancing at a party dressed in modern clothes, but there are also other women dressed in more traditional garments.

When Diabang first shoots Khady Sylla in the opening scene, she does so in a library, demonstrating the place of female creativity, learning, and teaching in Senegalese Muslim women's identities and experiences. Diabang does not provide details as to who Khady Sylla is—she appears just as another Muslim woman who is interviewed. Like the younger women, Sylla says that she also feels societal pressures to wear the veil: "I wear it sometimes, when I feel like it. But at other times I don't, simply because I've never done so. And now, because I've reached a certain age, I'm suddenly being told that I should keep my head covered at all times. I also find that many Muslims have taken up a more radical stance about it, and I don't quite know how to handle that." As she speaks, Diabang shoots women walking on a busy street with traffic in the background. Sylla believes that women should wear the veil out of personal choice, not to overtly show their faith or because they feel pressure to do so. "I think that faith is an intimate and personal thing. You don't really need to parade it on every street corner. If we were all to wear uniforms, we would all resemble one another. And I think that's wrong, as every individual is a unique human being." Again, as she speaks there are shots of women on the street in T-shirts and jeans and others in traditional African dresses. Through both images and words, Diabang shows the diversity of these individual choices in urban spaces. Sylla claims that women have won a lot of ground in Senegal and around the world but that at times Islam promotes the idea that women are inferior to men: "I think that's particularly regrettable, as Islam was initially a very progressive religion concerning women." She provides a counterpoint to Thiane, a woman dressed in a black burqa who says that Allah told women to stay at home and men to find food for their families.

Through her filmmaking practices in *Sénégalaises et Islam*, Diabang was evidently able to establish a creative social space in which all the women she interviewed and filmed felt respected, listened to, and safe enough to express themselves on a gamut of topics, many of which are sensitive. In turn, Diabang honors her interview subjects' honesty by documenting the full dimensions of their opinions on these topics and joining their individual voices into a strong, collective whole. This cinematic strategy can be seen as reflective of the intersecting religious and social experiences of Muslim Senegalese women themselves. Erin Augis writes of the importance of listening to Muslim women in Dakar as they narrativize their religious perspectives and experiences of veiling, prayer, and oneness with God, as this highlights the complex strategies they undertake to negotiate "important social conflicts in their changing city," which "expose the links between institutionalized liturgies and the women's appropriations of them for piety as well as debate within Senegalese Islam."[57] Furthermore, for Augis, such an approach underscores "the inherently contentious and global nature of Senegalese Islamic reform."[58] Diabang produces her film from a similar inclination of listening attuned to complex and multilayered experiences. At one point in the film, Thiane questions the global view on Osama bin Laden as a villain after his orchestrated attacks on the United States on September 11, 2001: "People always say that bin Laden kills innocent people and that that's not right. I don't have an opinion on this.... If bin Laden has a personal issue to settle with the Americans, such as showing them that they don't own the world or have total security, and he chooses to do that in his way, then I think that this is his business. God is the best judge." Despite the fact that the film was made in the early years of the war on terror, and Diabang could have felt either external or internal pressure to cut this footage, she instead refuses to demonize her interview subject and places Thiane's voice in dialogue with others'. The filmmaker portrays the heterogeneity of Muslim Senegalese women's perspectives, even at their most extreme.

Rather than condemn Thiane for her perspective, Diabang juxtaposes these more conservative views with comments by Maïmouna, Khady Sylla, Aïssatou, and Mame Marème Kara. Maïmouna claims, "I don't think it's allowed for a Muslim to kill in the name of religion." Khady Sylla similarly says, "Taking the lives of innocent people for an allegedly divine cause, is something for which you will be judged by the creator.... I think that these are people who have completely lost themselves, all their references and their identity." Aïssatou also has an opposing viewpoint to Thaine about violence: "I don't think that religion empowers someone to kill people, to make war.... No, it's not a way to resolve problems in the world." Finally, Mame Marème Kara explains, "We are not told to blow ourselves up and kill innocent people. No, we are being taught to forgive, to give and to share. We are being taught to become unified and trust in ourselves. That kind of confidence can also help in the development of a country. It is that kind of Islam we have been taught here in Senegal." It appears that the other women in the film directly oppose Thiane's lack of condemnation of Osama bin Laden and, as Kara's quotation demonstrates, anchor their personal understanding and expression of Islam in a national context, emphasizing the Senegalese nation as the moderating influence on extremist interpretations. Nevertheless, Diabang still includes Thiane's perspective within her portrayal of the intersection of gender and Islam in Senegal, allowing fellow Senegalese women's voices to contend with Thiane's, rather than excising this social dimension through directorial caveat.

Diabang reinforces the unique identity of each Muslim woman and cautions her viewers to avoid generalizing about Muslims. Several women interviewed blame stereotypes about Islam on negative representations circulating in Western media outlets. Khady Sylla claims that the violent extremists associated with Islam are an exception and result from a loss of identity. She encourages us to rethink our views toward Islam: "There is radicalism on both sides—in the West and in the Muslim world, and we need to meet somewhere in the middle. We need a conception of Islam that is simpler, less hardened, less ready to commit attacks à la bin Laden, and an understanding of the West that is more moderate, that doesn't try to oppose 'us, the civilized world' to 'you the savages.'" Along this same line, Mademoiselle Ndoye, wearing a dark burqa, declares that, rather than examining individual countries and individuals, people understand the religion of Islam very broadly, which leads to dangerous stereotypes. Diabang takes the opposite approach with her film, working against these misconceptions by interviewing a diverse group of Senegalese women.

Ndoye argues that women who wear a hijab are lumped together "in a bag" with other Muslim women, which creates misunderstandings. She says that when people meet her, they are surprised by her openness and often comment, "We thought that you would be much more closed, seeing that you're all covered up." In her view, it is "our duty" to show the beauty of Islam and to promote a human connection between individuals in order to break stereotypes. The possessive adjective *our* is important in showing this collective necessity of Muslim women and, even more specifically, Senegalese Muslim women to change the perception of their religion and how they practice and live out their faith. Diabang's documentation of Muslim women's varied experiences with veiling, one of the most overdetermined and controversial aspects of Islam for Western secularists, provides a simultaneously collective and individualized response to such ideas.

The women speak about the dominance of Islam in Senegal and its relationship with the other religions practiced. Sylla states, "As we live in a country where the majority of people are Muslim, Islam automatically

FIGURE 5.4. Three women walk through the Tilène Market in Dakar, 2023. Photo by Devin Bryson.

influences the minority religions." As Sylla refers to the "majority rule," Diabang cuts to a shot of a mosque full of people and a sign for the city of Tivaouane, a sacred site for the Tijaniyya brotherhood. Maïmouna then questions, "Why would there ever be fears that Islam is influencing the minority religions today, when we Muslims never asked ourselves that question when Senghor was in power? At that time, this was already a secular country led by a non-Muslim, and yet no one spoke of religious dominance." As she speaks, a street scene from the Grand Magal of Touba, an annual religious pilgrimage, is shown. The city of Touba is the holy seat of the Muridiyya brotherhood, another one of the most important Sufi Muslim brotherhoods in Senegal.

With its representation of the diversity of Muslim women in urban Senegal both visually and through interviews, the film becomes a documentation of the general issues of tolerance, acceptance, inclusion, difference, and understanding in Senegalese society and the unique ways those values can manifest themselves in urban contexts. At the end of the film, Khady Sylla says that the most important virtue is in fact tolerance, and if we aren't capable of tolerating others, then we are not worthy of living on this earth. The title of the film emphasizes the national dimension of its portrayal of Muslim women, yet the "and Islam" is particularly significant. Rather than call the film "Senegalese Muslim women" by employing the adjective *Muslim* to describe the women, the use of *Senegalese women* and *Islam* prioritizes their gender first and foremost, but it also clearly links them to their nationality. These are not just women but women from Senegal. The *and* illustrates the interplay between their gender, nationality, and religion, which creates a unique and multifaceted identity. These women's views on any of the topics they address in their interviews and the ways they present themselves in public as shown in the film cannot be detached from the national context in which they express themselves and carry out their daily lives. The multiplicity of the Muslim women in Diabang's film is due to Senegal's specific social, political, and cultural dynamics, whether that be for good or for bad. One of Diabang's goals in making the film was to "remind us that it's precious to have a space where each person can live their difference," and the visuals of the film emphasize that such a space is particularly urban.[59] As Nadine Sieveking writes, "In contemporary urban Senegal, diverging visions of development are negotiated by women's organisations, connecting globalised concepts to local discourses and practices.... Muslim women in Senegal are appropriating and 'translating' these concepts into local discourses in order to expand their room to manoeuvre and negotiate women's rights within their own cultural and religious context."[60] Diabang continues on in our interview to specify the contribution of Senegalese social cohesion to the creation of communal space in which such strategies and tactics can be enacted by Muslim women: "There is a truly good dialogue between Muslims and Christians that is long-standing and that creates a cohesion in Senegal that is envied by other countries."[61] However, Diabang points out that the dynamics of understanding and equality present in Senegalese interfaith relations have not been adequately applied to gendered relations and social roles. *Sénégalaises et Islam* portrays the intersections between gender, faith, and nationality that can, on one hand, lead to liberation and acceptance through women's own agency, narrativization of their experiences, and collectivity and, on the other, produce limitations and trepidation that women must continually negotiate. Diabang's film coherently accounts for this complexity, demonstrating the unique achievements in these areas in urban Senegal while still calling on Senegalese society to do better.

In *Cette couleur qui me dérange* and *Sénégalaises et Islam*, Pouye and Diabang depict Senegalese women in expansive, inclusive, and even confounding ways. They do not undertake simplistic, dishonest, or obfuscating representations of women's lived experiences in urban space in contemporary Senegal. Instead, these two filmmakers center the convoluted, contradictory, and interconnected strategies that Senegalese women undertake in the twenty-first century to achieve more equity, participation, and recognition within Senegalese communities. In this way, Pouye and Diabang exemplify the call of Fatou Kandé Senghor at the 2019 FESPACO to provide women greater access to the knowledge, tools, resources, and networks of filmmaking. As more women seize the camera in contemporary Senegal, they offer up more complex, diversified, and thought-provoking representations of women on-screen. This, in turn, provides Senegalese society as a whole and especially the young girls of Senegal, who will be the leaders of the future, with the feminine icons that they need to envision and create a more gender-equitable city, country, and world.

Conclusion

Cinematic Encounters in the City

Emergent Spaces of Collaboration and Exchange

At the opening of chapter 1, we described a 2018 screening of the documentary *Poisson d'or, poisson africain*. This event was organized by the Direction de la cinématographie to fete a recent film that had garnered international awards and was held at the most upscale and commercial theater in Dakar at that time. The audience was made up largely of members of the Dakar film industry, from administrators to filmmakers. This was an event primarily for insiders, meant to gather the community for recognition and networking. We were personally handed an invitation by the director of the Direction de la cinématographie because we were in the administration's office conducting research interviews and inquiring about access to films.

During a research trip to Dakar in 2021, we attended a film screening that was nearly a complete contrast to the aforementioned 2018 event. At the end of a hot June day, after a dinner of paella at a Senegalese friend's house, we decided to make our way to a double feature that was taking place at Kenu, a cultural center in Ouakam. Our initial problem was finding Kenu, as it was not easily accessible. We had only learned of it recently from the same friend who had served us the delicious paella but who had never been there. Kenu, called a LAB'Oratoire des imaginaires, was created in 2020 by the visual artist, musician, and filmmaker Saliou Sarr, who is also the brother of Felwine Sarr. After viewing posts for the event on Kenu's social media, we were curious to learn about the center that promotes interdisciplinary and collaborative artistic projects as well as to see the two films being shown that night. Our friend helped give directions to our cabdriver, and we set off through heavy traffic. Once the taxi finally arrived at what we thought based upon our friend's description would be Kenu's location, we got out and started wandering the sandy roads of Ouakam. It was dark, with few streetlights to guide our way. We eventually heard the loud sounds of what seemed like a movie soundtrack and tried to follow them to our desired destination. We circled around a couple of times, venturing down some small alleys, and eventually came into a courtyard in which an inflatable screen, a projector, and a few dozen plastic chairs had been set up. The screening had already begun; we were late.

We were surprised to see that the small audience primarily comprised children and their family members. Neighbors hung out of their windows to watch the films. Other community members who were walking by for other reasons would stop and watch for a bit. This was truly an open, accessible community screening. The two films featured that night were Fatou Kandé Senghor's *Donner naissance* (2015) and Iman Djionne's *La boxeuse* (2016), which exemplify so many of the aspects of twenty-first-century Senegalese cinema that we have studied in this book, from the documentary format of *Donner naissance*, to the midlength running time of *La boxeuse*, to the two women directors. As we highlighted in chapter 5, *Donner naissance* is a documentary on the Senegalese sculptor Seni Awa Camara, a woman from Casamance who has garnered international acclaim but who has remained in her small village in the southern region of Senegal for her life and career. While the film centers on Camara's artistic practices and theories, it references the connections that her sculptures have produced between her isolated, rural location and urban centers, in both Senegal and around the world. Despite the high-cultured dimension of *Donner naissance*, and the fact that Kenu only had a copy of the film dubbed in English, with no French or Wolof subtitles, the children and other audience members watched intently, perhaps recognizing a strong cultural heritage that transcended language in the shots of Camara's traditional artistic practices. The visuals of *La boxeuse* similarly transcended language for the audience, even as the dialogue was understandable. This fictional film depicts a young girl escaping the gendered confines of her family's hair salon by donning a pair of boxing gloves she finds in the street, which leads her on a series of adventures and journey of self-discovery through Dakar. The children laughed uproariously at the scenes from *La boxeuse* when the boxing gloves took on a life of their own and compelled the protagonist to speed down the streets and into parts of the city with which she was not previously familiar (fig. C.1). After the screening, Djionne came out to answer questions from the audience about her film, and a few young, brave souls asked about the story and why certain things occurred. The event was then over, lasting a relatively short time, and the audience dispersed into the dark streets of Ouakam and the rest of the city.

Although screenings like the one in 2018 at the Complexe Cinématographique Ousmane Sembène are evident and necessary symbols of the vibrancy of a national cinema, we contend that events such as

FIGURE C.1. Viewers watch the short film *La boxeuse*, directed by Iman Djionne, at an outdoor screening organized by Kenu, 2021. Photo by Molly Krueger Enz.

this screening at Kenu, hidden away in an everyday neighborhood of Dakar and attended by local residents, are equally representative of the life within contemporary Senegalese cinema. A luxurious edifice, like the Sembène cinema, and high-profile premieres might seem to decidedly symbolize stability in the film industry. By 2023, such events were ascendant in Dakar with the opening of the CanalOlympia Teranga and the Pathé Dakar multiplexes and the occurrence of consistent film premieres at the Daniel Sorano Theater. However, we have learned over our years of research in Dakar that such cinematic events and sites are only a very small part of the story of Senegalese film culture. Through our study of the various production, distribution, and screening innovations in Dakar, the filmmakers who live in and document the city, and their cinematic work that represents and reimagines urban life in Senegal, we argue that Senegalese cinema of the twenty-first century is vibrant, creative, and alive within the urban communities in the country. We posit that the constant circulation, movement, and exchange of cinema in contemporary Dakar, in both material form and conceptualization, open up paths of ongoing innovation and reinvention for Senegalese cinema itself and for urban life. Kenu promotes itself as a "laboratory of the imaginary" for a variety of cultural and artistic forms. On the night of that screening in June 2021, it was a site for the imaginative possibilities of Senegalese cinema. However, this wasn't due simply to the creative resources of Kenu itself. After all, temporary, communal screenings are constantly organized by other groups and individuals in the city. During a one-week period in May 2023, we attended five film events at five different venues in Dakar: two films that commemorated the death of Omar Blondin Diop at the Centre Ousmane Sembène and the Musée des Civilisations Noires; three short films by Awa Moctar Gueye at Centre Yennenga; the national premiere of Diabang's *Ma coépouse bien aimée* during the Salon du livre féminin at the Place du Souvenir; and four films around the theme of the banlieue at the Yoonir Ciné-Club's first meeting organized by Rama Thiaw and Mamadou Khouma Gueye at a restaurant in the Almadies neighborhood of Dakar. Like these 2023 events, Kenu was simply the latest site for the manifestation of the cinematic potential that is so active in Dakar. On that night in 2021, as during so many others, the city itself, the exchanges between urban residents, and the life of a local community were the true laboratories for cinematic imaginary, just as they have been throughout the early twenty-first century in Senegalese cinema.

The capital city of Dakar continues to give rise to such localized, modest sites for cinema. In 2021, the Centre Yennenga and École Kourtrajmé were the latest establishments to offer screenings and training of the next generation of filmmakers.[1] These sites represent the perpetual innovation and life, the continued renewal and dissemination of cinema in Dakar. They continue to be essential due to the challenges and limitations faced by official structures, institutions, and channels.[2] As mentioned in chapter 1, the Centre Yennenga was founded by director Alain Gomis and features not only film screenings but also panel discussions, exhibits, cultural activities, and workshops (fig. C.2). It is a center of exchange between local residents, cinephiles, and professionals in the film industry. Similar to Kenu, the Centre Yennenga organizes activities related to cinema for the local population. In addition to this social, communal role, the center also provides essential training and technical opportunities for African filmmakers. According to former director of the Direction de la cinématographie, Hugues Diaz, one reason for the

FIGURE C.2. The outdoor courtyard and screening area at the Centre Yennenga, 2023. Photo by Molly Krueger Enz.

Cinematic Encounters in the City   213

perceived crisis in Senegalese cinema is due to the absence of postproduction studios in the country. During a 2016 interview, he stated that it is critical to have postproduction options in Senegal so that this process does not need to be sourced abroad.[3] He also noted that many Senegalese filmmakers, even those who have gained international acclaim, were trained "on film sets" by observing and helping.[4] To change this and provide formal academic training, he argues that more cinema schools or programs, both public and private, are needed. The Centre Yennenga fulfills such needs in a variety of ways. It offers two-year training programs in postproduction work with high-quality equipment for sound and image editing and color grading (fig. C.3). Film students from

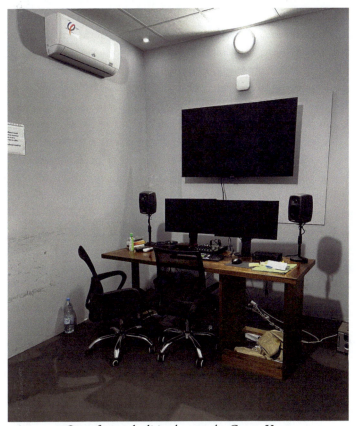

FIGURE C.3. One of several editing bays at the Centre Yennenga, 2023. Photo by Devin Bryson.

various African countries come to the center to benefit from this education. Filmmakers offer their films as material for the students to work on, which, in turn, offers them the chance to get high-quality postproduction work done on their films that they previously might have had to outsource to technicians outside of Africa. Experienced technicians come for periods of time to lend their expertise in training the students. When we visited the center in May 2023, we encountered students from Benin, Burkina Faso, and Senegal. A French sound editor was nearing the end of his several-week mentoring stay. Centre Yennenga itself was in the advanced stages of constructing a sound-mixing room, which would be the first in West Africa, according to those with whom we spoke. The new sound-mixing room at the Centre Yennenga would allow African filmmakers to avoid turning to outside sites and mixers to accomplish this essential stage of postproduction, thus rectifying the gap in postproduction identified by Diaz. Gomis states, "We hope to work with the neighborhood and its children through films that were made by them and projected here because we believe greatly in local cinema as an appeal and a tool for exchange."[5] Yet it is also clear from our visit that the center is looking to cultivate transnational exchanges for that local population with global actors. The multifaceted goals of the center include highlighting films from the African continent, teaching local populations about the language of cinema, and promoting the creative process for a young generation of directors in both localized and globalized dynamics.

The École Kourtrajmé is the first cinema school in Africa founded by the Franco-Malian directors Toumani Sangaré and Ladj Ly. Free and open to students of all levels of education, training, and experience, Ly says that the École Kourtrajmé wants to "break the rules."[6] An early project by some of the school's initial participants was inspired by a woman Senegalese colonial resistance fighter and set in the contemporary community of garbage pickers at the Dakar landfill. One of those students, Astou Diouf, says that the École Kourtrajmé is giving aspiring Senegalese filmmakers the tools necessary to tell their own stories, to revive important figures of Senegalese history, and to resist cultural appropriation and commodification through cinema. Sangaré, the director of the École Kourtrajmé, explains that establishing the school in this city was essential since there are so many high-quality technicians who could serve as instructors: "The country has become indispensable in audiovisual productions."[7] He continues on, "There's energy [here], things are moving."[8] The city of Dakar continues to give life to new generations of filmmakers who take on the responsibility, articulated by Felwine Sarr as cited in our introduction, of resisting distorted, globalized narratives of Africans and projecting accurate, honest depictions of African life and communities.

While governmental and industry centers of Senegalese cinema strive to improve and make genuine contributions to the betterment of the industry, they have not been and cannot be the only sources of change and development for cinema in Senegal. There might never be one central location or institution that stabilizes Senegalese cinema. One theater, film school, or office building cannot wholly represent the state of film in Senegal, whether its crises or its innovations. Instead, it is the city itself that has provided and will continue to provide the source of recreation and reimagination for Senegalese cinema, the means for the vibrant exchange and circulation of those innovations among Senegalese people, and the subjects that will populate its most vibrant cinematic creations. In this book, we have focused on filmmakers living and working in Dakar but whose work tends to be marginalized in scholarship and narratives about contemporary African cinema. Through their documentation of the city as a complex place of encounters between the local and global, between crises and solutions, between community and individuals, they represent and reimagine the vastness and potential of urban life in Senegal. Through their critical reflection on the current realities of Dakar and its habitants, as well as their place in the world, these innovative filmmakers reinforce Felwine Sarr's call to build an afrotopos and emphasize the African city as a place of possibilities.

Notes

Introduction: Beyond Senghor's Shadow

1. See Souleymane Bachir Diagne, "La leçon de musique: Réflexions sur une politique de la culture," in *Le Sénégal contemporain*, ed. Momar-Coumba Diop (Paris: Karthala, 2002), 243–60; Elizabeth Harney, *In Senghor's Shadow: Art, Politics, and the Avant-Garde in Senegal, 1960–1995* (Durham, NC: Duke University Press, 2004); Tracy D. Snipe, *Arts and Politics in Senegal, 1960–1996* (Trenton, NJ: Africa World Press, 1998).
2. Harney, *In Senghor's Shadow*.
3. Felwine Sarr, *Afrotopia*, trans. Drew S. Burk and Sarah Jones-Boardman (Minneapolis: University of Minnesota Press, 2019), ix.
4. Sarr, ix, xii.
5. Sarr, 99.
6. Mbye Cham, introduction to *African Experiences of Cinema*, ed. Imruh Bakari and Mbye Cham (London: BFI, 1996), 2.
7. Frieda Ekotto and Kenneth W. Harrow, "Introduction: Rethinking African Cultural Production," in *Rethinking African Cultural Production*, ed. Frieda Ekotto and Kenneth W. Harrow (Bloomington: Indiana University Press, 2015), 2.
8. Kenneth W. Harrow, introduction to *African Cinema: Postcolonial and Feminist Readings*, ed. Kenneth W. Harrow (Trenton, NJ: Africa World Press, 1999), xvii.
9. Harrow, *African Cinema*, xvii–xix.
10. Harney, *In Senghor's Shadow*, 49.
11. David Murphy, "The Performance of Pan-Africanism: Staging the African Renaissance at the First World Festival of Negro Arts," in *The First World Festival of Negro Arts, Dakar 1966: Contexts and Legacies*, ed. David Murphy (Liverpool: Liverpool University Press, 2016), 5.
12. Joanna Grabski, *Art World City: The Creative Economy of Artists and Urban Life in Dakar* (Bloomington: Indiana University Press, 2017), 7.

13. Vieux Savané and Baye Makébé Sarr, *Y'en a Marre: Radioscopie d'une jeunesse insurgée au Sénégal* (Paris: L'Harmattan, 2012), 15. "tente ainsi de masquer ses échecs dans la création d'emplois par une promotion de la lutte, de la danse et de la musique qui suscitent beaucoup d'engouement, notamment en banlieue." Unless otherwise specified, all translations into English are our own. In such cases, we provide the quote in the original language in the note.
14. Momar-Coumba Diop, "Introduction: Essai sur un mode de gouvernance des institutions et des politiques publiques," in *Sénégal (2000–2012): Les institutions publiques à l'épreuve d'une gouvernance libérale*, ed. Momar-Coumba Diop (Paris: Karthala, 2013), 67. "artistes, écrivains, ou 'parlementaires de la rue,' ces chanteurs populaires, ces nombreux 'porteurs de pancartes' (aux messages parfois fantaisistes) qui ont investi l'espace public pour bricoler des revendications arrimées à la demande politique centrale.... Cette nouvelle avant-garde se construit à partir des arts."
15. Savané and Sarr, *Y'en a Marre*, 8. "il a su fédérer toute une jeunesse broyée par le rouleau compresseur du chômage. Jeunes cadres dynamiques, journalistes, chômeurs, ouvriers, étudiants, musiciens, bref toutes les catégories sociales se sont identifiées à leur coup de gueule."
16. Sarr, *Afrotopia*, 106–7.
17. See, for example, Leslie J. Bank, *Home Spaces, Street Styles: Contesting Power and Identity in a South African City* (London: Pluto Press, 2011); Mamadou Diouf and Rosalind Fredericks, eds., *The Arts of Citizenship in African Cities: Infrastructures and Spaces of Belonging* (New York: Palgrave Macmillan, 2014); Achille Mbembe and Sarah Nuttall, "Writing the World from an African Metropolis," *Public Culture* 16, no. 3 (Fall 2004): 347–72; Garth A. Myers, *African Cities: Alternative Visions of Urban Theory and Practice* (London: Zed Books, 2011); Edgar Pieterse, *City Futures: Confronting the Crisis of Urban Development* (London: Zed Books, 2008); AbdouMaliq Simone, *City Life from Jakarta to Dakar: Movements at the Crossroads* (New York: Routledge, 2010).
18. See Catherine Appert, *In Hip Hop Time: Music, Memory, and Social Change in Urban Senegal* (Oxford: Oxford University Press, 2018); Diagne, "La leçon de musique"; Mamadou Diouf, "Wall Paintings and the Writing of History: Set/Setal in Dakar," *GEFAME: Journal of African Studies* 2, no. 1 (July 2005): 1–23; Mamadou Diouf and Rosalind Fredericks, eds., *Les arts de la citoyenneté au Sénégal: Espaces contestés et civilités urbaines* (Paris: Karthala, 2013); Rosalind Fredericks, *Garbage Citizenship: Vital Infrastructures of Labor in Dakar, Senegal* (Durham, NC: Duke University Press, 2018); Grabski, *Art World City*; Caroline Melly, *Bottleneck: Moving, Building, and Belonging in an African City* (Chicago: University of Chicago Press, 2016); Allen F. Roberts and Mary Nooter Roberts, *A Saint in the*

City: Sufi Arts of Urban Senegal (Los Angeles: UCLA Fowler Museum of Cultural History, 2003).
19. Mbembe and Nuttall, "Writing the World," 357, 360.
20. Sarr, *Afrotopia*, 107.
21. Grabski, *Art World City*, 3–4.
22. Aihwa Ong, "Introduction: Worlding Cities, or the Art of Being Global," in *Worlding Cities: Asian Experiments and the Art of Being Global*, ed. Ananya Roy and Aihwa Ong (Malden, MA: Wiley-Blackwell, 2011), 12.
23. Mamadou Diouf and Rosalind Fredericks, introduction to Diouf and Fredericks, *Arts of Citizenship*, 6.
24. Grabski, *Art World City*, 11.
25. Joseph Gaï Ramaka, interview with authors on Gorée Island, June 5, 2016. "Le cinéma global ne peut pas exister sans le particulier. Il faut penser aux deux."
26. Mbembe and Nuttall, "Writing the World," 348.
27. Mbembe and Nuttall, 348.
28. Mbembe and Nuttall, 351.
29. Achille Mbembe and Felwine Sarr, "Penser pour un nouveau siècle," in *Écrire l'Afrique-Monde*, ed. Achille Mbembe and Felwine Sarr (Dakar: Jimsaan, 2017), 8. "l'entrelacement et la communauté de sort entre l'Afrique et le monde" and "une séparation toujours déjà donnée et toujours tenue pour évidente entre le signe africain et le temps du monde." The inaugural event was held in 2016, but there have been subsequent Ateliers de la pensée workshops in the years following. More information about the public events, participants, and publications surrounding the workshops can be found at https://www.lesateliersdelapensee.org.
30. Mbembe and Nuttall, "Writing the World," 354, 355–56.
31. For an in-depth analysis of the social and individual life of cities, see AbdouMaliq Simone, "People as Infrastructure: Intersecting Fragments in Johannesburg," *Public Culture* 16, no. 3 (Fall 2004): 407–29, as well as Mbembe and Nuttall, "Writing the World" and Sarr, *Afrotopia*, especially the chapter "African Cities: Configurations of Possibles."
32. Diouf and Fredericks, introduction, 5.
33. While his birth name is Moussa Sène, the director added his mother's name, Absa, to his professional appellation. We recognize that there are important cultural distinctions between the United States and West Africa in naming practices and uses and that the director has been referred to in various ways depending upon the publication venue. The director himself indicated to us that we may use Sène Absa in the book when referring to his last name.
34. Sarr, *Afrotopia*, xv.

Chapter 1: Screening Urban Senegal

1. This expansive cinematic complex was constructed by the property development company le Groupe Saleh, directed by Youssef Saleh, who is Senegalese of Lebanese origin. Its official opening was March 31, 2018. See Amadou Oury Diallo, "Cinéma: À Dakar, les bienfaits de la concurrence," *Jeune Afrique*, September 27, 2018.
2. Fran Blandy, "Senegal Anguishes over 'Slow Death' of Its Film Industry," Modern Ghana, September 7, 2012, www.modernghana.com/.
3. Ashley Clark, "Making Waves: The New Senegalese Cinema," British Film Institute, January 17, 2013, https://www.bfi.org.uk/.
4. CGTN Africa, "Senegal Works to Restore Cinema Halls and Revive Movie Industry," March 25, 2017, YouTube video, 2:26, https://www.youtube.com/watch?v=LT8FcpevM6g; Avenel Rolfsen, "Senegalese Cinema Does Not Exist," Africa Is a Country, May 8, 2018, https://africasacountry.com/.
5. Manthia Diawara, "The Iconography of West African Cinema," in *Symbolic Narratives/African Cinema: Audiences, Theory and the Moving Image*, ed. June Givanni (London: BFI Publishing, 2000), 84.
6. Cinécole Sénégal, "Khady Sylla," October 13, 2013, YouTube video, 2:00, https://www.youtube.com/watch?v=DNCzF-MVvtY. "Le cinéma sénégalais est malade, c'est vrai, mais pas si gravement que ça. Il y a encore un espoir de guérison, je pense."
7. Cinécole Sénégal, "Khady Sylla." "Le cinéma c'est un art qui est long.... Si j'ai un conseil à donner c'est vraiment la patience et prendre le temps."
8. Caroline Melly, *Bottleneck: Moving, Building, and Belonging in an African City* (Chicago: University of Chicago Press, 2016), 15.
9. See Lifongo Vetinde, "Introduction: Cultural Politics in Senegal; A Quest for Relevance," in *Ousmane Sembène and the Politics of Culture*, ed. Lifongo Vetinde and Amadou T. Fofana (Lanham, MD: Lexington Books, 2015), ix–xxi. "[Sembène's] work is best appreciated through the lenses of a man who was committed to transforming his society through his work. Embedded in Sembène's ideological stance is his unwavering artistic militancy against oppression in all its forms and an insistence on identifying viable frameworks for the path of African liberation and progress through the deployment of culture" (Vetinde, xiv).
10. Manthia Diawara, *African Cinema: Politics and Culture* (Bloomington: Indiana University Press, 1992), 60.
11. Amadou T. Fofana, "A Critical and Deeply Personal Reflection: Malick Aw on Cinema in Senegal Today," *Black Camera* 9, no. 2 (Spring 2018): 351.
12. Fofana, 351.
13. James E. Genova, *Cinema and Development in West Africa*, (Bloomington: Indiana University Press, 2013), 163.

14. Diawara, *African Cinema*, 35.
15. Diawara, 36.
16. Elizabeth Mermin, "A Window on Whose Reality? The Emerging Industry of Senegalese Cinema," *Research in African Literatures* 26, no. 3 (1995): 121.
17. Françoise Pfaff, *À l'écoute du cinéma sénégalais* (Paris: L'Harmattan, 2010), 10. "Puis, le cinéma sénégalais se poursuit dans le changement et la continuité."
18. Genova, *Cinema and Development*, 163.
19. Genova, 163.
20. Fofana, "A Critical," 352.
21. FOPICA, accessed March 29, 2024, https://www.fopica.sn.
22. Pfaff cites Ramaka as an example in her discussion of filmmakers who seek funding from international sources. His 2001 film *Karmen Geï* cost fourteen million French francs. Pfaff, *À l'écoute*, 12.
23. FOPICA, accessed March 29, 2024, https://www.fopica.sn.
24. Alpha Molo, "Dakar va renouer avec le cinéma: 4 salles de ciné seront réhabilitées!," KoldaNews, May 29, 2014, https://www.koldanews.com/. "C'était un effort que l'on a fait pour permettre que les salles revivent. Ce qui va suivre, c'est qu'il faut aider les salles de cinéma à acquérir de nouvelles technologies. Mais cela se sera dans le cadre d'un partenariat public-privé."
25. Baba Diop, "Le Sénégal trace une nouvelle voie à son cinéma," *Senciné* 2 (2015): 4. "concrètes, planifiées, budgétisées sur la période 2016–2020."
26. The Direction de la cinématographie office is located in the neighborhood of Mermoz just off the VDN (voie de dégagement Nord) highway.
27. Abdoul Aziz Cissé, interview with Enz in Dakar, September 20, 2016. "Un fonds de mémoire."
28. Hugues Diaz, "2015: Réussir les chantiers du cinéma et baliser les sentiers du numérique," *Senciné* 2 (2015): 3. "Le cinéma, en tant qu'art, industrie et technique, a connu tout au long de son histoire des bouleversements nombreux.... Prévisible ou pas, la mutation liée au numérique s'inscrit donc dans la continuité d'une telle histoire de la technique."
29. Diaz, 3. "Interrogeons et décryptons l'ère numérique qui est la nôtre, dans une volonté commune d'être partie prenante et acteur de ce changement."
30. Lindiwe Dovey and Estrella Sendra, "Toward Decolonized Film Festival Worlds," in *Rethinking Film Festivals in the Pandemic Era and After*, ed. Marijke de Valck and Antoine Damiens (Cham, Switzerland: Palgrave Macmillan, 2023), 280.
31. Dovey and Sendra, 281.
32. Dovey and Sendra, 281.
33. See Mamadou Oumar Kamara, "Abdou Aziz Cissé, secrétaire permanent du FOPICA: 'Je ne comprends pas pourquoi Cinéseas parle d'exclusion de gestion...,'" *Le soleil*, May 9, 2022.

34. Frieda Ekotto and Kenneth W. Harrow, introduction to *Rethinking African Cultural Production*, ed. Frieda Ekotto and Kenneth W. Harrow (Bloomington: Indiana University Press, 2015), 1.
35. Fofana, "A Critical," 355–56.
36. Fofana, 355–56.
37. See Marijke de Valck, *Film Festivals: From European Geopolitics to Global Cinephilia* (Amsterdam: Amsterdam University Press, 2007); Marijke de Valck, Brendan Kredell, and Skadi Loist, eds., *Film Festivals: History, Theory, Method, Practice* (London: Routledge, 2016); de Valck and Damiens, *Rethinking Film Festivals*; Lindiwe Dovey, *Curating Africa in the Age of Film Festivals* (New York: Palgrave Macmillan, 2015); Winston Mano, Barbara Knorpp, and Añulika Agina, *African Film Cultures: Context of Creation and Circulation* (Newcastle upon Tyne, UK: Cambridge Scholars Publishing, 2017); Aida Vallejo and Ezra Winton, eds., *Documentary Film Festivals Vol. 1: Methods, History, Politics* (Cham, Switzerland: Palgrave Macmillan, 2020); Aida Vallejo and Ezra Winton, eds., *Documentary Film Festivals Vol. 2: Changes, Challenges, Professional Perspectives* (Cham, Switzerland: Palgrave Macmillan, 2020).
38. Beti Ellerson, "African Women on the Film Festival Landscape: Organizing, Showcasing, Promoting, Networking," *Black Camera* 11, no. 1 (Fall 2019): 430–31.
39. Dovey and Sendra, "Toward Decolonized Film Festival Worlds," 278.
40. Dovey and Sendra, 280.
41. Estrella Sendra, "Banlieue Films Festival (BFF): Growing Cinephilia and Filmmaking in Senegal," *Aniki: Portuguese Journal of the Moving Image* 8, no. 1 (2021): 247.
42. Sendra, 247.
43. Cinegal TV, "Khalilou Ndiaye, distributeur de films: Les jeunes ne doivent plus attendre...," November 14, 2019, YouTube video, 12:00, https://www.youtube.com/watch?v=ONKaWTBtPLY. "Les gens décident à notre place, font des choix qui nous concernent à notre place, et on reste un spectateur passif." See also the website of Image et vie, https://imagetvie.sn.
44. Ellerson, "African Women on the Film Festival Landscape," 425.
45. Films Femmes Afrique, https://www.filmsfemmesafrique.com.
46. Joseph Gaï Ramaka, interview with authors on Gorée Island, June 5, 2016.
47. Ramaka, interview. "un facteur de la paix."
48. Ramaka, interview. "là-bas."
49. Ramaka, interview. "un lieu d'échange."
50. Amadou T. Fofana, "'Cinefication' in West Africa," *Critical Interventions: Journal of African Art History and Visual Culture* 5, no. 1 (Spring 2011): 55.
51. Fofana, 55.

52. Ellerson, "African Women on the Film Festival Landscape," 431. This quotation from Ellerson's article is by former president of CNA, Rosalie N'Dah.
53. Coumba Sarr, interview with Enz in Dakar, December 14, 2016. "Leur donner la chance de découvrir le patrimoine et promouvoir le cinéma africain."
54. Sarr, interview. "Un débat communautaire . . . s'exprimer et s'enrichir . . . avec un sens de partage."
55. Sarr, interview. "Un esprit citoyen . . . une reconnaissance de la culture africaine par la population africaine."
56. In Senegal, the Wolof word *pencc* refers to a public gathering at which pertinent community issues are discussed. In the greater Dakar area, there are about twelve functioning semiofficial pencc in neighborhoods such as Yoff, Plateau, and Médina. Thanks to Kamir Délivrance Nzalé for the specifications about the socially institutionalized form of pencc.
57. Adams Sie, interview with authors in Dakar, June 6, 2016.
58. Sendra, "Banlieue Films Festival (BFF)," 247.
59. Sendra, 266.
60. Khady Sylla passed away in 2013 in Dakar.
61. See Pfaff, *À l'écoute* for more details on the career trajectories of each of these filmmakers.
62. Valérie Orlando, "Voices of African Filmmakers: Contemporary Issues in Francophone West African Filmmaking," *Quarterly Review of Film and Video* 24, no. 5 (2007): 452.
63. Aida Vallejo, "The Rise of Documentary Festivals: A Historical Approach," in Vallejo and Winton, *Documentary Film Festivals Vol. 1*, 89.
64. N. Frank Ukadike, "The Other Voices of Documentary: *Allah Tantou* and *Afrique, je te plumerai*," in *Focus on African Films*, ed. Françoise Pfaff (Bloomington: University of Indiana Press, 2004), 159.
65. Ukadike, 159.
66. Gerladine Pratt and Rose Marie San Juan, *Film and Urban Space: Critical Possibilities* (Edinburgh: Edinburgh University Press, 2014), 2.
67. Ukadike, "Other Voices of Documentary," 164.
68. Ukadike, 171.
69. Bertrand Cabedoche, "L'inscription du cinéma documentaire en Afrique dans le champ des sciences humaines et sociales," in *La diversité du documentaire de création en Afrique*, ed. François Fronty and Delphe Kifouani (Paris: L'Harmattan, 2015), 28–29. "accorde de plus en plus le 'je' social avec le 'je' individuel." "les normes sociales sont ainsi rediscutées." "Les identités hybrides provoquent ainsi perlocutoirement le collectif à interroger le retour aux sources."
70. Doris Posch refers to this concept being elaborated at the 2017 Documentary Filmmaking Practices in Africa conference held at the University of

Toronto. See Doris Posch, "Cultural Heritage and Popular Cultures: *The Revolution Won't Be Televised* and Its Global Reception," *Critical Interventions: Journal of African Art History and Visual Culture* 11, no. 3 (2017): 301–17.

71. See the chapter on Safi Faye in Françoise Pfaff, *Twenty-Five Black African Filmmakers: A Critical Study, with Filmography and Bio-Bibliography* (Westport, CT: Greenwood Press, 1988), 115–24.

72. Baba Diop, "Le cinéma au féminin," *Senciné* 4 (2018): 3. "balisait le chemin que devait prendre le cinéma au féminin: celui de l'engagement."

73. Beti Ellerson, "African Women and the Documentary: Storytelling, Visualizing History, from the Personal to the Political," *Black Camera: An International Film Journal* 8, no. 1 (Fall 2016): 223.

74. Ellerson, 223.

75. Beti Ellerson, "Cinémas documentaires en Afrique au féminin" in Fronty and Kifouani, *La diversité du documentaire*, 115. Since the publication of Ellerson's article, men have won for best documentary at FESPACO.

76. Emilie Ngo-Nguidjol, "Women in African Cinema: An Annotated Bibliography," in *African Cinema: Postcolonial and Feminist Readings*, ed. Kenneth Harrow (Trenton, NJ: Africa World Press, 1999), 305.

77. For recent work on African women filmmakers, see Ellerson, "African Women and the Documentary" and "Cinémas documentaires," as well as the *African Women in Cinema Blog*, which she's maintained since 2009; Elisabeth Lequert, "L'Afrique filmée par des femmes," *Le monde diplomatique*, August 1998; Orlando, "Voices of African Filmmakers"; Bronwen E. Pugsley, "Challenging Perspectives: Documentary Practices in Films by Women from Francophone Africa" (PhD diss., University of Nottingham, 2012).

78. Diop, "Le cinéma au féminin," 3. "la formidable cohorte, qui depuis le début des années 2000, étoffe les rangs et ose s'attaquer à des genres cinématographiques comme la comédie, ... la comédie musicale, ... la culture urbaine. Le cinéma sénégalais est désormais riche de ses réalisatrices."

79. Emeka Joseph Nwankwo, "White Eyes," Africa Is a Country, July 27, 2020, https://africasacountry.com/.

80. Hamidou Anne, *Panser l'Afrique qui vient* (Paris: Présence Africaine, 2019), 8. "la lucidité impose de sortir des catégories optimisme ou pessimisme et de photographier le continent tel qu'il est."

81. Felwine Sarr, *Afrotopia*, trans. Drew S. Burk and Sarah Jones-Boardman (Minneapolis: University of Minnesota Press, 2019), 104.

82. AbdouMaliq Simone, "On the Worlding of African Cities," *African Studies Review* 44, no. 2 (September 2001): 25.

83. Achille Mbembe and Sarah Nuttall, "Writing the World from an African Metropolis," *Public Culture*, 16, no. 3 (Fall 2004): 357.

84. Kenneth W. Harrow, *Trash: African Cinema from Below* (Bloomington: Indiana University Press, 2013), x.
85. Harrow, ix.
86. For a discussion of the critical and scholarly divide between these two categories of films in African cinema studies, see Mahir Saul and Ralph A. Austen, *Viewing African Cinema in the Twenty-First Century: Art Films and the Nollywood Video Revolution* (Athens: Ohio University Press, 2010).
87. James S. Williams, *Ethics and Aesthetics in Contemporary African Cinema: The Politics of Beauty* (London: Bloomsbury Academic, 2019).
88. Harrow, *Trash*, 3.

Chapter 2: Shaping the National Body

1. Caroline Melly, *Bottleneck: Moving, Building and Belonging in an African City* (University of Chicago Press, 2017). See in particular chapter 5, "Telling Tales of Missing Men."
2. Melly, 135.
3. *Yoolé*, dir. Moussa Sène Absa (Senegal: Absa Films, 2010). We received a DVD copy of *Yoolé* from African Film Festival, Inc., with the director's permission; *Boul fallé: La voie de la lutte*, dir. Rama Thiaw (Ivory Coast / France: Wassakara Productions / Banshees Films, 2009), DVD release by DocNet Films; *The Revolution Won't Be Televised*, dir. Rama Thiaw (Senegal: Boul Fallé Images, 2015). We viewed the film on YouTube in Senegal.
4. Moussa Sène Absa, interview with authors in Popenguine, June 17, 2021. "me fondre dans le pays, dans le peuple . . . montrer la société avec un regard qui permet de poser les enjeux, les contrastes, les paradoxes."
5. Sène Absa, interview. "anonymes, des héros de tous les jours, . . . de la chair et de l'esprit."
6. Rama Thiaw, "'The Revolution Won't Be Televised': An Interview with Rama Thiaw," interview by Marc Girardot, *Berlin Art Link*, March 11, 2016, https://www.berlinartlink.com/.
7. Benedict Anderson, *Imagined Communities: Reflections on the Origin and Spread of Nationalism* (London: Verso, 1983), 6.
8. Sidonie Smith and Gisela Brinker-Gabler, "Introduction: Gender, Nation, and Immigration in the New Europe," in *Writing New Identities: Gender, Nation, and Immigration in Contemporary Europe*, ed. Sidonie Smith and Gisela Brinker-Gabler (Minneapolis: University of Minnesota Press, 1997), 11.
9. Smith and Brinker-Gabler, 15.
10. George L. Mosse, *Nationalism and Sexuality: Middle-Class Morality and Sexual Norms in Modern Europe* (Madison: University of Wisconsin Press, 1985), 17.

11. Melly, *Bottleneck*, 158.
12. Stefan Helmreich, "Kinship, Nation, and Paul Gilroy's Concept of Diaspora," *Diaspora: A Journal of Transnational Studies* 2, no. 2 (Fall 1992): 245.
13. Melly, *Bottleneck*, 137.
14. A brief survey of the journalistic accounts of recent Senegalese migration places a strong emphasis on the masculine dimension. In 2015, a headline in the *Wall Street Journal* stated, "Young Men in Senegal Join Migrant Wave Despite Growing Prosperity at Home," suggesting that the crisis can be located within masculinity more than in economics or education. See Drew Hinshaw, June 12, 2015. In 2020, Emma Wallis reported in Info-Migrants that a Senegalese court sentenced three fathers to jail because it found them guilty of endangering the lives of others by pushing their sons to migrate across the Atlantic. See December 9, 2020, https://www.infomigrants.net/en/post/28998/fathers-in-senegal-sentenced-to-jail-for-pushing-their-sons-to-migrate. In *The Guardian*, Emmanuel Akinwotu observes the women who gather in Saint-Louis, sharing "memories of husbands, sons and brothers they have lost at sea." See "'I Woke Up, He Was Gone': Senegal Suffers as Young Men Risk All to Reach Europe," March 17, 2021. The headline from Reuters is succinct: "No Country for Young Men." See Kieran Guilbert, September 13, 2016.
15. Sebastian Prothmann, "Migration, Masculinity and Social Class: Insights from Pikine Senegal," *International Migration* 56, no. 4 (August 2018): 96.
16. Prothmann, 96.
17. Prothmann, 96.
18. Sène Absa, interview. "Toutes mes histoires racontent les histoires de ma jeunesse. Je les ramasse."
19. Sène Absa, interview. "En étant ici je deviens comme l'éponge qui prend toutes les histoires locales et ça me permet d'écrire. Je ne peux pas écrire ailleurs qu'ici."
20. Sène Absa, interview. "d'autres visions, d'autres univers, une rupture, un idéal à construire, un peu de rêve."
21. See, for example, Alain Gomis's *L'Afrance* (2001); El Hadji Samba Sarr's *Graines que la mer emporte* (2008); Idrissa Guiro's *Barcelone ou la mort* (2008); Merzak Allouache's *Harragas* (2009); Moussa Touré's *La pirogue* (2012); David Fedele's *The Land Between* (2014); Jonas Carpignano's *Mediterranea* (2015); Gianfranco Rosi's *Fire at Sea* (2016).
22. Dialogue in *Yoolé* is in English, French, and Wolof. Our quotations from *Yoolé* are from the film's English subtitles.
23. Véronique Corinus and Daniela Ricci, "Migration des hommes, des techniques et des imaginaires," in *Regards sur les migrations: Mobilités africaines entre écrit et écran*, ed. Véronique Corinus and Daniela Ricci (Paris: L'Harmattan, 2021), 7. "cherchent à faire contrepoids aux discours médiatiques

et politiques associant les migrants à des gueux, des délinquants ou des envahisseurs.'" "leur densité, leur fragilité et leur dignité humaines."
24. Sara Ahmed, *The Cultural Politics of Emotion* (Edinburgh: Edinburgh University Press, 2004), 12.
25. Ahmed, 12.
26. Melissa Thackway, "Migrations et traversées dans les cinémas d'Afrique," in Corinus and Ricci, *Regards sur les migrations*, 35. "Les circulations et les migrations donnent souvent lieu à une opposition ou à un contraste des espaces africains et européens."
27. Sène Absa, interview. "un vrai génocide de la jeunesse."
28. Sène Absa, interview. "Les gosses vont prendre le pouvoir et personne ne peut les arrêter."
29. Sabine Cessou, "Rama Thiaw, A Young Filmmaker in the Struggle," *African Women in Cinema Blog*, September 8, 2011, https://africanwomenincinema.blogspot.com/.
30. Cessou, "Rama Thiaw."
31. "La Chine offre une arène de lutte au Sénégal," BBC News Afrique, July 22, 2018, https://www.bbc.com/.
32. For important examples of the artistic expressions of wrestling, see Aminata Sow Fall's novel *L'appel des arènes* (Dakar: Nouvelles éditions africaines du Sénégal, 1982) and Cheikh Ndiaye's 2005 cinematic adaptation. For early academic work on the sport, see Ousseynou Faye, "Sport, argent et politique: La lutte libre à Dakar (1800–2000)," in *Le Sénégal contemporain*, ed. Momar-Coumba Diop (Paris: Karthala, 2002), 309–40; Jean-François Havard, "Ethos 'bul faale' et nouvelles figures de la réussite au Sénégal," *Politique africaine* 82, no. 2 (2001): 63–77.
33. For a good overview of these critical tensions within Senegalese wrestling scholarship and cultural productions, see Jonathon Repinecz, "Senegalese Wrestling between Nostalgia and Neoliberalism," *African Studies Review* 63, no. 4 (December 2020): 906–26.
34. Dominique Chevé et al., "Introduction: La lutte; Pratique sportive, phénomène socioculturel, prisme des croyances," in *Corps en lutte: L'art du combat au Sénégal*, ed. Dominique Chevé et al. (Paris: CNRS Editions, 2014), 55. "La société dakaroise est hybride, composite et complexe. Les enjeux actuels conjuguent donc individualisme émergeant et identités communautaires, recomposition et réinterprétation des rapports sociaux traditionnels. . . . la lutte à Dakar n'est pas seulement affaire sportive, culturelle, politique; elle est tout cela conjugué et encore autre chose."
35. Cessou, "Rama Thiaw."
36. Cheikh Tidiane Wane, "Techniques corporelles et différences ethnoculturelles dans la lutte sénégalaise," in Chevé et al., *Corps en lutte*, 98–99.

"le premier objet et moyen technique de l'homme, c'est son corps. C'est par les techniques du corps que l'homme va atteindre la totalité de sa personne."

37. For other studies of the body in Senegalese wrestling, see Alain Froment, "De graisse et de muscle: La corpulence ostentatoire en Afrique rurale," in Chevé et al., *Corps en lutte*, 119–26, and Dominique Chevé, "Corps construits, corps investis, corps effigies: Être lutteur à Dakar," in Chevé et al., *Corps en lutte*, 229–56.
38. Dialogue in *Boul fallé* is in French and Wolof. Quotations from *Boul fallé* are from the film's French subtitles or dialogue and are translated into English by the authors.
39. Babacar M'Baye, "Verbal and Acrobatic Strategies in Senegalese Wolof Wrestling," *Storytelling, Self, Society* 9, no. 2 (Fall 2013): 197.
40. Havard, "Ethos 'bul faale,'" 66.
41. Susann Baller, "Être jeune, masculin et sportif: Représentations urbaines de la masculinité au Sénégal," in *Perspectives historiques sur le genre en Afrique*, ed. Odile Goerg (Paris: L'Harmattan, 2007): 171. "une danse nouvelle, appellée 'danse bul faale' et exécutée au rythme du tam-tam."
42. Cessou, "Rama Thiaw."
43. See Havard, "Ethos 'bul faale'"; Jean-François Havard, "Par-delà le Bul Faale, la lutte continue! La lutte sénégalaise comme vecteur de mobilisation identitaire et d'une subjectivation générationnelle décalée," in Chevé et al., *Corps en lutte*, 163–76.
44. Havard, "Par-delà le Bul Faale," 174. "la lutte, notamment parce qu'elle est très faiblement institutionnalisée et encore peu contrainte par des normes extérieures, . . . s'est révélée être un terrain particulièrement performant pour justement donner prise à ce mouvement dialectique d'invention de la modernité par réinvention de la tradition."
45. Oumar Ndao, prologue to Chevé et al., *Corps en lutte*, 9. "avant toute autre chose, un art de l'approche et de la prévenance."
46. See Baller, "Être jeune"; Tshikala Kayembe Biaya, "Les plaisirs de la ville: Masculinité, sexualité et féminité à Dakar (1997–2000)," *African Studies Review* 44, no. 2 (September 2001): 71–85; Sebastian Prothmann, "Je suis sañse rëkk, mais auma xaalis (I'm dressed up, but I don't have money): Pretense, Camouflage, and the Search for a Lifestyle by Young Men in Pikine, Senegal," *Mande Studies* 22 (2020): 57–74.
47. Biaya, 84. "de nouveaux imaginaires de la masculinité sont en cours de formation dans les métropoles africaines."
48. Marianne Barthélémy, "Écuries et écoles de lutte à Dakar: Analyse et perspectives," in Chevé et al., *Corps en lutte*, 127–28. "le centre névralgique du quartier, foyer de socialisation et d'éducation. Elles représentent souvent pour les lutteurs une seconde famille."

49. Dialogue in *The Revolution Won't Be Televised* is in French and Wolof. Our quotations from *The Revolution Won't Be Televised* are from the film's English subtitles.
50. In this particular quotation from Sylla, the word *sittings* was used in the English subtitles. This seems to be a mistranslation, so we changed it to *sit-ins*.
51. Thiaw, interview.
52. Doris Posch, "Cultural Heritage and Popular Cultures: *The Revolution Won't Be Televised* and Its Global Reception," *Critical Interventions: Journal of African Art History and Visual Culture* 11, no. 3 (2017): 305.
53. Posch, 305.
54. Posch, 305.
55. Sarah Nelson, "The New Type of Senegalese under Construction: Fadel Barro and Aliou Sané on Yenamarreisme after Wade," *African Studies Quarterly* 14, no. 3 (2014): 22.
56. Nelson, 22.
57. It should be noted that Sylla states that "l'art est long," but the film's English subtitle reads "art is a long way." This seems to be a mistranslation, and we read the statement instead as "art is long."
58. Felwine Sarr, *Afrotopia*. trans. Drew S. Burk and Sarah Jones-Boardman (Minneapolis: University of Minnesota Press, 2019), 114.

Chapter 3: Community Responses to Peri-urban Water Mismanagement

1. "État des lieux du Plan 'Jaxaay,' après les inondations de 2005," New Humanitarian, December 21, 2006, https://www.thenewhumanitarian.org/fr/.
2. "État des lieux du Plan 'Jaxaay.'"
3. Al Jazeera English, "Senegal's Sinking Villages," July 25, 2018, YouTube video, 47:26, https://www.youtube.com/watch?v=0EdrRZvLXRQ.
4. Al Jazeera English, "Senegal's Sinking Villages."
5. Al Jazeera English, "Senegal's Sinking Villages."
6. Carl Söderbergh, "Senegal: The Impact of the Climate Crisis on the Fisher Community of St. Louis," Minority Rights Group International, November 13, 2019, https://minorityrights.org/.
7. *Plan Jaxaay!*, dir. Joseph Gaï Ramaka (Senegal: Colored People's Time / Observatoire Audiovisuel sur les Libertés /AfrikaDreaming, 2007), Vimeo, https://vimeo.com/26072579; *La brèche*, dir. Abdoul Aziz Cissé (Belgium/ Senegal: Gsara-Filmer à tout prix / Media Centre Dakar / Diwaan, 2007), OVNI—Desorg dot Org, https://www.desorg.org/titols/la-breche/.
8. Lindiwe Dovey, *Curating Africa in the Age of Film Festivals* (New York: Palgrave Macmillan, 2015), 21.
9. Michael T. Martin, "Joseph Gaï Ramaka: 'I Am Not a Filmmaker *Engagé*. I Am an Ordinary Citizen *Engagé*,'" *Research in African Literatures* 40, no. 3 (2009): 210.

10. Abdoul Aziz Cissé, interview with Enz in Dakar, September 20, 2016. "un instrument de transformation sociale."
11. Cissé, interview with Enz. "de souveraineté culturelle, économique, sociale et politique."
12. Abdoul Aziz Cissé, interview with Bryson in Dakar, June 13, 2016. "On fait des films pour changer la société. . . . Quand des jeunes cinéastes posent leurs caméras, ils sont conscients des enjeux politiques. . . . On ne filme pas tout simplement pour filmer. On filme pour un objectif précis."
13. Cissé, interview with Bryson. "la supériorité du documentaire."
14. Achille Mbembe and Sarah Nuttall, "Writing the World from an African Metropolis," *Public Culture* 16, no. 3 (Fall 2004): 368.
15. AbdouMaliq Simone, "People as Infrastructure: Intersecting Fragments in Johannesburg," *Public Culture* 16, no. 3 (Fall 2004): 407.
16. Simone, 407–8.
17. Rosalind Fredericks, *Garbage Citizenship: Vital Infrastructures of Labor in Dakar, Senegal* (Durham, NC: Duke University Press, 2018), 17.
18. Nikhil Anand, "PRESSURE: The PoliTechnics of Water Supply in Mumbai," *Cultural Anthropology* 26, no. 4 (November 2011): 545.
19. "Karmen Geï," California Newsreel, accessed November 9, 2017, www.newsreel.org/video/KARMEN-GEI.
20. Kenneth W. Harrow, introduction to *African Cinema: Postcolonial and Feminist Readings*, ed. Kenneth W. Harrow (Trenton, NJ: Africa World Press, 1999), xix. Harrow refers specifically to African women filmmakers, but this description can be aptly applied to the representation of female characters during the same time period.
21. Phil Powrie, "Politics and Embodiment in Karmen Geï," *Quarterly Review of Film and Video* 21, no. 4 (2004): 289.
22. There are forty-five departments in Senegal and four that comprise the Dakar region: Dakar, Guédiawaye, Pikine, and Rufisque.
23. Susann Baller, "Transforming Urban Landscapes: Soccer Fields as Sites of Urban Sociability in the Agglomeration of Dakar," *African Identities* 5, no. 2 (2007): 217.
24. Rosa Spaliviero, "Dakar's Ciné-Suburb: Young People Create a Ciné-Club in Pikine," Buala, April 14, 2010, https://www.buala.org/.
25. Marc Vernière, "Pikine, 'ville nouvelle' de Dakar, un case de pseudo-urbanisation," *L'espace géographique* 2, no. 2 (1973): 107. "surgie du néant."
26. Garth Myers, *Urban Environments in Africa: A Critical Analysis of Environmental Politics* (Bristol: Policy Press, 2016), 132.
27. Médina Gounass is one of five *communes d'arrondissement* (local municipalities) that form the department of Guédiawaye.
28. Dialogue in *Plan Jaxaay!* is in French and Wolof. Our quotations from *Plan Jaxaay!* are from the film's English subtitles.
29. Myers, *Urban Environments in Africa*, 136.

30. The acronym SONES stands for Société nationale des eaux du Sénégal.
31. Ramaka has posted over twenty videos of various sorts on Vimeo, including *Karmen Geï* and *Plan Jaxaay!*: https://vimeo.com/ramaka.
32. Mamadou Diouf and Rosalind Fredericks, introduction to *The Arts of Citizenship in African Cities: Infrastructures and Spaces of Belonging*, ed. Mamadou Diouf and Rosalind Fredericks (New York: Palgrave Macmillan, 2014), 9.
33. Cissé, interview with Enz. "Toute vie est vie. Aucune vie n'est plus vie qu'une autre vie."
34. Cissé, interview with Bryson. "Le cinéma sénégalais est génétiquement environnemental. . . . On ne peut pas éviter de parler de l'environnement."
35. Cissé, interview with Enz."nous mettre à la disposition de ces éléments. . . . Quel est le rapport que nous avons avec les lieux où nous vivons?"
36. Myers, *Urban Environments in Africa*, 23.
37. Myers, 21.
38. Dialogue in *La brèche* is in French and Wolof. Quotations from *La brèche* are from the film's French subtitles or dialogue and are translated into English by the authors.
39. Diouf and Fredericks, introduction, 12.
40. Diouf and Fredericks, 13.
41. Diouf and Fredericks, 6.
42. The statue and the square in which it sat, also named after Faidherbe, have been a site of resistance within the ongoing negotiation of the historical archive and memorialization of Senegal's colonized past and independent present. See "Dénomination des rues, places, . . . : STATUE QUO—Saint-Louis, Rufisque; Une décolonisation inachevée," *Le quotidien*, June 22, 2020; Aïssatou Diallo and Jules Crétois, "'Faidherbe doit tomber': Des collectifs français et sénégalais à l'assaut du mythe du colon bâtisseur," *Jeune Afrique*, April 10, 2018; "Sénégal: La place Faidherbe de la ville de Saint-Louis devient Baya Ndar," *Le point*, October 2, 2020. As of 2023, the square had been renamed Baya Ndar to express its indigenous realities, and the Faidherbe statue had been removed with no definitive decisions of when or if it will return to the square. The bridge is still named after the colonial administrator.
43. Munyaradzi Mawere, *Culture, Indigenous Knowledge, and Development in Africa: Reviving Interconnections for Sustainable Development* (Bamenda, Cameroon: Langaa Research & Publishing CIG, 2014), 23.
44. Theodore Trefon, "Hinges and Fringes: Conceptualising the Peri-urban in Central Africa," in *African Cities: Competing Claims on Urban Spaces*, ed. Francesca Locatelli and Paul Nugent (Leiden: Brill, 2009), 21.
45. Antina von Schnitzler, "Traveling Technologies: Infrastructure, Ethical Regimes, and the Materiality of Politics in South Africa," *Cultural Anthropology* 28, no. 4 (2013): 673.
46. Trefon,"Hinges and Fringes," 16.

47. Trefon, 16.
48. Trefon, 17.

Chapter 4: Urban Precarity, Voice, and Contingent Communities

1. *Voix silencieuses,* dir. Adams Sie (UK/Senegal: The British Council / Adams Sie, 2005), YouTube, 38:47, https://www.youtube.com/watch?v=olFZe7_wbQ8. *Le monologue de la muette,* dir. Khady Sylla (Senegal: Athénaïse / Iota Production / Karoninka, 2008), DVD release by Art-Mattan Productions.
2. Kenneth W. Harrow, *Trash: African Cinema from Below* (Bloomington: Indiana University Press, 2013), 2, 84.
3. Harrow, 84.
4. Harrow, 2.
5. Harrow, 1.
6. Mamadou Diouf and Rosalind Fredericks, introduction to *The Arts of Citizenship in African Cities: Infrastructures and Spaces of Belonging,* ed. Mamadou Diouf and Rosalind Fredericks (New York: Palgrave Macmillan, 2014), 5.
7. Harrow, *Trash,* 282.
8. Aihwa Ong, "Worlding Cities, or the Art of Being Global," in *Worlding Cities: Asian Experiments and the Art of Being Global,* ed. Ananya Roy and Aihwa Ong (Oxford: Wiley Blackwell, 2011), 3–4.
9. Bronwen Pugsley, "Ethical Madness? Khady Sylla's Documentary Practice in *Une fenêtre ouverte,*" *Nottingham French Studies* 51, no. 2 (July 2012): 212.
10. Keith Beattie points to how ethnographic documentary filmmaking has been especially contributive to these exploitative and power-imbalanced dynamics. See *Documentary Screens: Non-fiction Film and Television* (Basingstoke, UK: Palgrave Macmillan, 2004), 45–46.
11. Françoise Pfaff, *À l'écoute du cinéma sénégalais* (Paris: L'Harmattan, 2010), 203. "Everything began when I lived with the Caliph. He was very respected and I decided to make a film from his teachings. He always spoke about social questions, about how our cultural values were disappearing due to Western encroachment. That's how I decided to write a script about society, culture, Western influences and AIDS." (Original French: "Tout a commencé lorsque je vivais avec le calife. Il était très respecté et j'ai décidé de faire un film à partir de ses enseignements. Il parlait toujours de questions sociales, du fait que nos valeurs culturelles disparaissaient à cause de l'ascendant occidental. C'est ainsi que j'ai décidé d'écrire un script sur la société, la culture, les influences occidentales et le Sida.")
12. Adams Sie, interview with authors in Dakar, June 6, 2016.
13. Sie, interview with authors.
14. Adams Sie, interview with Bryson via email, March 2015.

15. Sie, interview with authors.
16. See "Les enfants des rues à Dakar," Le samu social Sénégal, accessed January 21, 2021, http://samusocialsenegal.com/.
17. See Samuel Nambile Cumber and Joyce Mahlako Tsoka-Gwegweni, "The Health Profile of Street Children in Africa: A Literature Review," *Journal of Public Health in Africa* 6, no. 2 (2015): 1–17.
18. Dialogue in *Voix silencieuses* is in French and Wolof. Quotations from *Voix silencieuses* are from the film's French subtitles or dialogue and are translated into English by the authors.
19. Khady Sylla, "Écrivain, cinéaste: Mme Khady Sylla," interview by Modibo S. Keïta, *Amina*, July 1999, https://aflit.arts.uwa.edu.au/AMINAScylla99.html. "J'ai pensé qu'en écrivant sur elle, je parviendrais à faire survivre quelque chose ... que j'arriverais à la faire sortir de ce qui pour moi était un anéantissement."
20. Sylla, interview. "une sorte de ville mythique du fait de mon exil."
21. Sylla, interview.
22. Pfaff, *À l'écoute*, 216.
23. Françoise Pfaff, "*Colobane Express* by Khady Sylla," *African Studies Review*, 56, no. 1 (2013): 224.
24. The feminine noun *la muette* is found in the French title of the film rather than the adjective *silent* employed in the official English translation of the title, *The Silent Monologue*.
25. Nicolas Azalbert, "Khady Sylla: Le 'tiers-oeil,'" *Cahiers du cinéma* 704 (2014): 40. "Le cinéma, pour Khady Sylla, consiste à dire l'invisible, à tenter de renouer un lien entre ce qui a été séparé, entre ce qui est et n'est pas (plus) là: les petits villages sénégalais et la capitale, l'enfance et l'âge adulte, les pratiques des ancêtres et l'économie libérale, la 'folie' et la 'normalité.'"
26. Dialogue in *Le monologue de la muette* is in French and Wolof. Quotations from *Le monologue de la muette* are from the film's English subtitles.
27. See Isabelle Chort, Philippe De Vreyer, and Thomas Zuber, "Gendered Mobility Patterns in Senegal," *Population* 75, nos. 2/3 (2020): 287–314.
28. Olga F. Linares, "Going to the City ... and Coming Back? Turnaround Migration among the Jola of Senegal," *Africa* 73, no. 1 (February 2003): 114–15.
29. Pfaff, *À l'écoute*, 222. "Quand on rentre dans une maison, on voit tout le monde mais on ne regarde pas la bonne. ... Elle fait partie des meubles! C'est une violence sociale terrible qui est faite à ces femmes-là!"
30. Pfaff, 222. "C'est quelque chose d'assez énorme ces femmes qui sont dans les maisons, qui assument toutes les tâches domestiques les plus dures et qui permettent, en fait, aux femmes sénégalaises de s'émanciper. ... Ma propre émancipation, je la dois aux bonnes!"

31. Odile Cazenave, "The Silent Monologue by Khady Sylla and Charlie Van Damme; Some (Not So New) Gendered Stories of Globalization," *Diogènes* 62, no. 1 (2017): 52, 55.

Chapter 5: Intersectionality, Complexity, and Contradictions

1. Mamadou Diouf and Rosalind Fredericks, introduction to *The Arts of Citizenship in African Cities: Infrastructures and Spaces of Belonging*, ed. Mamadou Diouf and Rosalind Fredericks (New York: Palgrave Macmillan, 2014), 5.
2. Mbye Cham, foreword to *Sisters of the Screen: Women of Africa on Film, Video, and Television*, ed. Beti Ellerson (Trenton, NJ: Africa World Press, 2000), xi.
3. Cham, xi.
4. Ellerson, *Sisters of the Screen*, 12.
5. "L'assemblée des Yennenga: Où sont les réalisatrices?," Africulturelle, February 22, 2019, https://www.africulturelle.com/. "C'est une fenêtre grande ouverte sur notre monde par laquelle l'imaginaire, l'idéologie de tous les autres peuples défilent sous le regard de nos enfants. L'accès à l'outil cinéma pour nous signifie l'accès aux moyens de production, de distribution, de diffusion de notre imaginaire, notre sensibilité, notre point de vue du monde. L'accès à l'outil cinéma c'est aussi une place aux centres de décisions traitant de notre profession et de sa pérennité. Et dans ce combat pour exister dans le monde, il faut de l'équité naturellement."
6. France 24 English, "Fespaco Meeting with Fatou Kandé Senghor," March 1, 2019, Facebook video, 5:30, https://www.facebook.com/watch/?v=780974968916843.
7. Lizelle Bisschoff and Stefanie Van de Peer, *Women in African Cinema: Beyond the Body Politic* (London: Routledge, 2020), 5.
8. On UNESCO's page "Women in African History," there was a module dedicated to Yennenga in both French and English. It included a comic strip, pedagogical lesson, quiz, and soundtrack. Accessed June 30, 2021, https://en.unesco.org/womeninafrica/yennega. This page can now be found in UNESCO's web archive.
9. See Alcyone Wemaëre, "Au Fespaco, après #MeToo, le #MemePasPeur du cinéma africain," France 24, March 2, 2019, https://www.france24.com/fr/; Léo Pajon, "Cinéma: #Memepaspeur, quand des femmes témoignent des agressions sexuelles dont elles ont été victimes," *Jeune Afrique*, February 28, 2019.
10. Sabbar artistiques, *Livret-Programme: Sabbar artistiques—ateliers réflexives féminins de Dakar*, March 1, 2019, https://issuu.com/yanisgaye/docs/livret-programme-sabbar_artistiques. "Quelle place pour les africains, les afro-descendantes et les femmes noires 50 ans après les révolutions de 68?"

A close-up, black-and-white photo of Davis lighting a pipe appears on the cover of the Sabbar artistiques flyer against a red background. The workshops aim to promote a discussion about Davis's conceptualization of the theory of race, which "encapsulates at once the notion of skin color and the pseudo-scientific category founded upon the supremacy of white European color on the rest of the world, legitimizing the exploitation of Humanity by the White Man, Capitalism, and Racism." (Original French: "qui englobe à la fois la notion de couleur de peau et l'organisation pseudo-scientifique de catégorie fondée sur la suprématie de la couleur blanche européenne sur le reste du monde, légitimant ainsi l'exploitation de l'Humanité par l'Homme Blanc, le Capitalisme et le Racisme.")

11. Sabbar artistiques, *Livret-Programme*. "Mais sur le Continent africain, qu'en est-il de ces résurgences du féminisme et des théories qui veulent repenser la femme noire africaine, arabo-africaine, touareg-africaine, berbère-africaine, blanche-africaine? Comment résonne la citation d'Angéla Davis dans un continent jeune, à l'orée du cinquantenaire des révolutions de 1968?"

12. This discrimination is even provoked, at times, by their own Black sisters living in Europe. Due to the fact that African women were born and live on the continent, "they do not have the right to speak, people speak for them.... They are not audible in their only country, nor on their continent, nor internationally. In their country, it is the Black intellectuals who speak for them if it is not their intellectual Black sisters of the Diaspora, Black European women or Black American women." (Original French: "elles n'ont pas le droit à la parole, on parle constamment pour elles.... Elles ne sont audibles ni dans leur pays, ni dans leur continent ni à l'international. Dans leur pays, ce sont les intellectuels noirs qui parlent pour elles, lorsque ce ne sont pas leurs consoeurs intellectuelles de la Diaspora, noires européennes ou noires américaines.") Sabbar artistiques, *Livret-Programme*.

13. Sabbar artistiques, *Livret-Programme*. "Cette première édition se veut comme le point Alpha d'un laboratoire féminin ... dans un esprit d'inclusivité." Senegalese participants include Aminata Sow Fall, Fatou Kandé Senghor, Ken Bugul, Ndeye Fatou Kane, Felwine Sarr, and Mohamed Mbougar Sarr.

14. *Cette couleur qui me dérange*, dir. Khardiata Pouye (Senegal: RTS-CIRTEF, 2012), Daily Motion, https://www.dailymotion.com/video/x3rg54n. *Sénégalaises et Islam*, dir. Angèle Diabang (Germany/Senegal: Goethe Institut Dakar / Karoninka, 2007), OVNI—Desorg dot Org, https://www.desorg.org/titols/mon-beau-sourire/. We accessed the film via two different formats: a DVD copy through the WorldCat database, and a streaming version with Spanish subtitles on OVNI—Desorg dot

Org. The site erroneously catalogs *Sénégalaises et Islam* under the entry for *Mon beau sourire*, Diabang's earlier film.
15. Diouf and Fredericks, introduction, 5.
16. Bisschoff and Van de Peer, *Women in African Cinema*, 2.
17. For more background on these women filmmakers, see the essential *African Women in Cinema Blog*, maintained by Beti Ellerson. The journal *Black Camera: An International Film Journal* also regularly features an *African Women in Cinema* dossier, written by Ellerson.
18. See the entry on Fatou Kandé Senghor in the *African Women in Cinema Blog* for a good overview of these shorts. Fatou Kandé Senghor, "My Work, My Passion," *African Women in Cinema Blog*, January 12, 2011, http://africanwomenincinema.blogspot.com/.
19. While Kâ doesn't appear in the cut of the film we viewed on the DVD obtained through WorldCat, the version of the film on OVNI includes interviews with Kâ.
20. Khardiata Pouye, interview with authors in Dakar, June 18, 2021. "carrément le réel." "partager le réel cru et des gens qui vivent ça.... on entre dans leur intimité."
21. Khardiata Pouye, interview with authors in Dakar, May 23, 2018. "a envie de dire des choses."
22. As of May 2023, *Élan brisé* was in postproduction, but Pouye wasn't yet certain of when the film would be completed or a release date.
23. The opening scene juxtaposes taller buildings, such as a mosque, with shacks that are described as being "au coeur du Plateau dakarois."
24. Pouye, 2018 interview.
25. Lynn M. Thomas, *Beneath the Surface: A Transnational History of Skin Lighteners* (Durham, NC: Duke University Press, 2020), 2.
26. Thomas, 6.
27. Diouf and Fredericks, introduction, 7.
28. D. Asher Ghertner, *Rule by Aesthetics: World-Class City Making in Delhi* (Oxford: Oxford University Press, 2015), 4.
29. Ghertner, 5.
30. Thomas, *Beneath the Surface*, 1.
31. "Khardiata Pouye Sall, réalisatrice: Le khessal, une pratique devenue inquiétante," Leral.net, September 14, 2012, https://www.leral.net. "Dans les télévisions, la majeure partie des animatrices ou présentatrices font du 'Khessal' et font des émissions qui passent à des heures de pointe."
32. Pouye, 2018 interview. "la beauté éphémère et abstraite."
33. Pouye, 2021 interview. "c'était de choquer des gens."
34. Dialogue in *Cette couleur qui me dérange* is in French and Wolof. Quotations from *Cette couleur qui me dérange* are from the film's French subtitles or dialogue and are translated into English by the authors.

35. Pouye, 2021 interview. "c'était le moment d'en parler."
36. Thomas, *Beneath the Surface*, 1.
37. Pouye, 2021 interview. "c'est la réalité; il n'y a aucune fiction."
38. Pouye, 2021 interview.
39. Thomas, *Beneath the Surface*, 207.
40. Thomas, 207.
41. Beti Ellerson, "African Women and the Documentary: Storytelling, Visualizing History, from the Personal to the Political," *Black Camera: An International Film Journal* 8, no. 1 (Fall 2016): 231–32.
42. Daniela Ricci, "La voix des femmes dans les documentaires d'Angèle Diabang," *Nouvelles Études Francophones* 33, no. 1 (2018): 75.
43. Françoise Pfaff, *À l'écoute du cinéma sénégalais* (Paris: L'Harmattan, 2010), 113. "Pour l'instant je désire parler de l'Afrique et de la femme africaine, de mon environnement immédiat. . . . L'histoire de l'Afrique a besoin d'être racontée par des Africains. Depuis toujours ce sont d'autres peoples qui viennent en Afrique et qui racontent l'Afrique comme ils la voient. Je pense que maintenant c'est à nous de raconter notre Afrique."
44. Angèle Diabang, "Senegalese Cinema" (lecture, West African Research Center, Dakar, Senegal, May 30, 2019).
45. Pfaff, *À l'écoute*, 113. "Je voulais montrer les réalités qui sont en train d'évoluer."
46. Pfaff, 115.
47. Angèle Diabang, interview with authors via email, August 2, 2018. "Mes choix de sujets ne sont, en réalité, pas pour des raisons de militantisme. Je traite le sujet proche de moi et qui, souvent, m'empêche de dormir à un moment donné. Mais, je suis consciente que le fait d'avoir jusque-là, fait des films qui traite de la femme me positionne comme étant une féministe. . . . Je suis juste une artiste qui apporte un regard sur l'environnement qui l'entoure et qui souhaite partager avec le monde entier la culture et la vraie histoire de son continent vu de l'intérieur."
48. Bisschoff and Van de Peer, *Women in African Cinema*, 5.
49. See *L'homme qui répare les femmes: La colère d'Hippocrate* (2015) and *City of Joy* (2018).
50. Diabang, "Senegalese Cinema."
51. Diabang, interview. "C'est cet amour inconditionnel d'une femme envers son conjoint qui donnera au film son caractère universel. Au-delà de la polygamie, 'Une si longue lettre' relate le positionnement d'une femme par rapport à la famille, à l'amour et cela concerne toutes les femmes du monde. Pour moi, il n'y a pas de distinguo entre femmes occidentales et africaines, il y a les femmes! Et la nécessité d'une solidarité entre femmes!"
52. Diabang, interview. "À travers ce roman, Mariama Bâ évoque la société sénégalaise avec rigueur, sévérité et tendresse sans jamais porter de

jugement de valeur. J'ai donc essayé de suivre cette sagesse dans mon écriture et cela même quand je sais que certaines réactions de mon héroïne seront déconcertantes pour un public occidental."

53. Diabang, interview:

> Adapter ce livre dans un Sénégal moderne relancerait le débat sur la polygamie et les exigences socioculturelles parfois trop contraignantes et inutiles, autant pour la cohésion sociale que pour les libertés individuelles. Bien que conscientes des progrès et de leur émancipation, les femmes sont encore prisonnières de stéréotypes qui sont autant d'obstacles à la concrétisation de leur rébellion intérieure. Le NOUS sociétal domine toujours sur le JE individuel.... Je voudrais que mon film aille au delà d'un simple pamphlet contre la polygamie, c'est une interrogation plus générale de la place de la femme dans la société sénégalaise et africaine d'aujourd'hui. Dans une Afrique partagée entre une modernité et une tradition qui s'influencent mutuellement, ce roman garde toute sa pertinence et sa justification tant les thèmes et faits évoqués sont encore contemporains.

54. Lucy Creevey, "Islam, Women, and the Role of the State in Senegal," *Journal of Religion in Africa* 26, no. 3 (1996): 302.
55. Diabang, interview. "Il me semblait important d'entendre la voix des femmes sur la question de l'islam. Cette voix qui, au Sénégal, s'exprimait rarement sur cette question. Également, il était novateur de montrer le positionnement de la femme musulmane face à sa religion. Le Sénégal est un pays où l'islam est arrivé par les confréries, c'était intéressant d'avoir une diversité de femmes venant chacune d'une confrérie différente."
56. Dialogue in *Sénégalaises et Islam* is in French and Wolof. Quotations from *Sénégalaises et Islam* are taken from the film's English subtitles.
57. Erin Augis, "Religion, Religiousness, and Narrative: Decoding Women's Practices in Senegalese Islamic Reform," *Journal for the Scientific Study of Religion* 51, no. 3 (2012): 430.
58. Augis, 430.
59. Diabang, interview. "nous rappeler que c'est précieux d'avoir un espace où chacun peut vivre sa différence."
60. Nadine Sieveking, "'We Don't Want Equality; We Want to Be Given Our Rights': Muslim Women Negotiating Global Development Concepts in Senegal," *Afrika Spectrum* 42, no. 1 (2007): 29.
61. Diabang, interview. "Il y'a un vrai et bon dialogue islamo—chrétien depuis toujours et c'est ce qui constitue un équilibre envié au Sénégal par rapport à d'autres pays."

Conclusion: Cinematic Encounters in the City

1. See Centre Yennenga, accessed May 17, 2022, https://www.centreyennenga.com/; and École Kourtrajmé, accessed May 17, 2022, https://ecolekourtrajmedakar.sn/.
2. See Malèye Mboup, "Opacité dans la distribution du Fopica de 2 milliards: Les cinéastes sénégalais vilipendent le ministre de la culture," PressAfrik, May 4, 2022, https://www.pressafrik.com/.
3. Hugues Diaz, interview with Enz in Dakar, December 9, 2016.
4. Diaz, interview. "sur les plateaux de tournage"
5. Sylvie Rantrua, "Centre Yennenga: Là où Dakar veut faire son cinéma," *Le point*, February 19, 2021. "On souhaite travailler avec le quartier et ses enfants à travers des films faits avec eux et projetés ici car nous croyons beaucoup au cinéma local comme outil d'interpellation et de rencontres."
6. Théa Ollivier, "Cinéma: À Dakar, l'école Kourtrajmé veut 'casser les codes,'" *Le Monde*, February 1, 2022. "casser les codes."
7. Ollivier, "Cinéma." "Le pays est devenu incontournable dans la production audiovisuelle."
8. Théo du Coëdic, "Sénégal: 'L'école de cinéma Kourtrajmé nous donne des armes pour raconter nos histoires par nous-mêmes," *Jeune Afrique*, March 9, 2022. "Il y a une ébullition, les choses sont en mouvement."

Bibliography

Africulturelle. "L'assemblée des Yennenga: Où sont les réalisatrices?" February 22, 2019. https://www.africulturelle.com/.

Ahmed, Sara. *The Cultural Politics of Emotion*. Edinburgh: Edinburgh University Press, 2004.

Al Jazeera English. "Senegal's Sinking Villages." July 25, 2018. YouTube video, 47:26. https://www.youtube.com/watch?v=0EdrRZvLXRQ.

Anand, Nikhil. "PRESSURE: The PoliTechnics of Water Supply in Mumbai." *Cultural Anthropology* 26, no. 4 (November 2011): 542–64.

Anderson, Benedict. *Imagined Communities: Reflections on the Origin and Spread of Nationalism*. London: Verso, 1983.

Anne, Hamidou. *Panser l'Afrique qui vient*. Paris: Présence Africaine, 2019.

Appert, Catherine. *In Hip Hop Time: Music, Memory, and Social Change in Urban Senegal*. Oxford: Oxford University Press, 2018.

Augis, Erin. "Religion, Religiousness, and Narrative: Decoding Women's Practices in Senegalese Islamic Reform." *Journal for the Scientific Study of Religion* 51, no. 3 (2012): 429–41.

Azalbert, Nicolas. "Khady Sylla: Le 'tiers-oeil,'" *Cahiers du cinéma* 704 (2014): 39–40.

Baller, Susann. "Être jeune, masculin et sportif: Représentations urbaines de la masculinité au Sénégal." In *Perspectives historiques sur le genre en Afrique*, edited by Odile Goerg, 165–90. Paris: L'Harmattan, 2007.

———. "Transforming Urban Landscapes: Soccer Fields as Sites of Urban Sociability in the Agglomeration of Dakar." *African Identities* 5, no. 2 (2007): 217–30.

Bank, Leslie J. *Home Spaces, Street Styles: Contesting Power and Identity in a South African City*. London: Pluto Press, 2011.

Barthélémy, Marianne. "Écuries et écoles de lutte à Dakar: Analyse et perspectives." In Chevé et al., *Corps en lutte*, 127–37.

BBC News Afrique. "La Chine offre une arène de lutte au Sénégal." July 22, 2018. https://www.bbc.com/afrique/.
Beattie, Keith. *Documentary Screens: Non-fiction Film and Television.* Basingstoke, UK: Palgrave Macmillan, 2004.
Biaya, Tshikala Kayembe. "Les plaisirs de la ville: Masculinité, sexualité et féminité à Dakar (1997–2000)." *African Studies Review* 44, no. 2 (September 2001): 71–85.
Bisschoff, Lizelle, and Stefanie Van de Peer. *Women in African Cinema: Beyond the Body Politic.* London: Routledge, 2020.
Blandy, Fran. "Senegal Anguishes over 'Slow Death' of Its Film Industry." *Modern Ghana,* September 7, 2012. www.modernghana.com/.
Cabedoche, Bertrand. "L'inscription du cinéma documentaire en Afrique dans le champ des sciences humaines et sociales." In *La diversité du documentaire de création en Afrique,* edited by François Fronty and Delphe Kifouani, 17–44. Paris: L'Harmattan, 2015.
California Newsreel. "Karmen Geï." Accessed November 9, 2017. www.newsreel.org/video/KARMEN-GEI.
Cazenave, Odile. "The Silent Monologue by Khady Sylla and Charlie Van Damme; Some (Not So New) Gendered Stories of Globalization." *Diogènes* 62, no. 1 (2017): 48–56.
Cessou, Sabine. "Rama Thiaw: A Young Filmmaker in the Struggle." *African Women in Cinema Blog,* September 8, 2011. https://africanwomenincinema.blogspot.com/.
CGTN Africa. "Senegal Works to Restore Cinema Halls and Revive Movie Industry." March 25, 2017. YouTube video, 2:26. https://www.youtube.com/watch?v=LT8FcpevM6g.
Cham, Mbye. Foreword to *Sisters of the Screen: Women of Africa on Film, Video, and Television,* xi–xii. Edited by Beti Ellerson. Trenton, NJ: Africa World Press, 2000.
———. Introduction to *African Experiences of Cinema,* 1–14. Edited by Imruh Bakari and Mbye Cham. London: BFI, 1996.
Chevé, Dominique. "Corps construits, corps investis, corps effigies: Être lutteur à Dakar." In Chevé et al., *Corps en lutte,* 229–56.
Chevé, Dominique, Cheikh Tidiane Wane, Marianne Barthélémy, Abdoul Wahid Kane, and Ibrahima Sow, eds. *Corps en lutte: L'art du combat au Sénégal.* Paris: CNRS Editions, 2014.
———. "Introduction: La lutte; Pratique sportive, phénomène socioculturel, prisme des croyances." In Chevé et al., *Corps en lutte,* 51–59.
Chort, Isabelle, Philippe De Vreyer, and Thomas Zuber. "Gendered Mobility Patterns in Senegal." *Population* 75, nos. 2/3 (2020): 287–314.
Cinécole Sénégal. "Khady Sylla." October 13, 2013. YouTube video, 2:00. https://www.youtube.com/watch?v=DNCzF-MVvtY.

Cinegal TV. "Khalilou Ndiaye, distributeur de films: Les jeunes ne doivent plus attendre..." November 14, 2019. YouTube video, 12:00. https://www.youtube.com/watch?v=ONKaWTBtPLY.

Cissé, Abdoul Aziz, dir. *La brèche*. Belgium/Senegal: Gsara-Filmer à tout prix / Media Centre Dakar / Diwaan, 2007.

Clark, Ashley. "Making Waves: The New Senegalese Cinema." British Film Institute, January 17, 2013. https://www.bfi.org.uk/.

Corinus, Véronique, and Daniela Ricci. "Migration des hommes, des techniques et des imaginaires." In *Regards sur les migrations: Mobilités africaines entre écrit et écran*, edited by Véronique Corinus and Daniela Ricci, 7–14. Paris: L'Harmattan, 2021.

Creevey, Lucy. "Islam, Women, and the Role of the State in Senegal." *Journal of Religion in Africa* 26, no. 3 (1996): 268–307.

Cumber, Samuel Nambile, and Joyce Mahlako Tsoka-Gwegweni. "The Health Profile of Street Children in Africa: A Literature Review." *Journal of Public Health in Africa* 6, no. 2 (2015): 1–17.

de Valck, Marijke. *Film Festivals: From European Geopolitics to Global Cinephilia*. Amsterdam: Amsterdam University Press, 2007.

de Valck, Marijke, and Antoine Damiens, eds. *Rethinking Film Festivals in the Pandemic Era and After*. Cham, Switzerland: Palgrave Macmillan, 2023.

de Valck, Marijke, Brendan Kredell, and Skadi Loist, eds. *Film Festivals: History, Theory, Method, Practice*. London: Routledge, 2016.

Diabang, Angèle, dir. *Sénégalaises et Islam*. Germany/Senegal: Goethe Institut Dakar / Karoninka, 2007.

Diagne, Souleymane Bachir. "La leçon de musique: Réflexions sur une politique de la culture." In *Le Sénégal contemporain*, edited by Momar-Coumba Diop, 243–60. Paris: Karthala, 2002.

Diallo, Aïssatou, and Jules Crétois. "'Faidherbe doit tomber': Des collectifs français et sénégalais à l'assaut du mythe du colon bâtisseur." *Jeune Afrique*, April 10, 2018.

Diallo, Amadou Oury. "Cinéma: À Dakar, les bienfaits de la concurrence." *Jeune Afrique*, September 27, 2018.

Diawara, Manthia. *African Cinema: Politics and Culture*. Bloomington: Indiana University Press, 1992.

———. "The Iconography of West African Cinema." In *Symbolic Narratives/African Cinema: Audiences, Theory and the Moving Image*, edited by June Givanni, 81–89. London: BFI Publishing, 2000.

Diaz, Hugues. "2015: Réussir les chantiers du cinéma et baliser les sentiers du numérique." *Senciné* 2 (2015): 3.

Diop, Baba. "Le cinéma au féminin." *Senciné* 4 (2018): 3.

———. "Le Sénégal trace une nouvelle voie à son cinéma." *Senciné* 2 (2015): 4.

Diop, Momar-Coumba. "Introduction: Essai sur un mode de gouvernance des institutions et des politiques publiques." In *Sénégal (2000–2012): Les institutions publiques à l'épreuve d'une gouvernance libérale*, edited by Momar-Coumba Diop, 33–84. Paris: Karthala, 2013.

Diouf, Mamadou. "Wall Paintings and the Writing of History: Set/Setal in Dakar." *GEFAME: Journal of African Studies* 2, no. 1 (July 2005): 1–23.

Diouf, Mamadou, and Rosalind Fredericks, eds. *The Arts of Citizenship in African Cities: Infrastructures and Spaces of Belonging*. New York: Palgrave Macmillan, 2014.

———. Introduction to *The Arts of Citizenship in African Cities: Infrastructures and Spaces of Belonging*, 1–23. Edited by Mamadou Diouf and Rosalind Fredericks. New York: Palgrave Macmillan, 2014.

———, eds. *Les arts de la citoyenneté au Sénégal: Espaces contestés et civilités urbaines*. Paris: Karthala, 2013.

Dovey, Lindiwe. *Curating Africa in the Age of Film Festivals*. New York: Palgrave Macmillan, 2015.

Dovey, Lindiwe, and Estrella Sendra. "Toward Decolonized Film Festival Worlds." In *Rethinking Film Festivals in the Pandemic Era and After*, edited by Marijke de Valck and Antoine Damiens, 269–89. Cham, Switzerland: Palgrave Macmillan, 2023.

du Coëdic, Théo. "Sénégal: 'L'école de cinéma Kourtrajmé nous donne des armes pour raconter nos histoires par nous-mêmes.'" *Jeune Afrique*, March 9, 2022.

Ekotto, Frieda, and Kenneth W. Harrow. "Introduction: Rethinking African Cultural Production." In *Rethinking African Cultural Production*, edited by Frieda Ekotto and Kenneth W. Harrow, 1–16. Bloomington: Indiana University Press, 2015.

Ellerson, Beti. "African Women and the Documentary: Storytelling, Visualizing History, from the Personal to the Political." *Black Camera: An International Film Journal* 8, no. 1 (Fall 2016): 223–39.

———. "African Women on the Film Festival Landscape: Organizing, Showcasing, Promoting, Networking." *Black Camera* 11, no. 1 (Fall 2019): 424–56.

———. "Cinémas documentaires en Afrique au féminin." In *La diversité du documentaire de création en Afrique*, edited by François Fronty and Delphe Kifouani, 115–35. Paris: L'Harmattan, 2015.

———, ed. *Sisters of the Screen: Women of Africa on Film, Video, and Television*. Trenton, NJ: Africa World Press, 2000.

Faye, Ousseynou. "Sport, argent et politique: La lutte libre à Dakar (1800–2000)." In *Le Sénégal contemporain*, edited by Momar-Coumba Diop, 309–40. Paris: Karthala, 2002.

Fofana, Amadou T. "'Cinefication' in West Africa." *Critical Interventions: Journal of African Art History and Visual Culture* 5, no. 1 (Spring 2011): 54–63.

———. "A Critical and Deeply Personal Reflection: Malick Aw on Cinema in Senegal Today." *Black Camera* 9, no. 2 (Spring 2018): 348–59.
France 24 English. "Fespaco Meeting with Fatou Kandé Senghor." March 1, 2019. Facebook video, 5:30. https://www.facebook.com/watch/?v=780974968916843.
Fredericks, Rosalind. *Garbage Citizenship: Vital Infrastructures of Labor in Dakar, Senegal*. Durham, NC: Duke University Press, 2018.
Froment, Alain. "De graisse et de muscle: La corpulence ostentatoire en Afrique rurale." In Chevé et al., *Corps en lutte*, 119–26.
Genova, James E. *Cinema and Development in West Africa*. Bloomington: Indiana University Press, 2013.
Ghertner, D. Asher. *Rule by Aesthetics: World-Class City Making in Delhi*. Oxford: Oxford University Press, 2015.
Grabski, Joanna. *Art World City: The Creative Economy of Artists and Urban Life in Dakar*. Bloomington: Indiana University Press, 2017.
Harney, Elizabeth. *In Senghor's Shadow: Art, Politics, and the Avant-Garde in Senegal, 1960–1995*. Durham, NC: Duke University Press, 2004.
Harrow, Kenneth W. Introduction to *African Cinema: Postcolonial and Feminist Readings*, ix–xxiv. Edited by Kenneth W. Harrow. Trenton, NJ: Africa World Press, 1999.
———. *Trash: African Cinema from Below*. Bloomington: Indiana University Press, 2013.
Havard, Jean-François. "Ethos 'bul faale' et nouvelles figures de la réussite au Sénégal." *Politique africaine* 82, no. 2 (2001): 63–77.
———. "Par-delà le Bul Faale, la lutte continue! La lutte sénégalaise comme vecteur de mobilisation identitaire et d'une subjectivation générationnelle décalée." In Chevé et al., *Corps en lutte*, 163–76.
Helmreich, Stefan. "Kinship, Nation, and Paul Gilroy's Concept of Diaspora." *Diaspora: A Journal of Transnational Studies* 2, no. 2 (Fall 1992): 243–49.
Kamara, Mamadou Oumar. "Abdou Aziz Cissé, secrétaire permanent du FOPICA: 'Je ne comprends pas pourquoi Cinéseas parle d'exclusion de gestion...'" *Le soleil*, May 9, 2022.
Le point. "Sénégal: La place Faidherbe de la ville de Saint-Louis devient Baya Ndar." October 2, 2020.
Lequert, Elisabeth. "L'Afrique filmée par des femmes." *Le monde diplomatique*, August 1998.
Le quotidien. "Cinema-19è festival image et vie: Un plaidoyer sur le droit à l'éducation pour tous." November 14, 2019.
Le quotidien. "Dénomination des rues, places,...: STATUE QUO – Saint-Louis, Rufisque; Une décolonisation inachevée." June 22, 2020.
Leral.net. "Khardiata Pouye Sall, réalisatrice: Le khessal, une pratique devenue inquiétante." September 14, 2012. https://www.leral.net/.

Le samu social Sénégal. "Les enfants des rues à Dakar." Accessed January 21, 2021. http://samusocialsenegal.com/.

Linares, Olga F. "Going to the City . . . and Coming Back? Turnaround Migration among the Jola of Senegal." *Africa* 73, no. 1 (February 2003): 113–32.

Mano, Winston, Barbara Knorpp, and Añulika Agina. *African Film Cultures: Context of Creation and Circulation*. Newcastle upon Tyne, UK: Cambridge Scholars Publishing, 2017.

Martin, Michael T. "Joseph Gaï Ramaka: 'I Am Not a Filmmaker *Engagé*. I Am an Ordinary Citizen *Engagé*.'" *Research in African Literatures* 40, no. 3 (2009): 206–19.

Mawere, Munyaradzi. *Culture, Indigenous Knowledge, and Development in Africa: Reviving Interconnections for Sustainable Development*. Bamenda, Cameroon: Langaa Research & Publishing CIG, 2014.

M'Baye, Babacar. "Verbal and Acrobatic Strategies in Senegalese Wolof Wrestling." *Storytelling, Self, Society* 9, no. 2 (Fall 2013): 188–216.

Mbembe, Achille, and Sarah Nuttall. "Writing the World from an African Metropolis." *Public Culture* 16, no. 3 (Fall 2004): 347–72.

Mbembe, Achille, and Felwine Sarr. "Penser pour un nouveau siècle." In *Écrire l'Afrique-Monde*, edited by Achille Mbembe and Felwine Sarr, 7–13. Dakar: Jimsaan, 2017.

Mboup, Malèye. "Opacité dans la distribution du Fopica de 2 milliards: Les cinéastes sénégalais vilipendent le ministre de la culture." PressAfrik, May 4, 2022. https://www.pressafrik.com/.

Melly, Caroline. *Bottleneck: Moving, Building, and Belonging in an African City*. Chicago: University of Chicago Press, 2016.

Mermin, Elizabeth. "A Window on Whose Reality? The Emerging Industry of Senegalese Cinema." *Research in African Literatures* 26, no. 3 (1995): 120–33.

Molo, Alpha. "Dakar va renouer avec le cinéma: 4 salles de ciné seront réhabilitées!" KoldaNews, May 29, 2014. https://www.koldanews.com/.

Mosse, George L. *Nationalism and Sexuality: Middle-Class Morality and Sexual Norms in Modern Europe*. Madison: University of Wisconsin Press, 1985.

Murphy, David. "The Performance of Pan-Africanism: Staging the African Renaissance at the First World Festival of Negro Arts." In *The First World Festival of Negro Arts, Dakar 1966: Contexts and Legacies*, edited by David Murphy, 1–43. Liverpool: Liverpool University Press, 2016.

Myers, Garth A. *African Cities: Alternative Visions of Urban Theory and Practice*. London: Zed Books, 2011.

———. *Urban Environments in Africa: A Critical Analysis of Environmental Politics*. Bristol: Policy Press, 2016.

Ndao, Oumar. Prologue to Chevé et al., *Corps en lutte*, 9–10.

Nelson, Sarah. "The New Type of Senegalese under Construction: Fadel Barro and Aliou Sané on Yenamarreisme after Wade." *African Studies Quarterly* 14, no. 3 (2014): 13–32.

New Humanitarian. "État des lieux du Plan 'Jaxaay,' après les inondations de 2005." December 21, 2006. https://www.thenewhumanitarian.org/fr/.

Ngo-Nguidjol, Emilie. "Women in African Cinema: An Annotated Bibliography." In *African Cinema: Postcolonial and Feminist Readings*, edited by Kenneth Harrow, 305–37. Trenton, NJ: Africa World Press, 1999.

Nwankwo, Emeka Joseph. "White Eyes." Africa Is a Country, July 27, 2020. https://africasacountry.com/.

Ollivier, Théa. "Cinéma: À Dakar, l'école Kourtrajmé veut 'casser les codes.'" *Le Monde*, February 1, 2022.

Ong, Aihwa. "Introduction: Worlding Cities, or the Art of Being Global." In *Worlding Cities: Asian Experiments and the Art of Being Global*, edited by Ananya Roy and Aihwa Ong, 1–26. Malden, MA: Wiley-Blackwell, 2011.

Orlando, Valérie. "Voices of African Filmmakers: Contemporary Issues in Francophone West African Filmmaking." *Quarterly Review of Film and Video* 24, no. 5 (2007): 445–61.

Pfaff, Françoise. *À l'écoute du cinéma sénégalais*. Paris: L'Harmattan, 2010.

———. "*Colobane Express* by Khady Sylla." *African Studies Review* 56, no. 1 (2013): 223–25.

———. *Twenty-Five Black African Filmmakers: A Critical Study, with Filmography and Bio-Bibliography*. Westport, CT: Greenwood Press, 1988.

Pieterse, Edgar. *City Futures: Confronting the Crisis of Urban Development*. London: Zed Books, 2008.

Posch, Doris. "Cultural Heritage and Popular Cultures: *The Revolution Won't Be Televised* and Its Global Reception." *Critical Interventions: Journal of African Art History and Visual Culture* 11, no. 3 (2017): 301–17.

Pouye, Khardiata, dir. *Cette couleur qui me derange*. Senegal: RTS-CIRTEF, 2012.

Powrie, Phil. "Politics and Embodiment in Karmen Geï." *Quarterly Review of Film and Video* 21, no. 4 (2004): 283–91.

Pratt, Geraldine, and Rose Marie San Juan. *Film and Urban Space: Critical Possibilities*. Edinburgh: Edinburgh University Press, 2014.

Prothmann, Sebastian. "Je suis sañse rëkk, mais auma xaalis (I'm dressed up, but I don't have money): Pretense, Camouflage, and the Search for a Lifestyle by Young Men in Pikine, Senegal." *Mande Studies* 22 (2020): 57–74.

———. "Migration, Masculinity and Social Class: Insights from Pikine Senegal." *International Migration* 56, no. 4 (August 2018): 96–108.

Pugsley, Bronwen. "Challenging Perspectives: Documentary Practices in Films by Women from Francophone Africa." PhD diss., University of Nottingham, 2012.

———. "Ethical Madness? Khady Sylla's Documentary Practice in *Une fenêtre ouverte.*" *Nottingham French Studies* 51, no. 2 (July 2012): 204–19.

Ramaka, Joseph Gaï, dir. *Plan Jaxaay!* Senegal: Colored People's Time / Observatoire Audiovisuel sur les Libertés / AfrikaDreaming, 2007.

Rantrua, Sylvie. "Centre Yennenga: Là où Dakar veut faire son cinéma." *Le point*, February 19, 2021.

Repinecz, Jonathon. "Senegalese Wrestling between Nostalgia and Neoliberalism." *African Studies Review* 63, no. 4 (December 2020): 906–26.

Ricci, Daniela. "La voix des femmes dans les documentaires d'Angèle Diabang." *Nouvelles Études Francophones* 33, no. 1 (2018): 73–87.

Roberts, Allen F., and Mary Nooter Roberts. *A Saint in the City: Sufi Arts of Urban Senegal*. Los Angeles: UCLA Fowler Museum of Cultural History, 2003.

Rolfsen, Avenel. "Senegalese Cinema Does Not Exist." *Africa Is a Country*, May 8, 2018. https://africasacountry.com/.

Sabbar artistiques. *Livret-Programme: Sabbar artistiques—ateliers réflexives féminins de Dakar*. March 1, 2019. https://issuu.com/yanisgaye/docs/livret-programme-sabbar_artistiques.

Sarr, Felwine. *Afrotopia*. Translated by Drew S. Burk and Sarah Jones-Boardman. Minneapolis: University of Minnesota Press, 2019.

Saul, Mahir, and Ralph A. Austen. *Viewing African Cinema in the Twenty-First Century: Art Films and the Nollywood Video Revolution*. Athens: Ohio University Press, 2010.

Savané, Vieux, and Baye Makébé Sarr. *Y'en a Marre: Radioscopie d'une jeunesse insurgée au Sénégal*. Paris: L'Harmattan, 2012.

Sendra, Estrella. "Banlieue Films Festival (BFF): Growing Cinephilia and Filmmaking in Senegal." *Aniki: Portuguese Journal of the Moving Image* 8, no. 1 (2021): 245–72.

Sène Absa, Moussa, dir. *Yoolé*. Senegal: Absa Films, 2010.

Senghor, Fatou Kandé. "My Work, My Passion." *African Women in Cinema Blog*, January 12, 2011. http://africanwomenincinema.blogspot.com/.

Sie, Adams, dir. *Voix silencieuses*. UK/Senegal: The British Council / Adams Sie, 2005.

Sieveking, Nadine. "'We Don't Want Equality; We Want to Be Given Our Rights': Muslim Women Negotiating Global Development Concepts in Senegal." *Afrika Spectrum* 42, no. 1 (2007): 29–48.

Simone, AbdouMaliq. *City Life from Jakarta to Dakar: Movements at the Crossroads*. New York: Routledge, 2010.

———. "On the Worlding of African Cities." *African Studies Review* 44, no. 2 (September 2001): 15–41.

———. "People as Infrastructure: Intersecting Fragments in Johannesburg." *Public Culture* 16, no. 3 (Fall 2004): 407–29.

Smith, Sidonie, and Gisela Brinker-Gabler. "Introduction: Gender, Nation, and Immigration in the New Europe." In *Writing New Identities: Gender, Nation, and Immigration in Contemporary Europe*, edited by Sidonie Smith and Gisela Brinker-Gabler, 1–27. Minneapolis: University of Minnesota Press, 1997.

Snipe, Tracy D. *Arts and Politics in Senegal, 1960–1996*. Trenton, NJ: Africa World Press, 1998.

Söderbergh, Carl. "Senegal: The Impact of the Climate Crisis on the Fisher Community of St. Louis." Minority Rights Group International, November 13, 2019. https://minorityrights.org/.

Sow Fall, Aminata. *L'appel des arènes*. Dakar: Nouvelles éditions africaines du Sénégal, 1982.

Spaliviero, Rosa. "Dakar's Ciné-Suburb: Young People Create a Ciné-Club in Pikine." Buala, April 14, 2010. https://www.buala.org/.

Sylla, Khady. "Écrivain, cinéaste: Mme Khady Sylla." Interview by Modibo S. Keïta. *Amina*, July 1999. https://aflit.arts.uwa.edu.au/AMINAScylla99.html.

Sylla, Khady, dir. *Le monologue de la muette*. Senegal: Athénaïse / Iota Production / Karoninka, 2008.

Thackway, Melissa. "Migrations et traversées dans les cinémas d'Afrique." In *Regards sur les migrations: Mobilités africaines entre écrit et écran*, edited by Véronique Corinus and Daniela Ricci, 17–39. Paris: L'Harmattan, 2021.

Thiaw, Rama. "The Revolution Won't Be Televised: An Interview with Rama Thiaw." Interview by Marc Girardot. *Berlin Art Link*, March 11, 2016. https://www.berlinartlink.com/.

Thiaw, Rama, dir. *Boul fallé: La voie de la lutte*. Ivory Coast / France: Wassakara Productions / Banshee Films, 2009.

———. *The Revolution Won't Be Televised*. Senegal: Boul Fallé Images, 2015.

Thomas, Lynn M. *Beneath the Surface: A Transnational History of Skin Lighteners*. Durham, NC: Duke University Press, 2020.

Trefon, Theodore. "Hinges and Fringes: Conceptualising the Peri-urban in Central Africa." In *African Cities: Competing Claims on Urban Spaces*, edited by Francesca Locatelli and Paul Nugent, 15–35. Leiden: Brill, 2009.

Ukadike, N. Frank. "The Other Voices of Documentary: *Allah Tantou* and *Afrique, je te plumerai*." In *Focus on African Films*, edited by Françoise Pfaff, 159–72. Bloomington: University of Indiana Press, 2004.

UNESCO. "Women in African History." Accessed June 30, 2021. https://en.unesco.org/womeninafrica/yennega (page discontinued).

Vallejo, Aida. "The Rise of Documentary Festivals: A Historical Approach." In *Documentary Film Festivals Vol. 1*, edited by Aida Vallejo and Ezra Winton, 77–100. Cham, Switzerland: Palgrave Macmillan, 2020.

Vallejo, Aida, and Ezra Winton, eds. *Documentary Film Festivals Vol. 1: Methods, History, Politics*. Cham, Switzerland: Palgrave Macmillan, 2020.

———, eds. *Documentary Film Festivals Vol. 2: Changes, Challenges, Professional Perspectives*. Cham, Switzerland: Palgrave Macmillan, 2020.

Vernière, Marc. "Pikine, 'ville nouvelle' de Dakar, un case de pseudo-urbanisation." *L'espace géographique* 2, no. 2 (1973): 107–26.

Vetinde, Lifongo. "Introduction: Cultural Politics in Senegal; A Quest for Relevance." In *Ousmane Sembène and the Politics of Culture*, edited by Lifongo Vetinde and Amadou T. Fofana, ix–xxi. Lanham, MD: Lexington Books, 2015.

von Schnitzler, Antina. "Traveling Technologies: Infrastructure, Ethical Regimes, and the Materiality of Politics in South Africa." *Cultural Anthropology* 28, no. 4 (2013): 670–93.

Wane, Cheikh Tidiane. "Techniques corporelles et différences ethnoculturelles dans la lutte sénégalaise." In Chevé et al., *Corps en lutte*, 89–118.

Williams, James S. *Ethics and Aesthetics in Contemporary African Cinema: The Politics of Beauty*. London: Bloomsbury Academic, 2019.

Index

Page numbers in italics refer to figures.

activism, 17, 58, 64, 102, 117; feminist, 190, 191, 195; of filmmakers, 104, 176, 190; and gender, 87, 90; and hip-hop, 87–90, 93, 95, 96; Pan-African, 88; against politicians, 95, 106, 119. *See also* protest; Sylla, Khady; Y'en a Marre

aesthetics, 51, 52, 58, 143, 183; and politics, 183; of self-reflexivity, 145; trashy, 51

African cinema, 37, 40, 47, 50–52; development of, 3, 36; and documentary film, 16, 44–47, 49; gender inequities in, 170–72, 175; and the Global North, 172; global value of, 3; history of, 25–26; innovation of, 19; and women filmmakers, 47, 170–72, 175. *See also* Sembène, Ousmane; Senegalese cinema

African cities, 10, 13–14, 19, 24–25, 49, 83, 103, 122; creativity in, 13–14, 25, 49; and imagination, 14, 50; inequities of, 24–25; possibilities of, 144, 215. *See also* Dakar, Senegal; Saint-Louis, Senegal; urban life

Afrotopia (Sarr), 2, 194, 215. *See also* Sarr, Felwine

agency: children's, 147, 151, 153–54; and disaster, 112; documentary subjects', 101, 109, 115, 117, 141, 144, 147, 151, 164, 189–90; and hip-hop, 59, 80; migrants', 67; rural residents', 134; and the urban periphery, 75, 87, 101, 104, 115, 137; urban residents', 75, 142, 144, 147, 153–54; women's, 164, 177, 189–90; and wrestling, 59, 75, 83, 85. *See also* voice(s)

Ahmed, Sara, 64–65

Anand, Nikhil, 104, 130

Anderson, Benedict: *Imagined Communities*, 55

Anne, Hamidou, 49

Augis, Erin, 202

Aw, Malick, 36

Awadi, Didier, 58, 76–79, 81, 87. *See also* hip-hop

Azalbert, Nicolas, 159

Ba, Cheikh Ngaïdo: *Xew xew*, 28

Bâ, Mariama: *Une si longue lettre*, 197–99

Bamba, Cheikh Amadou, 5, 6

Barbary peninsula, 100, 122, 127, 137

Barro, Fadel, 91

beauty, 45–46, 59, 61, 75, 115, 118, 201, 204; feminine, 185; practices, 174, 183, 195; standards, 19, 182–84, 186–89, 191–92. *See also* skin lightening

belonging: challenges of, 68; collective, 54; in Dakar, 10, 25; diasporic, 176; men's, 57, 58, 74, 76, 83, 84, 87; national, 17, 55, 57–59, 62, 64, 66–69, 71–72, 76, 80, 86, 90; in rural communities, 117; sites of, 13–15, 36, 60, 89; in urban communities, 104, 153, 183; women's, 69, 183. *See also* citizenship; collectivity; community

Benga, Sokhna, 180, 196

Biaya, Tshikala Kayembe, 83

Bisschoff, Lizelle, 171–72, 175, 196

bodies, 58, 63, 82–86, 132, 139, 184, 189; feminized, 183, 186, 192; masculine, 59, 75–76, 83, 84, 86; social, 59, 67, 75, 82–83, 86, 104, 143, 150, 154, 165. *See also* skin lightening; wrestling

boul fallé, 60, 76–81, 86. See also hip-hop
Boul fallé: La voie de la lutte (Thiaw), 17, 54, 56–60, 93, 95, 169; hip-hop in, 58–59, 73, 76–77, 81; masculinity in, 56–60, 75, 83, 84, 87; nationalism in, 54, 56; wrestling in, 58–59, 73–87
Brinker-Gabler, Gisela, 56

Cabedoche, Bertrand, 45
Camara, Seni Awa, 176, 209
care, 71, 154, 159, 197
Casamance (region), 39–40, 43, 155, 194, 209
Cazenave, Odile, 168
Centre Yennenga, 32–33, 42, 211–14
Cette couleur qui me dérange (Pouye), 18, 48, 179, 182–94, 207; aesthetic governmentality and, 183; domestic space in, 19, 174, 182, 192; *khessal* in, 19, 182; skin lightening in, 174, 180, 182–92, *193*; women's voices in, 174, 179
Cham, Mbye, 2, 170
Cheriaa, Tahar, 27
CinéBanlieue, 42
Cinéma numérique ambulant (CNA), 40
Cissé, Abdoul Aziz, 18, 31, 43, 101–4, 116, 136–37, 140, 143; *Aaru Mbèdd—les murs de Dakar*, 121; *Bët gaal*, 121; biography, 48, 120–22; *Renaissance*, 121. See also Fonds de promotion de l'industrie cinématographique et audiovisuelle (FOPICA); *La brèche* (Cissé)
citizenship, 14, 15, 104, 127, 129–30, 131; in African cities, 14; arts of, 15; contested, 129; hydraulic, 104, 130; practices, 104. See also belonging; nationalism
collaboration, 4, 9, 14, 25, 29, 103, 164, 179; between artists, 4, 9; between filmmakers, 173, 175–76, 178; between filmmakers and documentary subjects, 14, 155, 185; international, 29; and solidarity, 155, 170–73
collectivity, 83–84, 108–9, 122, 133–34, 207; female, 158–59, 162, 164, 168, 172, 202, 204–7; and film festivals, 38; masculine, 91; national, 66, 67; and precarity, 142, 152; in rural communities, 133; in wrestling, 60, 76, 83. See also belonging; solidarity
community: and *boul fallé*, 77–79;
contingent, 142, 147, 150, 153–55; in Dakar, 14, 36–37, 59, 143; dissolution of, 18; imagined, 55–56; international, 13; national, 57, 60, 62, 66, 69–70, 76, 154; of women, 157–58, 162, 164–68, 173, 175, 178, 196; and wrestling, 83, 84, 86, 87. See also belonging; solidarity
Creevey, Lucy, 199
crisis, 22, 33, 49, 54, 56, 60–61, 72, 73, 108, 146, 213; environmental, 98, 100, 101, 107, 112, 115, 118; of masculinity, 57; narratives of, 20, 24–25, 32, 56, 62; tropes of, 57
culture: cultural capital, 3, 34; cultural ideology, 2, 4, 5, 8, 37; cultural production, 3, 10, 12, 13, 16, 121; social change, 36, 46, 58, 89, 97, 140, 143, 158, 179, 192, 197, 199

Dakar, Senegal: as global cultural capital, 4–8; modern history of, 4–13; movie theaters in, 4–5, 15, 20, 22, 23–24, 26–32, 34–36, 40, 41, 43; as "palimpsest city," 8–11; and the world, 11–13. See also African cities
Davis, Angela, 173, 235n10
Diabang, Angèle, 18, 19, 43, 46, 173–75, 178–79, 193–99, 201–7, 211; biography, 48, 178, 194–95; *Congo, un médecin pour sauver les femmes*, 196; *Le revers de l'exil*, 196; *L'homme est le remède de l'homme*, 196; *Ma coépouse bien aimée*, 197, 211; *Mon beau sourire*, 194, 195; *Un air de kora*, 197; *Une si longue lettre*, 197, 198; *Yandé Codou: La griotte de Senghor*, 196. See also *Sénégalaises et Islam* (Diabang)
diaspora, 56, 70, 173, 176
Diawara, Manthia, 22, 26, 27
Diaz, Hugues, 31, 32, 212, 214. See also Direction de la cinématographie
Diop, Alioune, 4
Diop, Baba, 48
Diop, Moussa: *Poisson d'or, poisson africain*, 20, 22, 31, 208
Diop, Omar Blondin, 92, 211
Diouf, Abdou, 5
Diouf, Mamadou, 11
Direction de la cinématographie, 20, 22, 24, 29–33, 41, 47, 208, 212

Index

DJ Gadiaga, 87–88
Djily Bagdad, 91
Djionne, Iman: *La boxeuse*, 178, 209–10
documentary film, 16, 26, 43–52, 103; and collaboration, 179; ethics of, 145, 164; and exploitation, 144; forms of, 18, 19, 67, 81, 106, 155, 157, 179, 185, 188, 193; and global cinema, 12, 16; and self-reflexivity, 155; and women filmmakers, 177, 178. See also African cinema; ethnography; Senegalese cinema
Doune Baba Dieye (community), 100, 101, 103, 122, 127, 132
Dovey, Lindiwe, 32
dreams, 61, 152, 155, 161, 178, 181; deferment of, 177; of Europe, 171; of the future, 152, 171; of home, 161; of migration, 171; pursuit of, 155, 181; realization of, 155, 177. See also hope

École Kourtrajmé, 212, 214
economy: and *boul fallé*, 79; creative, 5, 11; crises, 27, 29, 53, 59, 63, 71, 101, 135, 139; and emasculation, 57; global, 19, 27, 68, 167, 182; growth, 167; informal, 139; and migration, 58, 66–70, 102, 161; Senegalese, 5, 18, 102, 159, 167; and urban maids, 161; and urban youth, 143; women's role in, 158. See also neoliberalism; poverty; precarity
education, 5, 18, 38, 40, 42, 51, 84, 121, 145, 154; of children, 139, 149, 154, 181–82; cinematic, 146, 194; in Dakar, 181–82; of filmmakers, 121, 145, 146, 194, 214; and marginalization, 139, 181; in rural communities, 125. See also Centre Yennenga; École Kourtrajmé
Ekotto, Frieda, 3, 34; *Rethinking African Cultural Production*, 3
Ellerson, Beti, 36, 47, 170, 192
embouteillages, 25
environment, 101, 107, 121, 122, 129, 132, 133. See also flooding; ocean; water
ethnography, 15, 20, 24, 25, 44, 232n10. See also documentary film
exclusion, 13, 15, 17, 18, 50, 54, 83, 145, 174; sites of, 14, 174; of urban children, 152; of women, 18, 46, 47, 158. See also invisibility; marginalization

Faye, Safi, 26, 46, 196; *Mossane*, 196
feminism, 173, 179, 192, 195, 237n47. See also gender; intersectionality; women filmmakers
film festivals, 32, 44, 48, 146, 178; in Africa, 37, 38, 170–72, 177; awards, 121, 170–71, 197; Berlin International Film Festival, 34, 197; Cannes Film Festival, 12, 34; in Dakar, 37, 39, 42; Festival du quartier, 48; Festival image et vie, 38, 121; Festival panafricain du cinéma et de la télévision de Ouagadougou (FESPACO), 12, 37, 47, 51, 170–72, 177, 197, 207; film culture, 37–38; Films Femmes Afrique, 38; Global North, 172; international festivals, 8, 12, 30, 34, 48, 194, 197; women, 38, 170–71
film industry: challenges of, 17, 22, 32–33, 44, 72; in Dakar, 208, 211; funding of, 28, 29, 31; innovations of, 40, 42, 44; and networking, 20, 36, 212; opportunities in, 146–47; women in, 41, 172, 174, 187. See also film festivals; movie theaters
First World Festival of Negro Arts, 4, 8, 37
flooding, 18; in Dakar, 98, 100, 101, 107, 109, 112–13; in Médina Gounass, 115; in Pikine, 99, 110; in Saint-Louis, 100, 103, 128, 132–33. See also environment; Médina Gounass (neighborhood); Pikine (neighborhood); Senegal River; water
Fofana, Amadou T., 26, 28, 35
Fonds de promotion de l'industrie cinématographique et audiovisuelle (FOPICA), 29–31, 34, 38, 42, 43, 48
Fredericks, Rosalind, 11, 104, 134
freedom, 10, 13, 79, 92, 105, 163, 198

gaze, 105, 137, 148, 187, 189, 195; female, 105; male, 105; white, 49
gender, 19, 56–60, 63, 91, 93, 105, 175, 178, 180, 182; and activism, 87, 89, 90, 191; equity, 11, 19, 39, 47, 158, 201, 207; inequity, 171, 172, 174; and Islam, 204, 206–7; and marginalization, 105, 158–59, 161, 165; and migration, 66, 69–70; and nationalism, 56–57, 63–64, 66, 90; and urban life, 157, 169–70. See also intersectionality; masculinity; women filmmakers

Genova, James, 27, 28
Ghertner, D. Asher, 183
global cinema, 3, 12, 16
globalization, 5, 34, 74, 129, 176, 192
Gomis, Alain, 32, 34, 212, 214; *Félicité*, 34; *Tey*, 179
Gorée Island, 39, 43
Grabski, Joanna, 5, 11–12; *Art World City: The Creative Economy of Artists and Urban Life in Dakar*, 5, 11
Grand, Thomas: *Poisson d'or, poisson africain*, 20, 22, 31, 208
Guédiawaye (neighborhood), 98, 106–8, 110
Gueye, Awa Moctar, 211

Harney, Elizabeth, 2
Harrow, Kenneth, 3, 34, 50, 52, 105; *African Cinema: Postcolonial and Feminist Readings*, 3, 47; *Rethinking African Cultural Production*, 3; *Trash: African Cinema from Below*, 50
Havard, Jean-François, 79–80
Helmreich, Stefan, 56
hip-hop, 8, 9, 16, 17, 58–59, 73, 76–77, 81; and activism, 87–90, 93, 95, 96, 140; and masculinity, 58–59, 78; and social change, 77; street art, 5, 7; and wrestling, 17, 58; and Y'en a Marre, 9, 87. See also *boul fallé*
hope, 46, 67, 72, 77, 80, 107, 115, 119, 181; of migrants, 61, 64; and the ocean, 93; and precarity, 155, 162, 166; for Senegalese cinema, 22, 24; for Senegalese men, 60. See also dreams
houseworkers, 18, 139–44, 158, 159, 161–68, 169, 179, 181. See also labor

ideology, 2, 4, 5, 8, 37, 63, 79, 81, 88, 171. See also nationalism
imperfect cinema, 51, 52
infrastructure, 3, 5, 13, 101, 104, 106, 107, 122, 132; artistic, 1, 121; cinematic, 15, 24, 29, 35–36, 44, 49; human, 103, 116, 118, 120; and politics, 120, 131; water, 124, 126, 129, 130, 131
inheritance, 58, 60, 63, 77, 80, 88–91, 92, 93, 95–96
intersectionality: and Islam, 199, 204, 207; and migration, 70; on-screen, 167, 173, 174, 180, 189, 199; and precarity, 139; and social problems, 90; and urban life, 145, 178; of women's experiences, 17–18, 175, 201; in women's expressions, 173, 174, 189. See also feminism; gender
invisibility, 18, 124, 140, 144, 150, 159, 165. See also exclusion
Islam, 19, 199, 202–4, 206; and gender, 19, 199, 201–4, 206

joy, 3, 46, 70, 145, 155, 164

Kâ, Marie: *L'autre femme*, 177–78
Kandé Senghor, Fatou, 170–73, 176, 207, 209; *Diola tigi*, 176; *Donner naissance*, 176, 209; *L'autre en moi*, 176; *Walabok: Une histoire orale du hip hop au Sénégal*, 177
Kenu, 208–12
Kesteloot, Lilyan, 180
Keur Gui, 58, 59, 60, 77, 87, 89, 90, 95–96
khessal, 19, 182. See also skin lightening
Kilifeu, 59, 87, 88, 90, 92–97, 99

labor, 97, 104, 159. See also houseworkers
La brèche (Cissé), 18, 120–22, 124–30; flooding in, 120–32; government mismanagement in, 101, 103, 120, 124; infrastructure in, 122, 124, 126, 129, 130–32
Le monologue de la muette (Sylla), 18, 138–45, 155–68; liminal existence in, 140, 159; urban maids in, 18, 139–44, 158, 159, 161–68, 169, 179, 181
lineage, 10, 17, 54, 55, 76, 78, 85, 89–93, 95, 97, 196
Lumumba, Patrice, 77, 87, 88, 90
Ly, Ladj, 214

Mambéty, Djibril Diop, 4, 26, 28, 30, 34, 41, 121, 157; *Touki bouki*, 4
Mame Coumba Bang, 122–30, 132, 136–37. See also myth
marginalization, 79, 105, 145, 175; in Dakar, 175; and gender, 18, 47, 83, 158–59; and precarity, 138; urban, 14, 141, 150–51, 158, 183; in urban periphery, 18, 40. See also exclusion; invisibility
Marx, Karl: *Das Kapital*, 92

Index 255

masculinity, 17, 56–61, 70, 71, 75, 83, 84, 87, 92; crisis of, 57, 226n14; and nationalism, 47, 56–59, 61, 70–71; tropes of, 17. *See also* gender
Mbembe, Achille, 50, 103, 134
Media Center of Dakar, 48, 146, 194
Médina Gounass (neighborhood), 108, 110, 113–17, 119–20, 124, 126, 130, 132
Melly, Caroline, 25, 54, 56
Mermin, Elizabeth, 28
migration, 55–59, 66–70; and belonging, 17, 55, 61, 65–66, 84, 93; of cultural capital, 34; internal, 161; and masculinity, 56–57, 59, 66, 69–70, 75, 226n14; narratives of, 53–54, 57–58, 61, 63–64, 71–72, 161; and urban life, 16; and women, 69–70, 90. *See also* dreams; pirogues
Mosse, George L., 56
movie theaters, 4–5, 15, 20, 22, 23–24, 26–32, 34–36; Bada Ciné, 22–24, 30, 34, 36; challenges of, 5, 24, 31, 32, 40, 41, 43; Cinéma Awa, 23, 24, 30, 34, 36; Cinéma Christa, 30, 36; Complexe Cinématographique Ousmane Sembène, 20–22, 210; funding of, 26–28, 30, 32, 34, 35; and local communities, 35–36; and programming, 27. *See also* film industry
"multiple elsewheres," 11, 12, 134, 135
Murphy, David, 4
Myers, Garth, 107, 110, 122, 124; *Urban Environments in Africa: A Critical Analysis of Environmental Politics*, 107
myth, 10, 54, 105, 124, 126, 136, 148, 156. *See also* Mame Coumba Bang

nationalism, 1, 54–56, 61, 63, 66, 72, 84, 90; and masculinity, 47, 56–59, 61, 70–71. *See also* belonging; citizenship; ideology
Ndiaye, Cheikh, 79
Ndiaye, Khalilou, 38
Ndiaye, Mamadou, 22, 28
Ndiaye, Samba Félix, 26, 179
N'Dour, Youssou, 196
Ndoye, Moustapha: *Sénégal salsa*, 194
Nelson, Sarah, 91
neoliberalism, 5, 80, 142. *See also* economy
Ngo-Nguidjol, Emilie, 47

Nguer, Cheick-Tidjane, 79–86, 93
Nollywood, 50
Nuttall, Sarah, 11, 12, 14, 50, 103, 134

ocean, 18, 53, 62, 80, 93, 98, 127–28; dangers of, 68, 93, 97; and fishing, 66, 128, 149, 154; and hope, 93, 152; and migration, 61, 65, 68, 97, 135. *See also* environment; water
Ong, Aihwa, 11
otherness, 13, 144, 145. *See also* exclusion; marginalization
Ouakam (neighborhood), 208–10

Pan-Africanism, 4, 87, 90
Pfaff, Françoise, 28, 157, 165, 194; *À l'écoute du cinéma sénégalais*, 28
Pikine (neighborhood), 200; cinema in, 23, 30; development of, 106–7; and flooding, 98, 99, 110, 111, 117; and hip-hop, 7, 78, 79, 80–81; and marginalization, 84–85, 87, 107, 110; and Rama Thiaw, 73, 83; and wrestling, 73–74, 78–79, 80–81, 82, 84–85
pirogues, 53, 54; and fishing, 53, 68, 121, 129; and migration, 55, 57–58, 61–63, 65–68, 70, 97, 135, 161; and national identity, 53–55, 57, 61–63, 65–68, 97; and rural communities, 134–35; and water, 97, 121, 128, 134
Plan Jaxaay! (Ramaka), 17, 18, 104–20, 124, 126, 132, 133; flooding in, 107–20; hyperlocalization in, 102, 104, 106, 109, 116, 119; water mismanagement in, 113, 115, 116, 118, 120, 124
Point E (neighborhood), 160
policy, 99, 101
Posch, Doris, 89
postcolonialism, 1, 2, 3, 4, 8, 15, 37, 47, 53, 56
Pouye, Khardiata, 18, 19, 43, 48, 173–75, 178–95, 207; biography, 48, 179–82; *Élan brisé*, 180; *La croisière des arts*, 180; *L'école espoir*, 180–82, 184; *Lilyan Kesteloot: Pionnière de la littérature africaine*, 180; *Obscure, clair-voyance*, 181, 184. See also *Cette couleur qui me dérange* (Pouye)
poverty, 49, 57, 73, 93, 140, 143, 146, 164, 167; *les déchets humains*, 141–42. *See also* economy; precarity

Powrie, Phil, 105
precarity: and the environment, 135; rural, 137; of street boys, 149–50, 152–55; urban, 17, 18, 138, 140–41, 143–44, 148–49, 158; of urban maids, 158, 164. *See also* economy; poverty
protest, 17, 60, 79, 94, 182; *See also* activism; revolution
Pugsley, Bronwen, 145

Ramaka, Joseph Gaï, 12, 30, 43, 48, 101–21, 124, 130, 137, 140, 143, 196; biography, 104–8; *Et si Latif avait raison!*, 105, 106, 107, 108; Gorée Island Cinema, 39–40, 43; *Karmen Geï*, 102, 104–5, 107–8, 117, 120, 196. See also *Plan Jaxaay!* (Ramaka)
religion, 73, 74, 199, 201–6
revolution, 89, 92, 173, 176. *See also* activism; protest
Revolution Won't Be Televised, The (Thiaw), 17, 49, 55–60, 87–97, 169, 178; activism in, 87, 89–90, 93, 95; masculinity in, 87, 92; Y'en a Marre, 59–60, 87–95
Rouch, Jean, 156
Roy, Ananya, 11
rural life, 5, 11, 17, 18, 40, 95, 100, 130–33, 159, 176; marginalization of, 137; in relation to urban life, 46, 127, 128, 135–37, 140, 161, 165–67, 209; and water, 130–33, 135–37

Sabbar artistiques, 172–73, 235n10
Saint-Louis, Senegal, 6, 13, 38, 103–4, 121–22, 125, 126–29, 131, 134–36; and infrastructure, 131, 132; myth in, 123, 124; and water, 18, 100–101, 103–4, 122, 123, 126–29, 134–36. *See also* African cities
Sall, Macky, 30, 74, 94, 95
Sané, Aliou, 91
Sangaré, Toumani, 214
Sankara, Thomas, 77, 87–92, 96, 97
Sarr, Baye Makébé, 9
Sarr, Coumba, 40
Sarr, Felwine, 2, 10, 11, 13, 17, 49, 97, 112, 194, 215; *Afrotopia*, 2, 194, 215
Sarr, Saliou, 209
Savané, Vieux, 9

Seck, Pape Goura, 194
Sembène, Ousmane, 4, 10, 20, 26, 27, 30, 102, 121, 220n9; *Borom sarret*, 4; and cinema infrastructure, 20, 21, 22, 24, 210, 211; *La noire de . . .*, 4; *Mandabi*, 4; *Xala*, 4. *See also* African cinema; Senegalese cinema
Sendra, Estrella, 32, 37, 42
Sène Absa, Moussa, 17, 30, 43, 54–55, 58, 60–66, 68–72, 92–93, 97, 137, 140, 143; biography, 60–61. See also *Yoolé* (Séne Absa)
Senegal: as conceptual site, 12; culture, 1–2, 10, 12, 16, 24, 26, 28, 32, 40, 44, 74; elections, 5, 8, 9, 63, 92, 94–96, 109–10, 118–20; independence, 1, 4, 10, 26, 63; inequity, 13, 14, 24, 40, 50, 51, 68, 116, 124, 138, 170; national identity, 1, 54–55, 61, 63, 72, 74, 84, 90. *See also* Dakar, Senegal; Saint-Louis, Senegal
Sénégalaises et Islam (Diabang), 18, 174, 178, 193, 196, 199, 201–4, 205–7; intersectionality in, 198–99, 204, 207; and perceptions of Islam, 199, 201, 202, 206; veiling in, 201, 202, 204
Senegalese cinema: and COVID-19 pandemic, 32–33, 41; and crisis, 1, 22, 24–25, 29, 30, 32, 146, 213; and distribution, 15, 16, 22, 25, 27, 28, 34, 40–44, 48, 146, 171, 172, 211; and environmentalism, 121–22; and financing, 4, 5, 15, 16, 22, 27, 29–30, 34–35, 43, 48, 146, 221n22; gender inequity in, 174–75, 177; and the global, 12–13, 102; history of, 26–27; infrastructure of, 15, 24, 29, 35–36, 44, 49, 215; innovations in, 15, 41–44, 51–52, 115, 147, 178, 211–12, 215; and production, 15–16, 22, 25, 27, 29, 42, 44, 48, 104, 146, 171, 194, 211; and viewership, 15–16, 25, 28, 40, 42, 48–49, 195. *See also* African cinema; documentary film; Sembène, Ousmane
Senegal River, 48, 100, 103, 121–22, 124–25, 127–28, 130–32, 136, 180
Senghor, Léopold Sédar, 10, 25–27, 61, 92, 176, 196, 206; and cinema, 26, 27, 37; and cultural ideology, 2, 8; and the First World Festival of Negro Arts, 8,

Index

37; and the Negritude movement, 1; and political conflicts, 26; and support for culture, 1, 4–5
sex, 153–54
Sie, Adams, 18, 41, 43, 48, 138, 140–54, 168, 179; biography, 48, 145–47; *Le cheval blanc*, 146; *Oumy et moi*, 148; *Summer pencc*, 41, 44. See also *Voix silencieuses* (Sie)
Sieveking, Nadine, 206
Simone, AbdouMaliq, 50, 103–4
Sita-Bella, Thérèse: *Tam-tam à Paris*, 46
skin lightening, 174, 180, 182–92, 193. See also beauty; bodies; *khessal*
Smith, Sidonie, 56
social impotence, 57, 58, 63–65, 70, 71, 73, 84, 92, 93, 97
Société de cinéma (SNC), 26
Société sénégalaise d'importation, de distribution et d'exploitation cinématographique (SIDEC), 27
solidarity, 53, 70, 89, 159, 164–66, 198. See also collectivity; community
Sow, Khadidiatou: *Une place dans l'avion*, 177–78
Spaliviero, Rosa, 106
stereotypes, 2, 182, 195, 198–99, 204
street art, 5, 7, 88, 123. See also hip-hop
Sy, Fatim Poulo, 163
Sy, Oumou, 180
Sylla, Khady, 24, 32, 41, 43–44, 46, 175, 178, 180, 195, 206; activism, 88–92, 96–97; biography, 155–58; *Colobane Express*, 156–58; *Le jeu de la mer*, 156; *Les bijoux*, 156; *The Revolution Won't Be Televised*, 87–92; *Sénégalaises et Islam*, 18, 178, 196, 201–4; *Une fenêtre ouverte*, 145; *Une simple parole*, 176. See also *Le monologue de la muette* (Sylla)
Sylla, Mariama, 175–76; *Derrière le silence*, 175; *Une simple parole*, 176

television: and career opportunities, 41, 73, 146–47; and cinema, 32, 41; during COVID-19 pandemic, 32; and film distribution, 41–42, 49; and RTS (channel), 32, 49, 179, 182; and skin lightening, 183, 184; and viewership, 42. See also Kandé Senghor, Fatou;

Pouye, Khardiata; Sie, Adams; Thiaw, Rama
Thackway, Melissa, 70
Thiaroye (neighborhood), 98
Thiat, 58, 59, 77, 81–97
Thiaw, Rama, 43, 46, 73–76, 137, 140, 143, 167; biography, 73; Sabbar artistiques, 172–73; Yoonir Ciné-Club, 211. See also *Boul fallé: La voie de la lutte* (Thiaw); *Revolution Won't Be Televised, The* (Thiaw)
Thomas, Lynn M., 182, 186, 190
Touré, Moussa, 30; *La pirogue*, 22, 62–63
Touré Ndiaye, Fatou: *La promesse*, 177, 178
trash, 50–51, 112, 118, 119, 141–42, 149. See also Harrow, Kenneth
Trefon, Theodore, 132
Tyson (Mohammed Ndao), 78–80, 85–86

Ukadike, N. Frank, 44, 45
urban life: challenges of, 14, 68, 141; creativity of, 14, 25, 211; in Dakar, 4, 16, 169; and gender inequity, 174, 183; and peripheral communities, 61, 112; potential of, 145, 215; and precarity, 18, 103, 143, 150; in relation to rural life, 45, 127, 128, 135–37, 140, 161, 165–67, 209; in Saint-Louis, 122; and urban space, 50, 143, 158, 199. See also African cities

Vallejo, Aida, 44
Van de Peer, Stefanie, 172, 175, 196
veiling, 19, 148, 201, 202, 204
Vernière, Marc, 107
violence, 40, 60, 149, 165, 203; sexual, 149, 197; state, 91, 93
voice(s): collective, 112, 133, 152, 158–59, 166, 202; marginalized, 18, 46, 95, 101, 102, 106, 107, 110, 120, 122; as trope, 143, 154, 158; and voice-over, 65–66, 81, 82, 85, 86, 106, 125, 159, 161–62, 164, 167, 175; of women, 19, 47, 86, 89, 158–69, 173, 174, 179, 191–96, 199, 203, 204; of youth, 38, 124, 147, 150–51, 154
Voix silencieuses (Sie), 18, 138–55, 158, 168; filmmaking process of, 148; precarity in, 148–50, 152–55; street boys in, 139, 140, 144, 147–54, 158; survival strategies in, 138, 142–44, 150, 153–54, 168

Wade, Abdoulaye, 104; and corruption, 105–7; and cultural projects, 8, 29; and flooding, 98–99, 104, 109–10, 119–20, 132; infrastructure projects of, 8, 98, 132; and migration, 17, 63–68; protests against, 9, 72, 87, 91, 93–95
water, 73, 98–137, 142, 149, 166; management, 17, 18, 108, 110, 132; mismanagement, 48, 101, 103, 112–16, 118, 120, 124, 142; spirit, 123, 125, 126. *See also* environment; flooding; ocean; Senegal River
Williams, James S.: *Ethics and Aesthetics in Contemporary African Cinema*, 51
women filmmakers, 18, 46–48, 169–75, 177–78, 180, 196. *See also* Diabang, Angèle; feminism; gender; Kandé Senghor, Fatou; Pouye, Khardiata; Sylla, Khady; Thiaw, Rama

world cinema. *See* global cinema
worlding, 11
wrestling, 8, 16, 17, 58–59, 73–87, 90, 95; and *bâkk*, 78; and the body, 76, 85; and neoliberalism, 80; popularity of, 59, 74, 78. *See also* collectivity; community; Nguer, Cheick-Tidjane; Tyson (Mohammed Ndao)

Y'en a Marre, 9–10, 59–60, 87–96, 120. *See also* activism; hip-hop; Wade, Abdoulaye
Yennenga, 33, 171
Yoolé (Séne Absa), 17, 54–72, 76, 85, 92, 93; Barbados in, 58, 63–65, 67, 70–71; masculinity in, 57–72; migration in, 17, 55–70, 93; nationalism in, 54–56, 61, 63, 66, 72; the ocean in, 61, 65, 66, 68; women in, 69–70